# Transfer Pricing in the US

# Transfer Pricing in the US

## A Practical Guide

Felix I. Lessambo

Wolters Kluwer

*Published by:*
Kluwer Law International B.V.
PO Box 316
2400 AH Alphen aan den Rijn
The Netherlands
Website: www.wolterskluwerlr.com

*Sold and distributed in North, Central and South America by:*
Wolters Kluwer Legal & Regulatory U.S.
7201 McKinney Circle
Frederick, MD 21704
United States of America
Email: customer.service@wolterskluwer.com

*Sold and distributed in all other countries by:*
Quadrant
Rockwood House
Haywards Heath
West Sussex
RH16 3DH
United Kingdom
Email: international-customerservice@wolterskluwer.com

ISBN 978-90-411-9196-0

e-Book: ISBN 978-90-411-9197-7
web-PDF: ISBN 978-90-411-9198-4

# About the Author

Felix Lessambo is Adjunct Associate Professor at The Peter J. Tobin College of Business at St. John's University, United States, where he teaches International Taxation, Corporate Tax, Individual Tax Planning, Specialized Topics in Federal Income Tax, Financial Reporting: Evaluation and Analysis, Intermediate Accounting 1&2. He specializes in International Transfer Pricing, International Finance, Alternative Investment Vehicles, International Banking System, International Corporate Governance System, and International Financial Institutions.

# Table of Contents

# Disclaimer

While the author has made every effort to ensure that the information in this book is correct at the time of publication, he does not assume and hereby disclaims any liability to any party for any loss, damage, or disruption caused by errors or omissions, whether such errors or omissions result from negligence, accident, or any other cause.

This publication is designed to provide accurate and authoritative information in regards to the subject matter covered. It is sold on the understanding that the publisher is not engaged in rendering professional services. If professional advice or other expert assistance is needed, the services of a competent professional should be sought.

# Foreword

Transfer pricing lies at the core of international taxation. International tax rules are ultimately about the division of the income from cross-border transactions among taxing jurisdictions, and transfer pricing is the most directly applicable set of rules that directly address this issue. In addition, it is a multi-billion dollar practice area, and the top tax concern of most multinationals.

Dr. Felix Lessambo's book on *Transfer Pricing in the US: A Practical Guide* is the best and most up-to-date summary of current transfer pricing practices available today. It begins with a general introduction to transfer pricing, and then discusses the current Organisation for Economic Co-operation and Development's (OECD) Transfer Pricing Guidelines, which form the basis for most transfer pricing rules around the world. Thereafter, Dr. Lessambo delves in depth into the US approach to transfer pricing, including practical case studies. He describes in detail the approved methods for tangible and intangible property, cost sharing, services, and the best method rule. Each of these includes detailed case studies as well. Dr. Lessambo then discusses functional analysis for the various methods, as well as the necessary documentation and penalty rules. Finally, the book addresses advance pricing agreements and current developments, including the OECD BEPS project, Country-by-Country reporting, European Union state aid, and business restructurings.

This book is an indispensable resource for practitioners and academics. There is no better short introduction to the subject.

*Reuven S. Avi-Yonah*

# List of Abbreviations

| | |
|---|---|
| AAS | Automated Assembly of Singapore |
| ADI | Apple Distributions International |
| ADR | Alternative Dispute Resolution |
| AOI | Apple Operations International |
| APA | Advanced Pricing Agreement |
| APMA | Advance Pricing Mutual Agreement |
| ARP | Average Realized Price |
| ASI | Apple Sales International |
| BEPS | Base Erosion and Profit Shifting |
| CA | Competent Authority |
| CbC Report | Country-by-Country Report |
| CCCTB | Common Consolidated Corporate Tax Base |
| CEM | Combination Export Manager |
| CP Method | Cost Plus Method |
| CPM | Comparable Profits Method |
| CPS Method | Comparable Profit Split Method |
| CPUs | Central Processing Units |
| CRDM | Cardiac Rhythm Disease Management |
| CSA | Cost Sharing Arrangement |
| CST | Cost Sharing Transaction |
| CTA | Compania Transporte Arroyo |
| CTI | Consolidated Taxable Income |
| CUP | Comparable Uncontrolled Price method |
| DHLI | Document Handling Limited, International |
| ECJ | European Court of Justice |

| | |
|---|---|
| ETR | Effective Tax Rate |
| EU | European Union |
| FMV | Fair Market Value |
| FY | Fiscal Year |
| GAAP | Generally Accepted Accounting Principles |
| GLAM | Generic Legal Advice Memorandum |
| IDA | Industrial Development Authority |
| IP | Intangible Property |
| IRC | Internal Revenue Code |
| IRS | Internal Revenue Service |
| JTC | Joint Tax Committee |
| LB&I | Large Business & International |
| LoB | Limitation-on-Benefits |
| MAP | Mutual Agreement Procedure |
| MAPS | Managed Account Product Structure |
| MCAA | Multilateral Competent Authority Agreement |
| MENA | Middle East and North Africa |
| MNE | Multinational Enterprise |
| NOPA | Notice of Proposed Adjustment |
| OECD | Organisation for Economic Co-operation and Development |
| PCT | Platform Contribution Transaction |
| PE | Permanent Establishment |
| PFRP | Purchased Finished Replacement Parts |
| PLDs | Programmable Logic Devices |
| PLI | Profit Level Indicator |
| PSM | Profit Split Method |
| QCSA | Qualified Cost Sharing Agreement |
| ROA | Return on Assets |
| ROCE | Return on Capital Employed |
| ROE | Return on Equity |
| ROS | Return on Sales |
| RPM | Resale Price Method |
| RPSM | Residual Profits Split Method |
| SCM | Service Cost Method |
| SFA | Sales Factor Apportionment |
| STI | Separate Taxable Income |

| | |
|---|---|
| T.C. | Tax Court |
| TEFRA | Tax Equity and Fiscal Responsibility Act |
| TFEU | Treaty on the Functioning of the European Union |
| TIEAs | Tax Information Exchange Agreements |
| TIN | Tax Identification Number |
| TPA | Transfer Pricing Operations |
| TPM | Transfer Price Methodology |
| TQM | Total Quality Management |
| TRA | Tax Reform Act |
| USNE | US Net Equity |
| USP | United States Parent |
| WQI | Withholding Qualified Intermediary |

# List of Figures

CHAPTER 1

# Overview of Transfer Pricing

## 1.1 INTRODUCTION

Transfer pricing is a method of pricing goods and services transferred within a multinational or transnational company in order to reduce tax burdens and maximize profits. The purpose of transfer pricing is to push profits into territories where either the tax rates are more favorable or more loopholes exist to be exploited.

Transfer pricing is not, per se, illegal or abusive.[1] Transfer pricing is portrayed as a technique for optimal allocation of costs and revenues amongst divisions, subsidiaries, and joint ventures within a group of related entities. In our twenty-first century economy, where multinational enterprises (MNEs) have become dominant players, transfer pricing has simultaneously become the new game. In 2010, 42 of the 100 largest economies in the world were MNEs, not countries. Total revenues of the five largest MNEs were larger than the combined gross domestic product of the world's poorest 110 countries. The top 100 largest MNEs controlled assets of USD 3,400 billion, of which 40 percent were located outside their home countries.

Of the USD 30 trillion in cross-border sales of goods and services that occur every year, about one-third is from intragroup transactions or transactions among members of the same corporate groups or multinational companies. A recent study by Professor Zdamowicz reveals that the US loses USD 2.3 trillion in tax revenue due to strategic mispricing of domestic trade goods and other criminal money laundering activities.[2]

By 2015, more than fifty countries had adopted transfer pricing rules based on the "Arm's Length" Principle (ALP).

Profit maximization seems to be the companies' ultimate goal. Meanwhile, national tax authorities, in both developed and developing, are struggling to keep their fair share of taxation from profits derived by MNEs. Transfer price manipulation defies

1. Tax justice network (2014) Transfer pricing background @ http://www.taxjustice.net.
2. Money News (Miami, August 2, 2016).

existing accounting, and auditing rules, since accounting and auditing programs have failed to include it in their curricula. Paradoxically, some auditing rules such as SAS 99 list transfer pricing among risk factors associated with fraud. Indeed, SAS 99 requires that auditors examine:

- significant related-party transactions not in the ordinary course of business or with related entities not audited or audited by another firm; and
- significant operations located or conducted across international borders in jurisdictions where differing business environments and cultures exist.

## 1.2 DOMESTIC AND INTERNATIONAL TRANSFER PRICING

Although transfer pricing can occur in a purely domestic transaction between related entities, the nature of international transactions between or among related entities from different countries or jurisdictions seems to encourage such type of manipulations.

Example of domestic transfer pricing

- Toys "R" Us is a global MNC incorporated in the state of New Jersey.
- Toys "R"Us sets up a subsidiary "Geoffrey Inc." and incorporates it in the state of Delaware.
- Toys "R" Us transfers some intangibles (trademarks) to Geoffrey inc.
- Geoffrey Inc. owns several trademarks—including Geoffrey, the Toys "R" Us giraffe—and trade names (including Toys "R" Us).
- Toys "R" Us pays royalties to Delaware-based Geoffrey Inc. to use the trademark and trade name. The tax impact of this is to reduce Toys "R" Us's taxable income in places where royalty payments are tax deductible, and shift it to Delaware, which does not tax royalty income.

MNEs engage in transfer pricing for multiple reasons, including: (i) reduction of transaction costs; (ii) cross-border shift of intangibles; (iii) maximization of the overall after-tax profit of the whole group; and (iv) tax loophole opportunities.

According to the last Transfer Pricing Report by the Auditing Firm—Ernst & Young—transfer pricing has become a multi-billion USD business industry. Many tax administrations, including the Internal Revenue Service (IRS) appear unequipped to face the worldwide transfer pricing machinery. The US Government Accountability Office states that:

> Two types of activities among related parties—cost-sharing arrangements and services transactions—were key sources of transfer pricing abuse.[3]

3. US Government Accountability Office, 2008, pp. 31-32.

The UK tax collection department (the "HRMC") estimates that around 25 percent or GBP 8 billion of the collectible tax revenues are not accounted for due to transfer pricing manipulation.

Among emerging economies (China, India, South Africa, and Brazil), tax authorities have complained about international transfer pricing manipulation. The Chinese government official stated that tax evasion through transfer pricing accounts for 60 percent of total tax evasion by multinational companies. Developing countries are even more exposed to transfer pricing manipulation as they are fighting to attract investments from MNEs within their respective boundaries tax. According to an NGO, Christian-Aid, around USD 365 billion a year is shifted from the richest MNEs to the poorest host countries.

Example of MNC transfer pricing abuse: IKEA

- The corporate structure is divided into two main parts: operations and franchising. Most of IKEA's operations, including the management of the majority of its stores, the design, and manufacture of its furniture, and purchasing and supply functions are overseen by INGKA Holding, a private, for-profit Dutch company.
- IKEA sells USD 28 billion furniture a year, making it the world's largest furniture company. But the retailer pays a small tax rate of just 3.5%—about a billion dollar—rather than the 18 percent rate it should pay. How? IKEA is a non-profit company dedicated to furthering the advancement of architecture and interior design—a cause to which they give a pittance of about USD 2 million per year.
- INGKA Holding is not an independent company, but is wholly owned by the Stichting INGKA Foundation, established in 1982 in the Netherlands as a tax-exempt, not-for-profit foundation.
- INGKA Holding is owned by the non-profit Stichting INGKA Foundation.
- While most IKEA stores operate under the direct purview of INGKA Holding and the INGKA Foundation, the IKEA trademark and concept is owned by an entirely separate Dutch company Inter IKEA Systems, headquartered in Delft. Every IKEA store, including those run by INGKA Holding, pays a franchise fee of 3% of revenue to Inter IKEA Systems.
- Inter IKEA Holding, in turn, belongs to an identically named company in the former Netherlands Antilles that is run by a trust company based in Curaçao.
- The royalties paid to Inter IKEA Systems are transferred through a chain of similarly named companies and eventually end up being administered by a trust company in Curaçao, an island in the Dutch Caribbean, which refuses to name the beneficiaries of the trust.

Although not properly discussed in accounting and auditing scandals, transfer pricing manipulation was present in Enron, or WorldCom financial scandals. Enron, with the advice of Arthur Andersen, Deloitte & Touche, Chase Manhattan, Deutsche Bank, Bankers Trust and major law firms, created 3,500 domestic and foreign subsidiaries and affiliates, including places such as Turks and Caicos, Bermuda, and Mauritius. A US Senate inquiry into Enron's tax avoidance strategies noted that Enron by designing such transfer pricing policies had shifted income to tax havens. However, the Senate report stated that one aspect of Enron's business did raise persistent and significant transfer pricing issues. These issues involved the treatment of services performed by Enron for the benefit of related foreign entities in connection with its foreign infrastructure development business. Likewise, WorldCom was involved in transfer pricing manipulation for a variety of trademarks, trade names, brands, service marks, and other types of Intellectual Properties (IP). WorldCom registered all these IP in low-tax jurisdictions and licensed them to several subsidiaries within the group. WorldCom's insolvency examiner found that in some cases the royalties charged actually exceeded the company's consolidated net income each from 1998 to 2001, and in other cases represented 80 percent–90 percent of a subsidiary's net income. Over a four-year period covering 1998–2001, more than USD 20 billion was accrued as royalty fees for use of the company's intangible assets and most of the fees resulted from the licensing of management foresight. To combat transfer pricing manipulation, the US IRS has added 1,200 examiners in 2009 and 800 in 2010 to scrutinize transfer pricing manipulations. Despite the addition, the IRS remains vulnerable to MNEs' transfer pricing strategies.

Although transfer pricing has become a dominant topic in management, accounting, and law debates, the challenge is not new.[4]

## 1.3 US DECADES OF TRANSFER PRICING LEGISLATIONS

In the US, for instance, the earliest response to transfer pricing problem came by the 1917 Regulation.

- The 1917 Regulation

The 1917 Regulation allowed the commissioner to require related corporations to file consolidated returns "whenever necessary to more equitably determine the invested capital or taxable income." These returns provided detailed information on the corporations' relationships with other affiliates.

- Section 240(d) of Revenue Act 1921

Four years later, in 1921, the IRS enacted section 240(d), which required consolidated accounts and authorized the Commissioner to request consolidated returns for commonly controlled trades or businesses in order to compute their tax liability.

- Section 45 of the 1928 Revenue Act

The Revenue Act of 1928 replaced the mandatory consolidation regime and introduced for the very first time, the concepts of "clear reflection of income" and "prevention of tax evasion." Section 45 of the 1928 Act expressly allowed the Commissioner to restate

4. According to a recent survey conducted by Ernst & Young (2015) more than 90 percent of the surveyed multinational companies listed transfer pricing as one of their key concerns, and the corporate tax directors of the companies named transfer pricing as the most important item on their agendas.

income to determine the "true tax liability" of related domestic and foreign corporations as an effort to prevent tax avoidance and to ensure clear reflection of the income of the related parties.

- The 1934 Regulations

In 1934, the Internal Revenue Code (IRC) published regulations that introduced the concept of "arm's length." However, those regulations provided no specific guidance as to the transfer pricing method(s) to be used. Rather, the matter or issue was left to the courts to decide. Inconsistencies were observed all along jurisdictions as judges struggled to determine appropriate transfer pricing methods under various circumstances.

- The 1986 Reform

In 1986, Congress amended section 482 by adding a second sentence to IRC section 482, which required related-party transfers of intangible property to yield income "commensurate with the income attributable to the intangible." The commensurate-with-income standard for the transfer of intangible property was added under the belief that MNCs were engaged in IP migration at the expense of the Treasury.

## 1.4 TRANSFER PRICING IN INTERNATIONAL FORA

In 1995, the Organisation for Economic Co-operation and Development (OECD) introduced its Transfer Pricing Guidelines. These rules provided guidelines on cross-border services, intangibles, costs contribution arrangements, and advance pricing arrangements. They were further modified in 2010 to provide guidance on what transfer pricing method would be appropriate in a variety of circumstances. The underlying philosophy is that pricing of transferred resources should reflect how prices might be determined if the parts of the multinationals were not connected—which can be summarized as the ALP. In a world where about 60 percent of international trade occurs within, rather than between multinationals, the determination of that ALP becomes hypothetical.

By 2014, over 50 countries had adopted some form of a transfer pricing rule based on the ALP. In the wake of considerable media attention (notably focusing on US giants, including Starbucks, Apple, Amazon and Google), the OECD continues to refine its approach to develop further guidelines and delivered a complete review in 2015.

## 1.5 REASONS FOR TRANSFER PRICING MANIPULATIONS

The increase in global trade provides plenty of opportunities for MNCs to craft transfer pricing strategies that aim to reduce their overall tax exposure. Further, the emergence of micro-jurisdictions commonly referred to as "tax heavens" or "offshore financial centers" allows MNCs to book and route their transactions so as to dodge taxation in many jurisdictions.

There are jurisdictions located outside the US with no tax or very low rates of taxation, strict bank secrecy provisions, a lack of transparency in the operation of its tax system, and a lack of effective exchange of information with other countries. There are several common legal strategies for sheltering corporate income in such jurisdictions. The 50 largest US corporations currently stash about USD 1.4 trillion in offshore tax havens. The Panama Papers Scandal reveals that about USD 2 trillion of transactions have passed through the firm's hands. Whereas those centers account for only about 3 percent of the world trade, it is often alleged that half of all the world trade transits through them. No country is exempt from transfer pricing manipulation. Transfer pricing is more art than science, more judgment than precision.[5]

5. Prysuski, Martin & Lalapet, Srini (2005): A Comprehensive Look at the Berry Ratio in Transfer pricing, Tax Notes International, Volume 40, Number 8, p. 762.

CHAPTER 2

# The OECD Transfer Pricing Guidelines

## 2.1 INTRODUCTION

The OECD Transfer Pricing Guidelines establish principles for establishing intercompany transfer prices. They are based on the ALP. That is, associated enterprises should price transactions and allocate income and themselves as unrelated parties would have done.[1]

## 2.2 STATEMENT OF THE ARM'S LENGTH PRINCIPLE

Article 9 of the OECD Model Tax Convention provides the statement of the ALP.[2]

Paragraph 1 of Article 9 of the OECD Model Tax Convention, which forms the basis of bilateral tax treaties involving OECD member countries and an increasing number of non-member countries, provides:

> [Where] conditions are made or imposed between the two [associated] enterprises in their commercial or financial relations which differ from those which would be made between independent enterprises, then any profits which would, but for those conditions have accrued to one of the enterprises but by reason of those conditions, have not so accrued, may be included in the profits of that enterprise and taxed in accordance.

Paragraph 1 of Article 9 of the OECD Model Tax Convention lays also the foundation for comparability analyses, as it requires:[3]

- a comparison between conditions (including prices, but not only prices) made or imposed between associated enterprises and those which would be made

1. Andrus, Joseph (2012): Transfer Pricing and the Arm's Length Principle, World Commerce Review, June 2012. p. 28.
2. OECD (2010) Transfer Pricing Guidelines, p. 33.
3. OECD (2010) Transfer Pricing Guidelines, p. 34.

between independent enterprises, in order to determine whether a rewriting of the accounts for the purposes of calculating tax liabilities of associated enterprises is authorized under Article 9 of the OECD Model Tax; and
- a determination of the profits which would have accrued at arm's length, in order to determine the quantum of any rewriting of accounts.

The application of the ALP is generally based on a comparison of the conditions in an intragroup transaction with the conditions in transactions between independent companies. For such comparisons to be useful, the economically relevant characteristics of the situations being compared must be sufficiently comparable. To be comparable means that none of the differences (if any) between the situations being compared could materially affect the condition being examined in the methodology (e.g., price or margin), or that reasonably accurate adjustments can be made to eliminate the effect of any such differences. To establish the degree of actual comparability and then to make appropriate adjustments to establish arm's length conditions (or a range thereof), it is necessary to compare attributes of the transactions or companies that would affect conditions in arm's length transactions. The OECD Guidelines list as attributes or "comparability factors" that may be important when determining comparability: the characteristics of the property or services transferred; the functions performed by the parties, taking into account assets used and risks assumed (functional analysis); the contractual terms; the economic circumstances of the parties; and the business strategies pursued by the parties.

## 2.3 THE OECD TRANSFER PRICING METHODS

The OECD Transfer Pricing Guidelines (hereinafter the "OECD Guidelines") provides five such methods to approximate an arm's length pricing of transactions and profit allocation between companies of the same corporate group: (i) the Comparable Uncontrolled Price Method (hereinafter "CUP Method"); (ii) the Cost Plus (CP) Method; (iii) the Resale Minus Method; (iv) the Transactional Net Margin Method (hereinafter "TNMM"); and (v) the Transactional Profit Split Method (PSM). The OECD Guidelines draw a distinction between traditional transaction methods (the first three methods) and transactional profit methods (the last two methods). Multinational corporations retain the freedom to apply methods not described in those guidelines to establish transfer prices provided those prices satisfy the ALP.

Traditional transaction methods are regarded as the most direct means of establishing whether conditions in the commercial and financial relations between associated enterprises are at arm's length. All three traditional transaction methods approximate an arm's length pricing of a specific intragroup transaction, such as the price of a certain good sold or service provided to a related company. In particular, the CUP method consists in observing a comparable transaction between two independent companies and applying the same price for a comparable transaction between group companies. The CP method consists in approximating the income from goods sold or services provided to a group company. The resale minus method consists in approximating the costs of goods acquired from or services provided by a group company. Other elements which enter into the profit calculation (such as personal costs or interest expenses) are calculated based on the price effectively paid to an independent company or are approximated using one of the three direct methods.

The transactional profit methods, by contrast, do not approximate the arm's length price of a specific transaction, but are based on comparisons of net profit indicators (such as profit margins, return on assets, operating income to sales, and possibly other measures of net profit) between independent and associated companies as a means to estimate the profits that one or each of the associated companies could have earned had they dealt solely with independent companies, and therefore the payment those companies would have demanded at arm's length to compensate them for using their resources in the intragroup transaction. For this purpose, the TNMM relies on a net profit indicator which refers, in principle, to the ratio of profit weighted to an item of the profit and loss account or of the balance sheet, such as turnover, costs, or equity. To this selected item, a margin is applied which is considered "arm's length" to approximate the amount of taxable profit. When the TNMM is used in combination with a net profit indicator based on costs, it is sometimes referred to as "cost plus" in exchanges between the taxpayer and the tax administration, but this should not be confused with the "cost plus method" described in the OECD Guidelines.

## 2.4 THE STRENGTHS OF THE ALP

The practicality of the ALP has come under ferocious attack. The integration—both horizontal and vertical—of MNEs has deprived the theory from its relevancy. Very often the transactions within a group of related entities are promoted, arranged, designed, and conducted by the parent entities, while the related get reduced to compliance activities. In doing so, there remains very little to argue in favor of the arm's length theory. However, the OECD is still of the opinion that "while it may not always be straightforward to apply in practice, it does generally produce appropriate levels of income between members of MNE groups, acceptable to tax administrations." This reflects the economic realities of the controlled taxpayer's particular facts and circumstances and adopts as a benchmark the normal operation of the market. The OECD member countries continue to believe and insist that the ALP should govern the evaluation of transfer prices among associated enterprises. That is, opponents of the arm's length theory still argue that the "theoretical benchmark" reflects the economic realities of the controlled taxpayer's particular facts and circumstances and sticks with the market considerations.

## 2.5 UPDATING THE ALP

The ALP was articulated almost a century ago and seems to not have kept track with our modern economy: production and distribution functions are no longer integrated in one foreign country; multinational activities are more integrated and operate often under common control with shared agreed upon strategies. This reality is often overlooked by tax administrations. Multinational companies operate as an economic unit and not "as if" they were unrelated to their foreign subsidiaries.

However, shifting from the ALP would not be easy. It requires a determination of how income should be allocated among several tax jurisdictions.

Proponents of the ALP still argue that the ALP is sound in theory since it provides the closest approximation of the workings of the open market in cases where property (such as goods, other types of tangible assets, or intangible assets) is transferred or services are rendered between associated enterprises. While it may not always be straightforward to apply in practice, it does generally produce appropriate levels of income between members of MNE groups, acceptable to tax administrations.[4] OECD members, proponents of the ALP allege several arguments in support of their views against global apportionment:[5]

- Global formulary apportionment is difficult to implement in a manner that both protect against double taxation and ensure single taxation.
- Global formulary apportionment would require substantial international co-ordination and consensus on the predetermined formulae to be used and on the composition of the group in question.
- With global formulary apportionment, each country would have a strong incentive to devise formulae or formula weights that would maximize that country's own revenue.
- In addition, tax administrations would have to consider jointly how to address the potential for artificially shifting the production factors used in the formula (e.g., sales, capital) to low-tax countries.
- Their incentives for tax avoidance could even be high to the extent that the components of the relevant formula can be manipulated (e.g., by entering into unnecessary financial transactions, by the deliberate location of mobile assets, by requiring that particular companies within an MNE group maintain inventory levels in excess of what normally would be encountered in an uncontrolled company of that type, and so on).
- The transition to a global formulary apportionment system therefore would present enormous political and administrative complexity and require a level of international cooperation that is unrealistic to expect in the field of international taxation.
- Global formulary apportionment may in fact present intolerable compliance costs and data requirements because information would have to be gathered

4. OECD (July 22, 2010): Review of Comparability and Profit Methods: Revision of Chapters I–III of the Transfer Pricing Guidelines, p. 8.
5. OECD (July 2010): Review of Comparability and Profit Methods: Revision of Chapters I–III of the Transfer Pricing Guidelines, pp. 8–9.

about the entire MNE group and presented in each jurisdiction on the basis of the currency and the book and tax accounting rules of that particular jurisdiction.

On the other side, opponents of the ALP often cite the global apportionment method as the credible alternative. Formulary Apportionment (FA) focuses on the worldwide net income of a business, regardless of where the income is earned, by taking a corporation's worldwide income and subtracting its worldwide expenses.[6]

Professors Avi-Yonah and Clausing, for instance, argued that the current inadequate system can be replaced by a FA:

> Under FA, a unitary business is defined based on whether the parent corporation exercises legal and economic control over its subsidiaries. That unitary business is treated as a single taxpayer and its income is calculated by subtracting worldwide expenses from worldwide income, based on a global accounting system, without regard to legal distinctions among units.[7]

The authors pursued that FA would eliminate the tax incentive to shift income to low-tax countries as MNEs are taxed on their global profits rather than on Country-by-Country (CbC) profits.[8] Simplicity is another advantage provided by the FA. In the complex field of transfer pricing, FA can accommodate the parties (IRS, MNEs) by: (i) determining which businesses are unitary, and (ii) establishing the destination of arm's length sales of goods or services.[9]

Notwithstanding the objections expressed by the proponents of the ALP, global apportionment has its distinctive advantages: (i) it reduces the emphasis on the corporate structure of a business, as illustrated with the IKEA corporate structure, (ii) it reduces the compliance cost, and (iii) it is administratively more efficient than the current status quo.

### 2.5.1 Sales Factor FA

Recently, a group of individuals interested in fixing the corporate tax system[10] submitted a proposal to the US Senate Finance Committee. The authors allege that the US should abandon the fictional ALP and shift toward Sales Factor Apportionment (SFA), which is a unitary system that uses apportionment. The SFA as a method of allocating earnings for income tax purposes is a sound alternative that would close

6. Osborne, David A. (2011): Deterring Transfer Pricing Abuse: Changing Incentives as a Practical Alternative to a Global Tax Regime, Washington University Global Studies Law Review, Volume 10- Issue 4-, p. 825.
7. Avi-Yonah, Reuven and Clausing, Kimberley (2007): Reforming Corporate Taxation in a Global Economy: A Proposal to Adopt Formulary Apportionment, The Hamilton Project, p. 12.
8. Avi-Yonah, Reuven & Clausing, Kimberley (2007): Reforming Corporate Taxation in a Global Economy: A Proposal to Adopt Formulary Apportionment, The Hamilton Project, p. 14.
9. *Idem.*, p. 15.
10. The group identifies itself as "Salesfactor.org" and is led by Jerry Wegman, Bill Parks & Walt Minnick.

existing loopholes, profit shifting, corporate inversion, and base erosion.[11] They view their approach as more rational and efficient relative to the ALP because it more closely corresponds to the economic reality.[12]

The authors point to other advantages of their approach, *inter alia*:

- it eliminates the international competitive disadvantage of US MNCs;
- it levels the playing field between US domestic companies and their MNC competitors;
- it eliminates the most egregious tax avoidance practices;
- it provides more efficient and transparent tax administration;
- it stimulates exports.

Among the different factors often used for global apportionment, the authors argued that a sales-only formula suits the US interests for four reasons:[13] (i) sales is the least fungible and is the factor that companies will be least likely to forgo. As a result, a formula based solely on sales causes the least amount of economic distortion, thus maximizing economic efficiency; (ii) it eliminates any competitive disadvantage that US multinationals face because of the US's relatively high corporate tax rate. Income from sales in foreign countries would be taxed at those countries' rates; (iii) it encourages exports because income from export sales is not taxed; and (iv) it levels the competitive playing field between US domestic and all multinational companies.

The cavalier approach alleged by the authors has no chance to get the acceptance of the international tax community as it fails to consider the multiple interests of the parties at stake. The unitary sale formula approach would trigger a war among various tax authorities, which would have interests to use FA factors distinct from sales.

### 2.5.2 The Compromise: Use of FA in the Context of the ALP

Although the OECD has never adopted the US Comparable Profit Methods (CPMs), it has recognized and adopted the TNMM, which requires a tougher comparability test than the US CPM.[14] Professor Avi-Yonah proposes that we combine the strengths and weaknesses of both the amorphous ALP and the FA. He noted that:

(i) ALS and formulary methods are not mutually exclusive.[15] The two can be integrated in order to strike a compromise.
(ii) The currently admitted practice of FA in the contest of residual profit under the PSM can be extended and enhanced. Rather than allocating the residual

11. Wegman, Jerry (2015): Sales Factor Formulary Apportionment of Global Profits as an Alternative System of Taxation of to the Current U.S. Federal Corporate Income Tax, p. 2.
12. *Idem.*, p. 12.
13. *Idem.*, p. 12.
14. Avi-Yonah, Reuven (2009): Between Formulary Apportionment and the OECD: A Proposal for Reconciliation, University of Michigan Law School Scholarship Repository, p. 13.
15. Avi-Yonah, Reuven (2011): Formulary Apportionment—Myths and Prospects- Promoting Better International Policy and Utilizing the Misunderstood and Under-Theorized Formulary Alternative, University of Michigan law School Scholarship Repository, p. 381.

profit based on each related-party contribution, the profit split of the remaining profit should better be split among related parties under a FA.[16]

### 2.5.3 The EU Common Consolidated Corporate Tax Base

Faced with a huge profit shifting among countries, the European Union (EU) is considering strengthening the Member States' territorial tax systems by adopting FA,[17] which would create a single set of rules for the EU companies in their determination and reporting income. Many EU MNCs operate through schemes structured to accommodate their frequent cross-border transactions, defeating the weak ALP.

Under the optional Common Consolidated Corporate Tax Base (CCCTB), a multinational corporation that operates in multiple EU countries would have to apportion its profits (or losses) among member countries based on a formula that would have to take into account the location of the assets, labor force, and sales. The EU's underlying thought is that those factors of production are harder to artificially shift easily through accounting maneuvers as opposed to IP or financing expenses. Each country would then tax its share of the profits at its corporate tax rate.[18] The main positive effect of the CCCTB proposal stems from the assumed reduction in compliance costs.[19]

Still, there is no such guarantee that Member States would agree upon.

16. *Idem.*, p. 383.
17. Kleinbard, Edward D. (2012): The Lessons of Stateless Income, Tax Law Review, Vol. 65, pp. 99–172.
18. Chye-Ching Huang (2013): The Fiscal and Economic Risks of Territorial Taxation, Center on Budget and Policy Priorities, p. 7.
19. European Commission (2011): Proposal for a Council Directive on a Common Consolidated Corporate Tax Base (WP), p. 6.

CHAPTER 3

# The US Transfer Pricing Approach

## 3.1 INTRODUCTION

IRC section 482 derives from section 45 of the Internal Revenue Code of 1928. The House report with reference to section 45 of the 1928 Code explained that its purpose was to allow the Commissioner to:

> distribute the income or deductions between or among [commonly controlled taxpayers] . . ., as may be necessary in order to prevent evasion (by the shifting of profits, the making of fictitious sales, and other methods frequently adopted for the purpose of 'milking'), and in order to clearly reflect their true tax liability.[1]

The caption of section 45 of the Revenue Act of 1928 was "Allocation of Income and Deductions." Its language is substantially identical to that in the present section 482.

IRC Section 482 authorizes the Secretary of the Treasury to allocate income, deductions, credits, or allowances among related business entities when necessary to clearly reflect income or otherwise prevent tax avoidance, and comprehensive Treasury regulations under that section adopt the arm's-length standard as the method of determining whether allocations are appropriate. Section 482 reads as follows:

> In any case of two or more organizations, trades, or businesses (whether or not incorporated, whether or not organized in the United States, and whether or not affiliated) owned or controlled directly or indirectly by the same interests, the Secretary may distribute, apportion, or allocate gross income, deductions, credits, or allowances between or among such organizations, trades, or businesses, if he determines that such distribution, apportionment, or allocation is necessary in order to prevent evasion of taxes or clearly to reflect the income of any of such organizations, trades, or businesses. In the case of any transfer (or license) of

1. H. Rep. No. 2, 70th Cong., 1st Sess., pp. 16–17 (1939-1 Cum. Bull. Part 2 384, 395).

> intangible property (within the meaning of Code Sec. 936(h)(3)(B)), the income with respect to such transfer or license shall be commensurate with the income attributable to the intangible.

The scope of IRC section 482 is very broad and covers almost all transactions.

A transaction between related parties meets the arm's-length standard if the results of the transaction are consistent with the results that would have been realized if unrelated taxpayers had engaged in the same transaction under the same circumstances. Because identical transactions between unrelated parties are rare, whether a transaction produces an arm's-length result generally is determined with reference to the results of transactions deemed to be comparable under circumstances. To evaluate comparability, the regulations require an analysis of all factors that could affect prices or profits in uncontrolled transactions. Each method requires an analysis of all the factors that affect comparability under that method, and a specific comparability factor may be particularly important to a particular method. The comparability factors include: (1) functions, (2) contractual terms, (3) risks, (4) economic conditions, and (5) the property or services transferred. Transfer pricing rules do not require that a comparable transaction be identical to the related-party transaction, but it must be sufficiently similar to the related-party transaction to provide a reasonable starting point for determining the arm's-length price. If there are material differences between the related-party transaction and the comparable transaction, adjustments are made to the relevant formulae, but only if it is possible to determine the impact of those differences on prices or profits with sufficient accuracy. If it is not possible to determine the impact of those differences on prices or profits with sufficient accuracy, the comparable transaction may be taken into account in establishing the arm's-length price, but it is considered a less-reliable measure of an arm's-length result.

In many cases, risk can be assigned by contract within an affiliated group to entities with the objective ability to bear such risk. However, whether the risks in the related-party transaction and in the comparable transaction are, in fact, comparable may be difficult to ascertain. Nonetheless, the respect given to contractual agreements between related companies is derived from the longstanding doctrine of Moline Properties v. Commissioner, in which the Supreme Court rejected the taxpayer's attempt to disregard the corporate form. Under the doctrine of corporate entity articulated in Moline Properties, the corporation remains a separate taxable entity.

## 3.2 IRC SECTION 482 PREREQUISITES

IRC section 482 states:

> In any case of two or more organizations, trades, or businesses (whether or not incorporated, whether or not organized in the United States, and whether or not affiliated) owned or controlled directly or indirectly by the same interests, the Secretary or his delegate may distribute, apportion, or allocate gross income, deductions, credits, or allowances between or among such organizations, trades, or businesses, if he determines that such distribution, apportionment, or allocation is necessary in order to prevent evasion of taxes or clearly to reflect the income of any such organizations, trades, or businesses.

To trigger IRC section 482, the Commissioner must establish three elements: (i) the existence of two or more organizations, trades/businesses; (ii) the common ownership or control; and (iii) his allocation determination is necessary to prevent tax evasion or to clearly reflect income.

### 3.2.1 Two or More Organizations, Trades, or Businesses

The terms "organization," "trade," and "business" are broadly defined in Treasury Regulation section 1.482-1(a)(1) and (2). In Borge v. Commissioner, the Tax Court (T.C.) found that an individual stockholder and his wholly owned corporation satisfied the two or more business prerequisites of section 482.

### 3.2.2 Common Ownership or Control

For section 482 to be applied, there must be two or more organizations, trades, or businesses owned or controlled directly or indirectly by the same interests. No definition of control is contained in section 482. However, it has been opined that this omission was intentional in order to allow for flexibility of administration. Guidelines for determining control are contained in Treasury Regulation 1.482-1(a)(3), which defines the term "controlled" to include:

> Any kind of control, direct or indirect, whether legally enforceable, and however exercisable or exercised. It is the reality of the control which is decisive, not its form or the mode of its exercise. A presumption of control arises if income or deductions have been arbitrarily shifted.

Actual control and not recorded ownership determine whether the statute applies. In order to find control, no percentage requirements are specified nor are any precise requirements necessary.

In using the term "same interests," Congress apparently intended to include more than "the same persons" or "the same individuals." Likewise, different persons with a common goal or purpose for artificially shifting income can constitute the "same interests" for the purposes of section 482.

By using the standards of an uncontrolled taxpayer to determine the controlled taxpayer's true taxable income, section 482 equalizes the treatment of controlled and uncontrolled taxpayers and prevents the artificial shifting of income between related businesses.

### 3.2.3 The Allocation Necessary to Prevent Tax Evasion or to Clearly Reflect Income

IRC section 482 gives the IRS (Service or Commissioner) broad authority to act when in his judgment it is necessary to prevent tax evasion or clearly to reflect income, and, accordingly, it has been uniformly held that a section 482 allocation will not be modified unless the petitioner proves that the allocation was arbitrary, unreasonable, or capricious. Whether the Service has inappropriately allocated items under section 482 is usually a question of fact. In reviewing the reasonableness of the Service's section 482 allocations, courts focus only on the reasonableness of the result and not on the details of the methodology employed. When allocating income within a consolidated group, the Service considers each corporation as a separate standalone taxpayer. Although section 1.482-1(b)(2)(ii) requires that the arm's length allocation be calculated by separately applying one or more methods in the case of interrelated transactions, the aggregation of these transactions may sometimes be more appropriate.[2] That is, the Service can evaluate the arm's length results by applying the appropriate methods to the overall results for product lines or other groupings, whenever it may be impractical to analyze the arm's length price of individual transactions. Further, IRC section 1.482-1T(f)(2)(i) provides that the combined effect of two or more separate transactions may be considered, if such transactions, taken as a whole, are so interrelated that consideration of multiple transactions is the most reliable means of determining the arm's length consideration for the controlled transactions.

## 3.3 THE ARM'S LENGTH STANDARD

While the OECD guidelines require that taxpayers use the traditional methods before considering the transactional ones, the US transfer pricing rules under section 482 and the regulations thereof require that taxpayers use the best method rule. That is taxpayers can use whatever admissible methods they see fit, provided that the methods provide the best arm's length, under the circumstances.

Section 1.482-1(a)(1) explains the purpose of section 482 as follows:

> The purpose of section 482 is to ensure that taxpayers clearly reflect income attributable to controlled transactions and to prevent the avoidance of taxes with respect to such transactions. Section 482 places a controlled taxpayer on a tax parity with an uncontrolled taxpayer by determining the true taxable income of the controlled taxpayer.

And IRC Section 1.482-1(b)(1) goes on to add:

> In determining the true taxable income of a controlled taxpayer, the standard to be applied in every case is that of a taxpayer dealing at arm's length with an uncontrolled taxpayer. A controlled transaction meets the arm's length standard if the results of the transaction are consistent with the results that would have been realized if uncontrolled taxpayers had engaged in the same transaction under the same circumstances (arm's length result). However, because identical transactions can rarely be located, whether a transaction produces an arm's length result generally will be determined, by reference, to the results of comparable transactions under comparable circumstances.

The OECD guidelines are used to provide a specific order in the choice of the arm's length methods. Recently, it has aligned its position within the US transfer

2. IRC sections 1.482-1(f)(2)(iv) and 1.482-1(f)(2)(i)(B).

pricing guidelines, which relies upon the arm's length best method(s). However, the best method can be a combination of more than one applicable method.

Treasury Regulation 1.482-1(d)(3) provides factors that taxpayers should consider in determining comparability. Taxpayers are allowed to make adjustments in order to improve the comparability of the controlled transactions with the asserted comparables.

These factors are described in the below sections.

### 3.3.1 Functions of the Parties

Determining the degree of comparability between controlled and uncontrolled transactions requires a comparison of the functions performed, and associated resources employed, by the taxpayers in each transaction. The comparison is based on a functional analysis that identifies and compares the economically significant activities undertaken, or to be undertaken, by the taxpayers in both controlled and uncontrolled transactions. A functional analysis should also include consideration of the resources that are employed, or to be employed, in conjunction with the activities undertaken, including consideration of the type of assets used, such as plant and equipment, or the use of valuable intangibles. A functional analysis is not a pricing method and does not itself determine the arm's length result for the controlled transaction under review. Functions that may need to be accounted for determining the comparability of two transactions include:

(a) research and development;
(b) product design and engineering;
(c) manufacturing, production, and process engineering;
(d) product fabrication, extraction, and assembly;
(e) Purchasing and materials management;
(f) marketing and distribution functions, including inventory management, warranty administration, and advertising activities;
(g) transportation and warehousing; and
(h) managerial, legal, accounting and finance, credit and collection, training, and personnel management services.

### 3.3.2 Contractual Terms

Determining the degree of comparability between the controlled and uncontrolled transactions requires a comparison of the significant contractual terms that could affect the results of the two transactions. When a written agreement does exist between the parties, the IRS will respect the contractual terms as long as they are consistent with the economic substance of the underlying transactions. In the absence of a written agreement, the district director may impute a contractual agreement between the controlled taxpayers consistent with the economic substance of the transaction.

In considering the economic substance of the transaction, the following facts are relevant:

(1) whether the pattern of the controlled taxpayer's conduct over time is consistent with the purported allocation of risk between the controlled taxpayers; or where the pattern is changed, whether the relevant contractual arrangements have been modified accordingly;
(2) whether a controlled taxpayer has the financial capacity to fund losses that might be expected to occur as the result of the assumption of a risk, or whether, at arm's length, another party to the controlled transaction would ultimately suffer the consequences of such losses; and
(3) the extent to which each controlled taxpayer exercises managerial or operational control over the business activities that directly influence the amount of income or loss realized. In arm's length dealings, parties ordinarily bear a greater share of those risks over which they have relatively more control.

These most relevant contractual terms include:

(1) the form of consideration charged or paid;
(2) sales or purchase volume;
(3) the scope and terms of warranties provided;
(4) rights to updates, revisions, or modifications;
(5) the duration of relevant license, contract, or other agreements, and termination or renegotiation rights;
(6) collateral transactions or ongoing business relationships between the buyer and the seller, including arrangements for the provision of ancillary or subsidiary services; and
(7) extension of credit and payment terms.

### 3.3.3 Assignment Risks

Determining the degree of comparability between controlled and uncontrolled transactions requires a comparison of the significant risks that could affect the prices that would be charged or paid, or the profit that would be earned, in the two transactions. Relevant risks to consider include:

(1) market risks, including fluctuations in cost, demand, pricing, and inventory levels;
(2) risks associated with the success or failure of research and development activities;
(3) financial risks, including fluctuations in foreign currency rates of exchange and interest rates;
(4) credit and collection risks;

(5) product liability risks; and
(6) general business risks related to the ownership of property, plant, and equipment.

### 3.3.4 Economic Conditions

Determining the degree of comparability between controlled and uncontrolled transactions requires a comparison of the significant economic conditions that could affect the prices that would be charged or paid, or the profit that would be earned in each of the transactions. These factors include:

(a) the similarity of geographic markets;
(b) the relative size of each market, and the extent of the overall economic development in each market;
(c) the level of the market (e.g., wholesale, retail);
(d) the relevant market shares for the products, properties, or services transferred or provided;
(e) the location-specific costs of the factors of production and distribution;
(f) the extent of competition in each market with regard to the property or services under review;
(g) the economic condition of the particular industry, including whether the market is in contraction or expansion; and
(h) the alternatives realistically available to the buyer and seller.

### 3.3.5 Property or Services Rendered by Either Party

Evaluating the degree of comparability between controlled and uncontrolled transactions requires a comparison of the property or services transferred in the transactions. This comparison may include any intangibles that are embedded in tangible property or services being transferred. The relevance of product comparability in evaluating the relative reliability of the results will depend on the method applied.

## 3.4 THE ARM'S LENGTH RANGE

In some cases, application of a pricing method will produce a single result that is the most reliable measure of an arm's length result. In other cases, application of a method may produce a number of results from which a range of reliable results may be derived. A taxpayer will not be subject to adjustment if its results fall within such range (arm's length range). Thus, the arm's length price may not be a single price. Rather, it is a price within a bracket. The arm's length range is ordinarily determined by applying a single pricing method selected under the best method rule to two or more uncontrolled transactions of similar comparability and reliability.

Uncontrolled comparables must be selected based upon the comparability criteria relevant to the method applied and must be sufficiently similar to the controlled transaction that they provide a reliable measure of an arm's length result. If material differences exist between the controlled and uncontrolled transactions, adjustments must be made to the results of the uncontrolled transaction if the effect of such differences on price or profits can be ascertained with sufficient accuracy to improve the reliability of the results.[3]

### 3.4.1 The Full Range

The full range can be used if the transactions meet all the following criteria:[4]

- when the controlled and uncontrolled transactions are sufficiently similar;
- all material differences have been identified; and
- adjustments are made to eliminate the effect of such differences.

In the event there are no uncontrolled comparables, the arm's length range is derived from the results of all the uncontrolled comparables that achieve a similar level of comparability and reliability. In such cases the reliability of the analysis must be increased. The reliability of the analysis is increased when statistical methods are used to establish a range of results in which the limits of the range will be determined such that there is a 75 percent probability of a result falling above the lower end of the range and a 75 percent probability of a result falling below the upper end of the range.

Example 1: Determination of the AL range on a full range

- Alexandra Corp. ("AlCorp") is a US domestic corporation based in Florida. AlCorp manufactures and sells wigs worldwide.
- AlCorp has two wholly owned subsidiary based in Brussels ("AlBruss") and Paris ("AlPar").
- In 2015, AlCorp sold 10,000 wigs (at USD 5 each) to AlBruss and Alpar, respectively.
- AlCorp also sold to unrelated corporations in Middle East and North Africa (MENA), the same wigs for USD 4.5 each. In 2015, the proceeds from the MENA equaled USD 450,000.
- Assuming that all the transactions are sufficiently similar, and small marketing differences have identified and adjusted accordingly, AlCorp may determine its AL range on a full range.

### 3.4.2 The Interquartile Range

The interquartile range (IQR) is the difference between the highest and lowest figures in the price data set. The IQR represents the range from the 25th percentile to the 75th

3. IRC section 1.482-1(d)(2).
4. IRS-ISI/9422.09_06(2013).

percentile. For this purpose, the 25th percentile is the lowest result derived from an uncontrolled comparable such that at least 25 percent of the results are at or below the value of that result. However, if exactly 25 percent of the results are at or below a result, then the 25th percentile is equal to the average of that result and the next higher result derived from the uncontrolled comparables. The 75th percentile is determined analogously." Regulation section 1.482-1(e)(2)(iii)(C).

It is often seen as more effective the full range as it shows the dispersion range rather than just one number.

Formulae:

- Upper quartile (UQ) = $(n + 1) / 4$
- Lower quartile (LQ) = $((n + 1) / 4) \times 3$
- IQR = UQ - LQ
- N = number of items in the data set

Several steps must be considered in order to determine the IQR:

- Step 1: Put the data in rank order from the smallest to the largest.
- Step 2: Calculate the demarcation value for the first quartile.
- Step 3: Calculate the demarcation value for the third quartile.
- Step 4: Calculate the interquartile range.

Example: Interquartile range

(a) US Corp. is a US Manufacturing Corporation based in Seattle, Washington.
(b) US Corp. has five wholly owned subsidiaries in (i) London, (ii) Paris, (iii) Geneva, (iv) Brussels, and (v) Prague.
(c) US Corp. sold and delivered the wigs it produces to the five subsidiaries as well as to other unrelated entities worldwide.
(d) From 2013 to 2015 the subsidiaries have reported the following gross profit margin:
    (i) London: 3.5%
    (ii) Paris: 3.8%
    (iii) Geneva: 4.0%
    (iv) Brussels: 45%
    (v) Prague: 5.0%
(e) During the same period (2013–2015) US Corp. sold to three unrelated entities which reported the following gross profit margins:
    (i) Yunok (Vietnam): 2.2%
    (ii) Chin (China): 2.4%
    (iii) Irishgates (Ireland): 2.5%
(f) The IRS is challenging the range price of the transactions between US Corp. and its European subsidiaries under IRS section 482.

Task: Compute the IQR

- Step 1: put the data in rank order from the smallest to the largest
  2.2, 2.4, 2.5, 3.5, 3.8, 4.0, 4.5, 5.0
- Step 2: calculate the demarcation value for the first quartile
  LQ = (n + 1)/ 4 = (8 + 1)/4 = 9/4 = 2.25
  Since 2.25 falls between 2.2 and 2.4, we compute the average of the two numbers, which is 2.3.
- Step 3: calculate the demarcation value for the third quartile
  UQ = (n + 1 / 4) × 3 = 2.25 × 3 = 6.75
  Since the upper quartile falls between 4.0 and 4.5, we compute the average of the two numbers, which is 4.25
- Step 4: calculate the interquartile range
  IQR = UQ – LQ = 4.25 – 2.25 = 2.0

## 3.5 COURT CASES

### 3.5.1 Two or More Organizations, Trades, or Businesses

#### *3.5.1.1 Rubin v. Commissioner, 460 F.2d 1216 (2nd Cir. 1972)*

- Rubin Bros. was incorporated in New York in the early 1940s and was in the business of purchasing and reselling of wool waste. Rubin Bros. purchased wool waste throughout the world, doing 80 percent–90 percent of its purchasing in Europe.

- Rubin Bros. had three wholly owned subsidiaries: Wythe Fiber Corp. ("Wythe"), Milford Processing Co., Inc. ("Milford"), and Delaware Wool Co.
- Delaware Wool Co. was a broker of virgin-wool fiber. Wythe purchased orlon and nylon waste and paid Milford to reprocess the waste into fiber. Wythe then sold the fiber to textile mills throughout the country.
- Beginning in 1941, Dorman Mills was a customer of Rubin Bros. Dorman Mills purchased approximately 50 percent of its fiber requirements from Rubin Bros. Sales to Dorman Mills accounted for approximately 10 percent of the annual wool fiber sales of Rubin Bros.
- As an employee and officer of Rubin Bros., a creditor and supplier of Dorman Mills, Richard Rubin was contemporaneously aware of the unprofitable operating situation at Dorman Mills.
- Due to the feud between the Estate of Thomas Dorman and the CEO of Dorman Mills, Rubin Bros. offered to buy one-half of the shares owned by the estate. Accordingly, on August 13, 1956, Rubin Bros. purchased from the estate 1,050 shares of Dorman Mills for USD 42,000 or USD 40 per share.
- As of December 1956 the Rubin interests controlled 1,182 of the 6,000 outstanding shares of Dorman Mills. Their block was comprised of Richard's 132 shares and Rubin Bros.' 1,050 shares.
- On February 25, 1957, Richard, among others, was elected to the board of directors of Dorman Mills. In this capacity he represented his interests as well as those of Rubin Bros.
- On June 27, 1957, Richard Rubin, in his efforts to revitalize Dorman Mills, executed a four-year option to purchase Franklin Dorman's 3,142 shares of Dorman Mills for USD 102,000.
- On June 27, 1957, a contract was executed between Dorman Mills, Franklin Dorman, and Richards Associates, Inc. ("Park"). The contract provided that Park would manage Dorman Mills for four years at a compensation equal to 25 percent of the net profits of Dorman Mills in excess of USD 25,000. In addition, the contract provided that Richard would personally receive an expense allowance of USD 100 per week.
- Park agreed to loan USD 20,000 to Dorman Mills. The agreement further provided that Dorman Mills would attempt to obtain additional financing, not in excess of USD 150,000, to which the USD 20,000 indebtedness to Park would be subordinated. Finally, the agreement provided that Dorman Mills would hire Franklin Dorman as a management consultant for four years at a fixed salary plus a percent of its profits. Richard signed the contract as president of Park.
- Throughout the course of the Park-Dorman Mills management-service relationship, Richard worked for Rubin Bros. and some of its subsidiaries in addition to doing his work for Dorman Mills.
- From July 1, 1957, to December 31, 1961, the last day of the last taxable year involved herein, Richard, William, and Larry were the three directors of Park.

- In July 1957, Dorman Mills obtained a USD 100,000 loan commitment from the First National Bank of Baltimore. The loan was secured by corporate machinery and by Richard's personal assets. Dorman Mills received USD 50,000 of the loan on July 31, 1957, and the remaining USD 50,000 on January 13, 1958.
- On or about September 24, 1958, The SBA extended a loan of USD 250,000 to Dorman Mills. As finally negotiated, Richard was required to personally guarantee 50 percent of the loan and to assign as security a USD 50,000 life insurance policy on his life.
- On November 10, 1958, Richard purchased from the Estate of Franklin Dorman the 3,112 shares of Dorman Mills that the decedent had owned. As of November 10, 1958, the Rubin interests controlled 4,324 of the 6,000 outstanding shares of Dorman Mills. On December 20, 1958, Richard acquired 122 shares of Dorman Mills from four minority stockholders for a total of USD 2,440.
- In his employment agreement of July 1, 1963, with Dorman Mills, Richard agreed to act as chairman of the board and chief executive officer of Dorman Mills and to receive an annual salary of USD 35,000. By its terms, the employment agreement was not assignable. Since United Merchants acquired Dorman Mills, Richard has managed Dorman Mills as an employee-officer. Effective December 1, 1965, Richard was appointed director of a new office for Market Planning and Analysis for United Merchants.
- All management fees received by Park were attributable to services performed for Dorman Mills or its subsidiary, Bradfield Mills. Richard performed all the management services for which fees were paid to Park.
- On its Federal corporate income tax returns during the years relevant hereto, Park consistently reported as part of its gross income the fees received from Dorman Mills and deducted the expenses allocable thereto. On his Federal individual income tax returns for the taxable years 1960 and 1961, Richard reported as salary received from Park USD 8,750 and USD 6,900, respectively.
- The Commissioner issued a statutory notice of deficiency for the taxable years 1960 and 1961 that income reported as management fees by Park International, Inc. and related expenses deducted by Park International, Inc. should have been allocable to Richard.
- Rubin contended that section 482 was inapplicable, primarily because of the absence of any organization, trade, or business other than Park.
- The T.C. held Rubin's furnishing of management services to Dorman constituted an organization, trade, or business separate from that of Park. That Richard controlled Park by virtue of his 70 percent ownership of its stock... That he also controlled Dorman Mills through the combination of his outright ownership of its stock and his option to purchase its stock which gave him voting power during the option period... That after acquiring the shares of Franklin Dorman and Mary Dorman, Richard controlled Dorman Mills through outright ownership of stock alone.
- The Circuit Court upheld the T.C. decision on the basis that:

Rubin's rendition of management services to Dorman, for which Park was paid sums largely in excess of Rubin's salary and any associated expenses, was as much a trade or business as Borge's furnishing entertainment services for which his controlled corporation was paid sums far greater than it paid him. It is immaterial that Borge had been in the entertainment business long before the formation of the controlled corporation whereas Rubin, although engaged in the textile business for many years, began his services to Dorman concurrently with the formation of Park. It is likewise immaterial that tax avoidance loomed large in Borge's plan; existence of such a motive is not a prerequisite for application of Sec. 482. Save in this last respect, the case seems a fortiori to Ach, where the taxpayer simply continued to render services to her former dress business whose assets had been acquired by a corporation under common control.

### 3.5.1.2 *Cooper v. Commissioner, 64 T.C.576 (1975)*

- R. D. Cooper Construction Co., Inc., was a corporation organized under the laws of Louisiana.
- Prior to July 1, 1967, the Coopers were the proprietors of a construction firm established by Revel in 1945 and styled "R. D. Cooper Construction Co."
- On its returns filed for the fiscal years ended June 30, 1968, September 30, 1968, and September 30, 1969, the corporation reported gross profits derived from construction contracts in the following amounts: USD 237,132, USD 161,632, and USD 693,706, respectively.
- Both the Coopers and the corporation reported income derived from construction contracts in accordance with the completed contract method of accounting.
- The Coopers entered into no new construction contracts personally; but they did retain ownership of 56 contracts which were in the process of completion on June 30, 1967. As of that date, the Coopers had earned USD 463,172 in gross profits on these contracts, but they had not as yet been required to report these amounts under the completed contract method of accounting.
- Services performed by the corporation in connection with these contracts constituted 75 percent of the corporation's work in the second half of 1967 and 10.4 percent in the first half of 1968. By June 30, 1968, the 56 contracts were completed. The Coopers recognized gross profits of USD 830,945 on them.
- The corporation was not compensated by the Coopers for the services it performed in connection with the 56 contracts.
- On their joint Federal income tax returns filed for 1967 and 1968 the Coopers reported taxable income of USD 239,953 and USD 131,130.
- On its US Corporation income tax returns filed for its fiscal years ended June 30, 1968, September 30, 1968, and September 30, 1969, the corporation reported taxable income of USD 26,570, USD 9,896, and USD 46,864.
- The Commissioner contended that a material distortion in the petitioners' income resulted when the corporation used assets belonging to the Coopers on

jobs which it was engaged to perform, without having to pay rent. The Commissioner proposed to impute to the Coopers a reasonable rental for the corporation's use of their assets on jobs which it had contracted to perform and to allow the corporation a commensurate rental expense deduction.

- The Coopers contended that during the years in issue, the corporation did not have sufficient income to pay such rentals; and in consequence, that adjustment based upon them would result in the creation rather than the mere allocation of income.
- Looking at the record, the T.C. found that:

> When the corporation was organized to carry on the Coopers' pre-existing construction business, the Coopers did not supply it with all the resources which would have enabled it to conduct that business independently. Rather the Coopers retained ownership of all the depreciable assets which were essential to the conduct of the business and permitted the corporation to use those assets without charge on jobs which the corporation contracted to perform. By virtue of this arrangement, the Coopers continued to participate in a business enterprise within the intendment of section 482.

- Therefore, pursued the T.C., the Commissioner was authorized by section 482 to make an allocation such as he had proposed to ensure that the Coopers recognize the income derived from their assets. That, upon due consideration of the entire record, the T.C. decided that USD 18,572 represented a reasonable rental for 1967, and that USD 84,948 and USD 94,386 represented reasonable rentals for the first and second halves of 1968, respectively.

### 3.5.2 Common Ownership or Control

#### *3.5.2.1 Kerry Investment Co., v. Commissioner, 58 T.C. 479 (T.C. 1972)*

- Kerry Investment Co. ("Kerry"), was a Washington corporation having its office in Seattle, Washington. Kerry was a personal holding company with its assets consisting primarily of stocks, bonds, debentures, and notes and contracts receivable.
- Since its organization in 1929, Kerry has been owned and controlled by Albert S. Kerry, Sr., his wife, his children, and their families.
- At least since April 30, 1942, the Kerry family has also, directly or indirectly, controlled Kerry Timber Co. ("Timber"), and until its liquidation in 1948 the Seattle Medical Arts Building Co. ("Medical Arts"). From October 28, 1943 to December 29, 1948 Kerry owned all the outstanding capital stock of Medical Arts, and since December 29, 1950, it has owned all the outstanding capital stock of Timber.

- Timber was a Washington corporation engaged in the business of owning, leasing, and operating various commercial office buildings, apartment houses, and other real estate. Prior to its liquidation, Medical Arts operated the Medical Arts Building in downtown Seattle as lessee and owned and leased the South Court Apartments in Bremerton, Washington.
- On December 23, 1948, Medical Arts sold the Southcourt Apartments and the Medical Arts Building leasehold and equipment to Timber for USD 127,609.54. Kerry has held the contract since that time and had received no payments upon the deferred balance of the purchase price. Similarly, no interest had ever been paid on this indebtedness.
- On July 15, 1956, Timber purchased the First and Seneca Building for a purchase price of USD 169,000. In order to finance this purchase, Timber borrowed USD 18,000 from Kerry and USD 150,000 from the Washington Mutual Savings Bank. The loan from the bank has been repaid in full, but no payment of interest or principal has been made on the note payable to Kerry.
- On May 22, 1957, the petitioner sold to Timber certain common stock, preferred stock, and promissory notes of the Wilkeson Cut Stone Co. (Wilkeson). The total purchase price of USD 24,500.
- In 1958, Wilkeson paid in full the promissory notes and redeemed the preferred stock. No payments of interest or principal have ever been made on the demand note payable to Kerry.
- On September 18, 1957, Kerry sold debentures of General American Industries (General debentures), which had a face value of USD 45,000, to Timber for USD 24,617.50. No payments of interest or principal have been made on the note payable to Kerry.
- On October 13, 1959, Timber borrowed USD 20,000 from Kerry for the purpose of making a loan to Wilkeson. The loan from Kerry to Timber bore no interest, and the loan from Timber to Wilkeson bore 6 percent interest. Sometime before June 30, 1968, Wilkeson repaid the loan from Timber. No payments of interest or principal have been made on the loan from Kerry.
- On or around January 24, 1961, Timber purchased a parking lot situated adjacent to the Southcourt Apartments for a cash purchase price of USD 38,887.60. In order to finance the purchase, Timber borrowed USD 30,000 from Kerry. No payments of principal or interest have been made on the note.
- In 1966, Timber purchased the Colonial Building and the Grand Pacific Building for a total purchase price of USD 208,901 payable in cash. To finance this purchase, Timber borrowed USD 100,000 from Kerry on June 7, 1966, and USD 110,000 from the Washington Mutual Savings Bank on August 29, 1966. The loan from the bank was at 6.5 percent interest and was secured by a real and chattel mortgage covering the Medical Arts Building and the First and Seneca Building. Timber had made regular payments of principal and interest to the bank, but has not made any payments of interest or principal to Kerry.
- During the period from February 13, 1951 to April 3, 1958, Timber borrowed USD 57,500 from Kerry for the purpose of making improvements to the

Medical Arts Building and USD 36,000 for the purpose of making improvements to the First and Seneca Building. An additional USD 16,000 was borrowed from Kerry for the purpose of making improvements to both buildings. No interest or principal payments have been made on any of the notes.

- From September 23, 1948 to July 31, 1966, Kerry made open account advances of USD 255,888 to Timber for the purposes of providing Timber with funds for current operations, advances to tenants, and investments. Timber had repaid all but USD 59,000 of these advances. None of the open account advances bore interest.
- During the period from December 23, 1948 to December 10, 1957, Kerry also made interest-free loans of USD 88,021.98 to Timber for current operations, for improvements to real estate, and for other purposes. These loans had been repaid in full prior to January 1, 1966.
- During 1966 and 1967, Kerry extended several noninterest-bearing loans to Timber.
- Timber had not claimed any deductions for interest as the result of the loans to it by Kerry, and Kerry had not received or accrued any interest income from these loans. However, Timber, which computed its income on the basis of a fiscal year ending June 30, claimed deductions for interest paid on the loan by the Washington Mutual Savings Bank in the amounts of USD 479.57, USD 5,921.58, and USD 6,909.35, for its fiscal years ended in 1966, 1967, and 1968, respectively. Timber received interest income of USD 4,441.13, USD 4,223.32, and USD 3,682.83, for its fiscal years 1966, 1967, and 1968, respectively.
- For the calendar years 1966 and 1967, it timely filed its Federal income tax returns, using the accrual method of accounting, with the IRS office at Ogden, Utah.
- The Commissioner issued a statutory notice of deficiency, alleging that under section 482, Kerry's income should be increased for the years 1966 and 1967 by an amount equal to 5 percent of the interest-free indebtedness owed by Timber. That such adjustments were necessary to prevent the evasion of tax or clearly to reflect Kerry's income, and that correlative adjustments would be made in the returns of Timber.
- Kerry contended that: (i) such allocations constituted "income creation," (ii) the income tax liability of Timber and the petitioner would have been less if they did business as one corporation and that, therefore, no allocation is needed to prevent the evasion of taxes or to properly reflect income, and (iii) expenses must be allocated with gross income and that because Timber had net losses in 1966 and 1967, the allocation from Timber to the petitioner should reduce rather than increase the petitioner's taxable income.
- The T.C. found that:

> when a related party makes an interest-free loan, it has done all that is necessary to realize interest income, except charge interest; and some of the gross income which the borrower realizes from the use of the proceeds of

> the loan has, in reality, been earned by the funds of the lender. The regulations under section 482 provide for adjustments when one related person makes an interest-free loan to another related person, as well as when there are bargain sales between related persons.

- The T.C. held that the Commissioner was authorized to allocate gross income or deductions after he determined that such allocation was necessary clearly to reflect the income of the related persons. In this case, profits of Kerry were artificially shifted to Timber by making loans to it, without charging an arm's-length interest for the loans, to acquire or improve the rental properties.

### 3.5.3 Clearly Reflection of Income

#### *3.5.3.1 Philipp Brothers Chemicals, Inc. (N.Y.) v. Commissioner, 52 T.C. 240, 241 (T.C. 1969)*

- Philipp Bros., Inc., was a corporation engaged in extensive business activities involving metals and chemicals.
- In 1945 or 1946 Charles H. Bendheim ("Bendheim") acquired the chemicals department or business of that corporation. His father (S. Bendheim) and another person each owned 50 percent of the stock of Philipp Bros., Inc., and Bendheim's acquisition of the chemicals business was a consequence of his father's decision to retire and withdraw from the corporation.
- In May 1946 Bendheim formed Philipp Bros. Chemicals, Inc. (N.Y.), a New York corporation.
- Philipp Bros. Chemicals, Inc. (Mass.) ("Massachusetts") was organized on May 27, 1946 under the laws of Massachusetts as a wholly owned subsidiary of New York to conduct the chemicals business in the New England area.
- In July 1946, New York acquired all the stock of Philipp Bros. Chemicals, Inc. (Pa.) ("Pennsylvania"), and all the stock of Philipp Bros. Chemicals, Inc. (Md.) ("Maryland").
- Pennsylvania and Maryland had each been incorporated on March 22, 1944, under the laws of Pennsylvania and Maryland, respectively, as affiliates of Philipp Bros., Inc.
- In 1950, Philipp Brothers Chemicals, (NY) formed three more corporations: (i) Philipp Bros. Chemicals, Inc. ("Connecticut"); (ii) Philipp Bros. Chemicals Export Corp. ("Export"); and (iii) Philipp Bros. Chemicals, Inc. (R.I.) ("Rhode Island").
- In 1951, Philipp Brothers Chemicals, (NY) formed four other corporations: (i) Philipp Bros. Chemicals Pan-American Corp. ("Philipp Bros. Chemicals Pan-American Corp"); (ii) Philipp Bros. Chemicals International Co., Inc. ("International"); (iii) Philipp Bros. Chemicals Trans-America Corp. ("Trans-America"), and Phibro International Corp. ("Phibro").

- The bookkeeping and the shipping arrangements for all the petitioners were handled in the office of New York in New York City. None of the petitioners but New York had bookkeeping or traffic departments.
- Each petitioner served, or was formed to serve, a different selling function.
- Each petitioner filed a separate Federal income tax return, and each availed itself in computing its tax liability of the surtax exemption provided in section 11, I.R.C. 1954.
- The Commissioner issued a statutory notice of deficiency to Philipp Brothers Chemicals, (NY) and made an adjustment relating to a leasehold expenditure, and other adjustments under the authority of sections 482 and 61(a) reallocated to New York the gross income and deductions of the 10 corporations for the 12-month period ended June 30, 1960, June 30, 1961, and June 30, 1962 with certain adjustments for inter-corporate payments. The determination for the year ending June 30, 1961 was asserted under the provisions of section 6501(e).
- Phillip Brothers Chemicals and the other 10 corporations ("petitioners") argued that section 482 cannot be applied to corporations formed for a valid business purpose. Further, Philipp Brothers Chemical (New York) argued that since all the gross income was reported by the petitioners taken as a group, it cannot be said that such income was omitted.
- The T.C., for clarity sake split the 11 corporations in two groups: international sales and domestic sales. It went on to find that the Commissioner allocation to New York was sustainable as to the net income of the foreign sales corporations, but not of that of the domestic sales corporations.

### *3.5.3.2 PPG Industries, Inc., v. Commissioner, 55 T.C. 928*

- PPG Industries, Inc. ("PPG"), a manufacturer of glass, fiberglass, and paint products, was incorporated under the laws of Pennsylvania in 1883. Its principal office and place of business at the time the petition, in this case, was filed was Pittsburgh, Pennsylvania.
- In 1955 and 1956 PPG Industries bought more glass from foreign suppliers than it sold to foreign customers. Prior to 1957, PPG's physical facilities and the domestic demand for glass limited the amount of glass products it could export.
- PPGI was incorporated in July 1958 as a wholly owned foreign subsidiary of PPG Industries, Inc. for the purpose of: (1) expanding the sale of PPG's products outside the United States (US), (2) developing opportunities outside the US for the exploitation of PPG's technology in the glass, paint, and chemical fields, and (3) developing opportunities outside the US for investments where equity interests could be built around the manufacture of products using PPG's technology.

- A detailed basic agreement was executed between petitioner and PPGI (effective as of January 1, 1959) establishing prices, terms, and discounts in the sale of glass and paint products to PPGI and defining the obligations, rights, and duties of each party. A similar basic agreement was executed between Columbia-Southern and PPGI covering all facets of the sales of chemical products to PPGI.
- The Commissioner issued a statutory notice of deficiency, making allocations of gross income from PPGI to PPG Industries, Inc., for fiscal years 1960 and 1961 in the respective amounts of USD 1,032,999 and USD 866,749. In making these allocations, the Commissioner relied upon the Source Book of Statistics of Income compiled by the U.S. Treasury Department for 1960 and 1961.
- The Commissioner computed a net profit of 3.59 percent of gross sales in 1960 and 2.43 percent of gross sales in 1961. He then applied these percentages to gross sales figures for PPGI for 1960 and 1961 in the respective amounts of USD 17,793,900 and USD 12,989,000 and obtained the amounts of USD 638,801 and USD 315,632 which he regarded as appropriate net profits for PPGI in the years 1960 and 1961.
- Subtracting USD 638,801 from PPGI's income of USD 1,671,800 for 1960, the Commissioner determined that the difference, or USD 1,032,999, was allocable under section 482 to the petitioner in 1960. Similarly the respondent subtracted USD 315,632 from PPGI's income of USD 1,182,381 for 1961 and determined that the difference, or USD 866,749, was allocable under section 482 to the petitioner in 1961.
- However, on trial, the Commissioner announced a new position to the effect that (1) PPGI's activities were comparable to those of a Combination Export Manager (CEM) with a nominal net profit margin of 2 percent of sales, and (2) PPGI's sales of petitioner's glass products to petitioner's two Canadian subsidiaries (CPI and Duplate) were merely "paper shuffling" and in effect share transactions. The net result of this new position was that all of PPGI's income from the Canadian sales would be allocated to PPG Industries, Inc., and that any earnings of PPGI in excess of 2 percent on its remaining sales would also be allocated to the PPG Industries, Inc.
- The T.C. found that:

> The Commissioner's original allocation of income based upon the Source Book of Statistics of Income was arbitrary and unreasonable...That there was no indication in the record to show that the operations of the unnamed corporations in the $10 to $25 million asset category were in any way comparable to the operations of PPGI and, in fact, the evidence that does appear in the record emphasizes this lack of comparability.
> That in computing the 3.59 percent and the 2.43 percent as the proper return on gross sales in 1960 and 1961 he misapplied the statistical information appearing in the compilation so that the lack of comparability with PPGI, both as to its operations and to its capital structure, was aggravated.

That there was also evidence that in 1960 and 1961 petitioner sold a substantial amount of plate glass products to the Franklin Glass Co. at prices lower than those it charged PPGI.
That the record also established that most of PPGI's net profits in 1960 and 1961 were earned from the sale of glass products, that the sales of both glass and paint products made by petitioner to PPGI were at arm's-length prices and that substantially all of PPGI's net profits were earned from the resale of products purchased at arm's-length prices.

CHAPTER 4

# Transfer Pricing for Tangible Property

## 4.1 INTRODUCTION

The arm's length amount charged in a controlled transfer of tangible property must be determined under one of the six available methods. Each of the methods must be applied in accordance with all of the provisions of section 1.482-1, including the best method rule of section 1.482-1(c), the comparability analysis of section 1.482-1(d), and the arm's length range of section 1.482-1(e).

## 4.2 TRANSFER PRICING METHODOLOGY

Several methods available to taxpayers in addressing their tangible property transfer pricing are discussed in the following sections.

### 4.2.1 The Comparable Uncontrolled Price Method

The CUP method evaluates whether the amount charged in a controlled transaction is arm's length in reference to the amount charged in a Comparable Uncontrolled Transaction (CUT). The results derived from applying the CUP method generally will be the most direct and reliable measure of an arm's length price for the controlled transaction if an uncontrolled transaction has no differences with the controlled transaction that would affect the price, or if there are only minor differences that have a definite and reasonably ascertainable effect on price and for which appropriate adjustments are made. If there are differences between the controlled and uncontrolled transactions that would affect price, adjustments should be made to the price of the uncontrolled transaction according to the comparability provisions of section 1.482-1(d)(2). The reliability of the results derived from the CUP method is affected by the completeness and accuracy of the data used and the reliability of the assumptions made to apply the method.

Factors that may be particularly relevant to this method include:

- quality of the product;
- contractual terms (e.g., scope and terms of warranties provided, sales or purchase volume, credit terms, transport terms);
- level of the market (i.e., wholesale, retail, etc.);
- geographic market in which the transaction takes place;
- date of the transaction;
- intangible property associated with the sale;
- foreign currency risks; and
- alternatives realistically available to the buyer and seller.

#### 4.2.1.1 *The Following Example Derived from Regulation 1.482-3 Illustrates the Aforementioned Principles*

USM, a US manufacturer manufactures business machines. USM makes minor modifications to the physical properties of the machines to satisfy specific requirements of a customer in controlled sales, but does not make these modifications in uncontrolled sales. If the minor physical differences in the product have a material effect on prices, adjustments to account for these differences must be made to the results of the uncontrolled transactions according to the provisions of section 1.482-1(d)(2), and such adjusted results may be used as a measure of the arm's length result.

I should stress that CUP may be derived from data from public exchanges or quotation media, but only if the following requirements are met:

- the data is widely and routinely used in the ordinary course of business in the industry to negotiate prices for uncontrolled sales;
- the data derived from public exchanges or quotation media is used to set prices in the controlled transaction in the same way it is used by uncontrolled taxpayers in the industry; and
- the amount charged in the controlled transaction is adjusted to reflect differences in product quality and quantity, contractual terms, transportation costs, market conditions, risks borne, and other factors that affect the price that would be agreed to by uncontrolled taxpayers.

Also, the use of data from public exchanges or quotation media may not be appropriate under extraordinary market conditions.

### 4.2.2 The Resale Price Method

The Resale Price Method (RPM) arrives at an arm's-length price by measuring the value of the distribution function where a controlled taxpayer buys goods from a related supplier and sells them to unrelated buyers. The RPM is usually used in situations where the reseller performs merely a simple processing or resale of goods. Use of the

RPM is inappropriate if the buyer/reseller has added more than an insubstantial amount to the value of the property by physically altering the product before resale or by the use of intangible property.[1]

In short, the RPM can be expressed in this formula:

| |
|---|
| Arm's Length Purchase Price = Resale price to unrelated parties × (1 – Gross margin of comparable uncontrolled transaction. |

The RPM evaluates whether the amount charged in a controlled transaction is arm's length by reference to the gross profit margin realized in CUTs. The RPM measures the value of functions performed and is ordinarily used in cases involving the purchase and resale of tangible property in which the reseller has not added substantial value to the tangible goods by physically altering the goods before resale. The RPM is not ordinarily used in cases where the controlled taxpayer uses its intangible property to add substantial value to the tangible goods. The RPM measures an arm's length price by subtracting the appropriate gross profit from the applicable resale price for the property involved in the controlled transaction under review. The appropriate gross profit is computed by multiplying the applicable resale price by the gross profit margin (expressed as a percentage of total revenue derived from sales) earned in CUTs. Whether results derived from applications of this method are the most reliable measure of the arm's length result must be determined using the factors described under the best method rule in section 1.482-1(c). Comparability under this method is less dependent on close physical similarity between the products transferred than under the CUP method. For example, distributors of a wide variety of consumer durables might perform comparable distribution functions without regard to the specific durable goods distributed. Substantial differences in the products may, however, indicate significant functional differences between the controlled and uncontrolled taxpayers. Finally, the reliability of profit measures based on gross profit may be adversely affected by factors that have less effect on prices. If there are material differences between the controlled and uncontrolled transactions that would affect the gross profit margin, adjustments should be made to the gross profit margin earned with respect to the uncontrolled transaction according to the comparability provisions of section 1.482-1(d)(2).

The following factors may be particularly relevant to this method include for comparability sake:

- inventory levels and turnover rates, and corresponding risks, including any price protection programs offered by the manufacturer;
- contractual terms (e.g., scope and terms of warranties provided, sales or purchase volume, credit terms, transport terms);
- sales, marketing, advertising programs, and services (including promotional programs, rebates, and co-op advertising);
- the level of the market (e.g., wholesale, retail); and
- foreign currency risks.

1. Section 1.482-2(e)(3)(ii).

Further, the degree of consistency in accounting practices between the controlled transaction and the uncontrolled comparables that materially affect the gross profit margin would also affect the reliability of the result. Thus, for example, if differences in inventory and other cost accounting practices would materially affect the gross profit margin, the ability to make reliable adjustments for such differences would affect the reliability of the results. Further, the controlled transaction and the uncontrolled comparable should be consistent in the reporting of items (such as discounts, returns and allowances, rebates, transportation costs, insurance, and packaging) between cost of goods sold and operating expenses.

The following example illustrates the aforementioned principles:

Example 1

- ParCo is a US parent company of Sub 1, Sub 2, and Sub 3.
- In 2015, Sub 1 sold (from its existing inventory) wigs to Sub 2 for USD 1,000.00 making a gross profit margin of 20%.
- Sub 2 later on sold the same wigs (without any alteration) to an unrelated company (ForCo) for USD 1,500.00 realizing a 50% gross profit margin.
- In the absence of any transfer pricing manipulation the gross profit margin would be the same (50%), with an arm's length resale around USD 1,500.00.
- As the products (wigs) had not been altered or modified, the resale price between Sub 1 and Sub 2 shall not be different from the resale price between Sub 2 and ForCo.

### 4.2.3 The Cost Plus Method

The CP method evaluates whether the amount charged in a controlled transaction is arm's length by reference to the gross profit mark up realized in CUTs. The CP method is ordinarily used in cases involving the manufacture, assembly, or other production of goods that are sold to related parties. The CP method measures an arm's length price by adding the appropriate gross profit to the controlled taxpayer's costs of producing the property involved in the controlled transaction. The appropriate gross profit is computed by multiplying the controlled taxpayer's cost of producing the transferred property by the gross profit markup, expressed as a percentage of cost, earned in CUTs.

The CP arm's length can be derived using this formula:

Arm's Length Price = reasonable cost × (1 + cost plus margin of comparable uncontrolled transaction.

Comparability under this method is less dependent on close physical similarity between the products transferred than under the CUP method. Substantial differences in the products may, however, indicate significant functional differences between the controlled and uncontrolled taxpayers. If there are material differences between the controlled and uncontrolled transactions that would affect the gross profit markup, adjustments should be made to the gross profit markup earned in the CUT according to the provisions of section 1.482-1(d)(2). If there are differences in functions performed, however, the effect on gross profit of such differences is not necessarily equal to the differences in the amount of related operating expenses. Specific examples of the factors that may be particularly relevant to this method include:

- the complexity of manufacturing or assembly;
- manufacturing, production, and process engineering;
- procurement, purchasing, and inventory control activities;
- testing functions;
- selling, general, and administrative expenses;
- foreign currency risks; and
- contractual terms (e.g., scope and terms of warranties provided, sales or purchase volume, credit terms, transport terms).

The degree of consistency in accounting practices between the controlled transaction and the uncontrolled comparables that materially affect the gross profit markup affects the reliability of the result.

### 4.2.4 The Comparable Profit Method

The CPM differs from traditional methods in that the analysis is not necessarily based on particular CUTs. Rather, the analysis is based on the return realized by various companies engaged in a particular line of business or, as it is more commonly called, a "function" (i.e., a series of transactions that are appropriate to be aggregated).

The CPM evaluates whether the amount charged in a controlled transaction is arm's length based on objective measures of profitability (Profit Level Indicators (PLIs)) derived from uncontrolled taxpayers that engage in similar business activities under similar circumstances. The determination of an arm's length result is based on the amount of operating profit that the tested party would have earned on related-party transactions if its profit level indicator were equal to that of an uncontrolled comparable (comparable operating profit). Comparable operating profit is calculated by determining a profit level indicator for an uncontrolled comparable, and applying the profit level indicator to the financial data related to the tested party's most narrowly identifiable business activity for which data incorporating the controlled transaction is available (relevant business activity). To the extent possible, PLIs should be applied solely to the tested party's financial data that is related to controlled transactions. The tested party's reported operating profit is compared to the comparable operating profits derived from the PLIs of uncontrolled comparables to determine whether the reported operating profit represents an arm's length result. The tested party will be the participant in the controlled transaction whose operating profit attributable to the controlled transactions can be verified using the most reliable data and requiring the fewest and most reliable adjustments, and for which reliable data regarding uncontrolled comparables can be located. The tested party's operating profit must first be adjusted to reflect all other allocations under section 482, other than adjustments pursuant to this section. For purposes of the CPM, the arm's length range will be established using comparable operating profits derived from a single profit level indicator. PLIs are ratios that measure relationships between profits and costs incurred or resources employed. A variety of PLIs can be calculated in any given case. Whether use of a particular profit level indicator is appropriate depends upon a number of factors, including the nature of the activities of the tested party, the reliability of the available data with respect to uncontrolled comparables, and the extent to which the profit level indicator is likely to produce a reliable measure of the income that the tested party would have earned had it dealt with controlled taxpayers at arm's length, taking into account all of the facts and circumstances. The PLIs should be derived from a sufficient number of years of data to reasonably measure returns that accrue to uncontrolled comparables. Generally, such a period should encompass at least the taxable year under review and the preceding two taxable years. This analysis must be applied in accordance with section 1.482-1(f)(2)(iii)(D). PLIs that may provide a reliable basis for comparing operating profits of the tested party and uncontrolled comparables include the following.

#### *4.2.4.1 Rate of Return on Capital Employed*

The return on capital employed is an important measure of a company's profitability. It is especially useful in comparisons between certain types of businesses. The Return on Capital Employed (ROCE) ratio, expressed as a percentage, complements the Return on Equity (ROE) ratio by adding a company's debt liabilities, or funded debt, to capital equity to reflect a company's total capital employed.

#### *4.2.4.2 The Berry Ratio*

The US applied the Berry ratio since the 1990s. The Berry ratio is the ratio of gross profit to operating expenses. The use of this ratio as profit indicator was introduced, first, by an American economist professor, Charles Berry, in the transfer pricing court case E.I du Pont de Nemours.[2] The Berry ratio is often used to test the profits of limited-risk distributors or service providers that do not own or use any intangible assets. Originally, the Berry ratio was developed, in fact, just as a variant of the CP. A Berry ratio uses the level of operating costs, in the case of a distributor, as a measure of the extent, or amount, of the services in fact provided. A Berry ratio has no justification in the case of a firm that combines distribution with other functions.

#### *4.2.4.3 Financial Ratios*

Several financial ratios can be used as profit indicators. The US regulations outline these primary PLIs, besides the Berry ratio. Profitability ratios must be properly analyzed before comparing firms' or related entities operational efficiency and

2. E.I du Pont de Nemours & Co. v. US, 608 F. 2d 445 (Ct. Cl. 1979).

profitability. However, these ratios can be affected by estimates, assumptions, accounting policies use by the comparable entities. If these differences are not dealt with properly, comparability can be impaired leaving the analysis useless.

#### *4.2.4.3.1 Return on Assets*

Return on Assets (ROA) is a profitability ratio that measures the net income produced by total assets during a period by comparing net income to the average total assets. It is an indicator of how profitable a company is relative to its total assets. ROA is computed by dividing a company's annual earnings by its total assets and is expressed in percentage. As company's asset total varies over time due to the purchase or sale, land or equipment, inventory changes, or seasonal sales fluctuations. It is important to find the average total for the period in at stake. As a PLI, ROA is often used to compare the performance of two different companies. Some industries and businesses require large amounts of fixed assets to produce goods and services for sale. Thus the comparison must take into consideration all the relevant facts of each terms of the comparison. However, ROA taken in silo provides an incomplete picture of the capital base that management has at its disposal; it considers only total assets.

#### *4.2.4.3.2 Return on Capital Employed (ROCE)*

ROCE is a financial ratio that measures a company's profitability and the efficiency with which its capital is employed. ROCE is a useful measure for comparing the relative profitability of companies after taking into account the amount of capital used. The higher the return on capital, the greater the company's ability to expand in order to grow earnings. ROCE uses the pre-tax operating earnings of a company instead of net income. ROCE focuses on profitability from operations relative to the cost of the assets used to produce those profits. Like the ROA, this ratio (ROCE) also provides an incomplete picture as the levels of firms' debts and tax rates vary within and across industries.

#### *4.2.4.3.3 Return on Sales (ROS)*

Return on sales (also known as "the operating profit margin") is a financial ratio that measures a company's performance by analyzing what percentage of total company revenues is actually converted into company profits. ROS is often used to compare the profitability of companies and industries of differing sizes. ROS can also be applied to industry analysis to determine which companies within an industry are being most efficiently run.

#### *4.2.4.3.4 Return on Total Costs*

"Return on costs" is a term that refers to the ratio of the total costs to the sales of the enterprise. In managerial accounting, the total cost concept is one of the cost-plus pricing methods used to determine the selling price of a product. Cost-plus pricing methods determine the selling price of a product as the total cost per unit plus the markup.

### 4.2.5 The Profit Split Method

The PSM is typically applied when both sides of the controlled transaction own significant intangible properties. The PSM evaluates whether the allocation of the combined operating profit or loss attributable to one or more controlled transactions is arm's length by reference to the relative value of each controlled taxpayer's contribution to that combined operating profit or loss. The relative value of each controlled taxpayer's contribution to the success of the relevant business activity must be determined in a manner that reflects the functions performed, risks assumed, and resources employed by each participant in the relevant business activity, consistent with the comparability provisions of section 1.482-1(d)(3). Such an allocation is intended to correspond to the division of profit or loss that would result from an arrangement between uncontrolled taxpayers, each performing functions similar to those of the various controlled taxpayers engaged in the relevant business activity. The allocation of profit or loss under the PSM must be made in accordance with one of the following allocation methods: (i) The Comparable Profit Split (CPS); or (ii) The Residual Profit Split (RPS), described in paragraph (c)(3) of this section.

- The Comparable Profit Split Method

A comparable profit split is derived from the combined operating profit of uncontrolled taxpayers whose transactions and activities are similar to those of the controlled taxpayers in the relevant business activity. Under this method, each uncontrolled taxpayer's percentage of the combined operating profit or loss is used to allocate the combined operating profit or loss of the relevant business activity. The CPS compares the division of operating profits among the controlled taxpayers to the division of operating profits among uncontrolled taxpayers engaged in similar activities under similar circumstances. Comparability under this method also depends particularly on the degree of similarity of the contractual terms of the controlled and uncontrolled taxpayers. If there are differences between the controlled and uncontrolled taxpayers that would materially affect the division of operating profit, adjustments must be made according to the provisions of section 1.482-1(d)(2). The reliability of the results derived from the CPS is affected by the quality of the data and assumptions used to apply this method. In particular, the following factors must be considered:

- the reliability of the allocation of costs, income, and assets between the relevant business activity and the participants' other activities will affect the accuracy of the determination of combined operating profit and its allocation among the participants;

- the degree of consistency between the controlled and uncontrolled taxpayers, in accounting practices that materially affect the items that determine the amount and allocation of operating profit, affects the reliability of the result.

- The Residual Profit Split Method

Under the RPS method, the combined operating profit or loss from the relevant business activity is allocated between the controlled taxpayers following the two-step process: (i) the first step allocates operating income to each party of the controlled transactions to provide a market return for its routine contributions to the relevant business activity. Routine contributions are contributions of the same or of a similar kind to those made by uncontrolled taxpayers involved in similar business activities for which it is possible to identify market returns, and (ii) the second step is the allocation of the residual profit.

### 4.2.6 Unspecified Methods

Consistent with the specified methods, an unspecified method should take into account the general principle that uncontrolled taxpayers evaluate the terms of a transaction by considering the realistic alternatives to that transaction, and only enter into a particular transaction if none of the alternatives are preferable to it.

In establishing whether a controlled transaction achieved an arm's length result, an unspecified method should provide information on the prices or profits that the controlled taxpayer could have realized by choosing a realistic alternative to the controlled transaction.

## 4.3 CASE STUDY

### 4.3.1 E.I. Dupont de Nemours & Co, v. Commissioner (RPM)

- Du Pont de Nemours ("Du Pont"), the American chemical concern, created early in 1959 a wholly owned Swiss marketing and sales subsidiary for foreign sales—Du Pont International S.A. ("DISA") to perform substantial commercial functions needed within the European market.
- Most of the Du Pont chemical products marketed abroad were first sold by Du Pont to DISA, which were then arranged for resale to the ultimate consumer through independent distributors. Du Pont's internal memoranda were replete with references to tax advantages, particularly in planning prices on Du Pont goods to be sold to the new entity. The profits on these Du Pont sales were divided for income tax purposes between and DISA via the mechanism of the prices plaintiff charged DISA.
- DISA accumulated profits would be used to finance further foreign investments. For its technical service function, DISA did not develop its own

extensive laboratories (with resulting costs and risks), but could rely on its parent's laboratory network in the US and England.

- In operating DISA, Du Pont also maximized its subsidiary's income by funneling a large volume of sales through DISA which did not call for large expenditures by the latter. Many of the products Du Pont sold through DISA required no special services, or already had ample technical services provided. Du Pont routed sales to Australia and South Africa through DISA although the latter provided no additional services to sales in these non-European countries.
- Du Pont also routed all European sales of Elastomers through DISA, even though the parent had a well-established English subsidiary which had all the necessary technical services and marketing ability.
- For 1959 and 1960 the Commissioner of Internal Revenue found these divisions of profits economically unrealistic as giving DISA too great a share. Accordingly, he reallocated a substantial part of DISA's income to Du Pont, thus increasing the latter's taxes for 1959 and 1960 by considerable sums. The additional taxes were paid and this refund suit was brought in due course. Du Pont assailed the Service's reallocation, urging that the prices plaintiff charged DISA were valid under the Treasury regulations implementing section 482.
- For sales of tangible goods, as here, IRC section 482 and the regulations thereof mandate determination of an arm's length price for the sale by one controlled entity to the other, and then sets out (in order of preference) four methods for calculating such an arm's length price: the CUP method, the RPM, the CP method, and any other appropriate method. The parties correctly agree upon the inapplicability of the CUP method as they could not find comparable transactions.
- The Commissioner argued that DISA's gross profit margin for resale was 35 percent and the prevailing margin for comparable uncontrolled resellers was 25 percent, the Commissioner. He introduced evidence that the six companies Du Pont had identified most closely with DISA all had average selling costs much higher than DISA.
- Du Pont alleged that a group of 21 distributors, whose general functions were similar to DISA's, provided the proper base of comparison. However, no data was available to establish similarity of products (with associated marketing costs), comparability of functions, or parallel geographic (and economic) market conditions. Further, Du Pont alleged that DISA was exposed to all normal risks, including shipping and warehouse risks, sudden European market declines, or termination by manufacturing departments of Du Pont. Requiring it to prove the proper amount of adjustment is an unfair burden.
- The trial judge premised his rejection of Du Pont's case on the failure to suggest appropriate adjustments under this subpart, particularly for DISA's lack of "entrepreneurial risk."

- The Court of Claims, on appeal rejected the IRS arguments founding that:

> they may have made gross profits comparable to DISA's but their selling costs, reflecting the greater scale of their services or efforts, were much higher in each instance. Moreover, the record shows that these companies dealt with quite different products (electronic and photographic equipment) and functioned in different markets (primarily the United States).

- The Court also found that the lack of any significantly comparable resale (or group of resales) underscored by Du Pont's failure to suggest any means of adjusting for differences between DISA and the uncontrolled resellers. Further, Du Pont proposed no adjustments for differences in marketing locations, selling functions, or production differences between DISA and the "comparable" 21 distributors.
- Therefore, said the Court of Claims, Du Pont has failed to bring itself within the RPM. Du Pont's prices to DISA were set wholly without regard to the factors which normally enter into an arm's length price.
- Finally, after rejecting the alleged "resale price method" the Court of Claims agreed with the trial judge determination as appropriate and reasonable. In determining reasonableness, the court relied on ratios of gross income to total operating costs for functionally similar corporations, and on rates of return for 1,100 corporations in general.

### 4.3.2 Bausch & Lomb v. Commissioner, 92 T.C. 525 (1989)

- Bausch & Lomb Inc. was a New York corporation with principal corporate offices at Rochester, New York. B&L first entered the contact lens business on a national level in May 1971, when B&L began to manufacture and sell "soft" contact lenses throughout the US on a commercial basis.
- During late 1971 and throughout 1972, B&L and its subsidiaries began to market soft contact lenses in various foreign countries in the Western Hemisphere, Europe, and the Pacific Basin region.
- In 1978, B&L was a major participant in the soft contact lens industry, controlling upwards of 50.6 percent of the US market. Between 1978 and 1980, B&L prepared long-range forecasts that predicted increasing demand for soft contact lenses in international markets, particularly in Europe.
- In 1978, B&L began to investigate the possibility of an overseas manufacturing facility to complement its existing plant in Rochester, New York. Responding to various incentives offered by the Industrial Development Authority of the Republic of Ireland ("IDA"), including a tax holiday on all export profits through 1990, B&L determined to establish a manufacturing facility in Waterford, Ireland.
- Accordingly, B&L Ireland was incorporated on February 1, 1980. B&L Ireland agreed, *inter alia*, not to enter into any royalty commitments, except that B&L

Ireland could pay royalties to B&L or any subsidiaries in an amount not to exceed 5 percent of B&L Ireland's annual net sales.

- Through 1982, B&L was the only manufacturer in the US using the cost effective spin cast method. Thus, B&L was able to produce lenses at a cost of USD 1.50 each, which was far below its competitors' costs. During 1981 and 1982, for example, a competitor of B&L had per unit costs of over USD 4.00 using a cast molding process and over USD 6.00 using a lathing process.
- In January 1981, B&L granted B&L Ireland a nonexclusive license to manufacture lenses using B&L's spin cast technology. In addition, the license agreement entitled B&L Ireland to any improvements resulting from B&L's ongoing research and development in the manufacture of contact lenses, and permitted B& L Ireland to sell soft contact lenses anywhere under B&L's trademarks. In exchange, B&L was to receive a royalty of 5 percent of the subsidiary's net contact lens sales. The agreement was terminable upon the written notice of either party.
- B&L was under no contractual obligation to purchase any lenses from B&L Ireland, but 61 percent of B&L Ireland's total sales in 1981 and 56 percent in 1982 were to be given to B&L for resale in the US.
- The balance of B&L Ireland's sales went to overseas affiliates of B&L.
- Throughout that two-year period, the intercompany transfer price was USD 7.50 per lens. The purchasers also paid the duty and freight charges, which in the case of B&L were USD 0.62 per lens.
- In 1980, 1981, and 1982, B&L sold approximately 4,148,000, 5,354,000, and 5,264,000 daily wear soft contact lenses in 1980, 1981, and 1982, respectively, in the US. The Average Realized Price (ARP) for sales of daily wear soft contact lenses to unrelated parties in the US was USD 16.74 and USD 15.25 in 1981 and 1982, respectively. B&L's foreign subsidiaries sold approximately 1,474,000 and 1,803,000 daily wear soft contact lenses in 1981 and 1982 at ARP's of USD 22.03 and USD 18.41, respectively.
- The Commissioner contended that: (i) neither the comparable uncontrolled price method or RPMs are applicable, (ii) the sales by manufacturers to distributors cited by petitioners on the one hand, and the sales by B&L Ireland to B&L on the other, were not sufficiently similar to function as comparables, (iii) dissimilarities between B&L and the distributors cited by B&L rendered inappropriate reference to the markup percentages of these distributors in application of the RPM. He went on to argue on disparities in the volumes of lenses sold and functions performed.
- B&L contended that: (i) they had presented ample evidence of comparable, uncontrolled sales of soft contact lenses which establish that the USD 7.50 per lens price charged by B&L Ireland to B&L was at or below the price which would have been charged by uncontrolled manufacturers to distributors for similar lenses; (ii) B&L pointed to sales to distributors by Lombart, American Hydron, American Optical, and Hydrocurve of soft contact lenses during 1980 through 1982. No sale cited by petitioners took place for a price less than the

USD 7.50 charged by B&L Ireland. Alternatively, petitioners argue that application of the RPM to the facts of this case lends further support to the arm's-length nature of the USD 7.50 transfer price.

- The T.C. found that the third-party purchase agreements identified by B&L qualified as comparable-uncontrolled-sales for purposes of application of the CUP method. However, it had made some adjustments for differences that existed between sales performed by B&L Ireland and those of B&L to unrelated buyers.
- The T.C. held that:

> The third-party transactions identified by petitioner provide ample evidence that the $7.50 per-lens price charged by B&L Ireland is equal or below prices which would be charged for similar lenses in uncontrolled transactions. When conditions for use of the comparable-uncontrolled-price method are present, use of that method to determine an arm's-length price is mandated.

## Chapter 5
# Transfer Pricing for Intangible Property

### 5.1 INTRODUCTION

IP and other intangible assets are key drivers for corporate success in our modern economy. Intangibles can be anything—rights for exclusivity, patents, trade names—and are internationally highly mobile. MNCs exploit this mobility and strategically locate ownership of their intangibles at low-cost affiliates. Transfers of a company's core intangibles outside of a corporate group rarely occur in the market, so comparable transactions are difficult, if not impossible, to find. In 1988, the US Treasury released a study on transfer pricing, commonly referred to as "The White Paper," in which it recognized that the application of transfer pricing for intangible property was challenging due to the fact that it is not easy to identify appropriate comparables. In the unavailability of proper comparables, the Treasury came with the theory of "commensurate-with-income standard" which departs a bit from the regular ALP. It was not until 1994, when the Treasury issued regulations that set forth the basic rules for determining income in connection with a transfer of intangible property. These regulations generally provide that the arm's length consideration for the transfer of an intangible in a controlled transaction (i.e., a transaction between related entities) must be commensurate with the income attributable to the intangible, and it requires taxpayers to apply one of four methods to meet this requirement. Unfortunately, a substantial proportion of MNCs has concluded that they can only successfully exploit the IP they developed by transferring them across national boundaries within their own organizations rather than by selling their right of use to foreign-based enterprises.

For purposes of section 482, an intangible is an asset that comprises any of the following items and has substantial value independent of the services of any individual:

- patents, inventions, formulae, processes, designs, patterns, or know-how;
- copyrights and literary, musical, or artistic compositions;
- trademarks, trade names, or brand names;

- franchises, licenses, or contracts;
- methods, programs, systems, procedures, campaigns, surveys, studies, forecasts, estimates, customer lists, or technical data; and
- other similar items. For purposes of section 482, an item is considered similar to those listed in paragraph (b)(1) through (5) of this section if it derives its value not from its physical attributes but from its intellectual content or other intangible properties.

## 5.2 METHODS OF TRANSFERRING INTANGIBLE PROPERTY

A US person that develops or purchases intangible property generally can make that intangible property available to a related person in one of the four ways.[1]

- The first is through an outright transfer of all substantial rights in the intangible property, either by sale or through a non-recognition transaction.
- The second is through a license of the intangible property, in which the US person transfers less than all substantial rights in the intangible property to the foreign affiliate.
- The third is the provision of a service using the intangible property, rather than a direct transfer of the property.
- The fourth, intangible property is made available through a cost sharing arrangement.

## 5.3 INTANGIBLE PROPERTY VALUATION METHODOLOGY

It is common for the licensee to pay a rolling royalty based on its performance. Royalties are usually either a percentage of the licensee's net sales or an amount per unit of licensed product sold.

Related parties involved in a license arrangement have to establish the basis for royalty payment at arm's length. Two factors influence the determination of a royalty rate: (i) the earnings generated by the IP, and (ii) how this is shared between the owner and the licensee.[2] Several methods can be considered.

### 5.3.1 Established Reasonable Royalty

A reasonable royalty may be based upon an established royalty, if there is one, or if not upon a hypothetical royalty resulting from arm's length negotiations between a willing

1. US Joint Committee on Taxation (2010): Present Law and Background Related to Possible Income Shifting and Transfer Pricing, p. 20.
2. Heberden, Tim (2011) Intellectual Property Valuation and Royalty Determination, Wolters Kluwer Law & Business, p. 8.

licensor and a willing licensee.[3] Reasonable royalty is essentially a function of multiple fact determinations. To show that a royalty is established, "it must be paid by enough different licensees to indicate a general acquiescence in its reasonableness."[4] A single licensing agreement, without more, is insufficient proof of an established royalty. In the absence of a reasonable royalty, which often is the case, the court will have to compute one. The obvious flaw with this approach is that it is not always evident to find or identify current, reliable data for deals and technologies that are truly comparable.

### 5.3.2 Arm's Length Determination

The arm's length determination of royalty payment can be computed using several methods: (i) income approach, (ii) transactional approach, (iii) return on R&D costs, (iv) return on market value, and the 25 percent rule.

#### *5.3.2.1 Income Approach*

In general, under the income approach, the royalty is a share of the profit the licensee is expected to receive as a result of taking the license and selling the licensed products. As Heberden pointed out:[5]

> The appropriate point within the earnings spectrum is function of market forces such as: (i) the uniqueness of the IP, (ii) the number of suitable licenses, (iii) the risks born by two parties and their respective level of investment, and (iv) each party's rights and responsibilities in terms of the license.

Further, most IP are integrated or combined with other assets in order to generate the expected flows of income. Under such circumstances, a split of revenue between those generated through the IP and other assets must be performed either through a PSM or any residual method. The starting point for the divide between income from the IP and income from other assets is the determination of the routine profit of the business.

#### *5.3.2.2 Transactional (Market) Approach*

The transactional approach determines the actual price paid for a similar intangible under similar circumstances. It can be used either for direct acquisition or purchase or for the right to use, a license. It is often considered to be the most reliable of methods

3. Anders E. Trell, Plaintiff-appellee, v. Marlee Electronics Corporation, Defendant-appellant, 912 F.2d 1443 (Fed. Cir. 1990).
4. Tj Smith Nephew Ltd v. Parke Davis & Company, 9 F. 3d 979, Nos. 92-1240, 92-1241, United States Court of Appeals, Federal Circuit.
5. Heberden, Tim (2011) Intellectual Property Valuation and Royalty Determination, Wolters Kluwer Law & Business, p. 9.

when it can be performed credibly.[6] The key to performing a successful transactional approach is to ensure comparability between the outside evidence and the subject asset. Adjustments are also conducted for comparability sake.

#### *5.3.2.3 Cost Approach or Return on R&D*

Under the cost approach, the royalty is set at a level that would allow the IP owner to recoup all the costs related to the IP over the lifespan of the license. The cost approach has limited use as it fails to take into account the actual market value of the IP. Nonetheless, there are circumstances where the cost approach provides a relevant reference point for the computation of the royalty payment, when the IP is replicable.

#### *5.3.2.4 Return on Market Value*

The return on market value approach considers factors that might increase or decrease the value of the technology in the hands of the licensee. Such factors include: (i) the unique features of the assets, (ii) the easiness of replication, and (iii) the potential income.

#### *5.3.2.5 The 25 Percent Rule of Thumb*

The 25 percent rule is a variant of the income approach aforementioned. This rule of thumb states that the IP owner is entitled to 25 percent of the licensee's long-term pre-tax operating profit made from sales of the licensed products. The 25 percent share is often expressed in the license agreement either as a percentage of net sales, or a price per unit of licensed product sold.

Example

- Lin Corp. licenses to Zyco LLC to make, use and sell a new type of calculator. Lin Corp. has a patent for the calculator.
- Zyco's long-term projections indicate that: (i) Zyco LLC expects to sell the calculators for USD 200 plus GST each, (ii) projected costs per unit over the long term are approximately USD 120, leaving a pre-tax operation profit per unit of USD 80.
- Under the 25% rule, 25% of Zyco LLC USD 80 per unit profit should go Lin Corp. That is, 20% of the unit's USD 200 sale price. So Lin Corp. and Zyco LLC agree that Zyco LLC will pay a royalty of 20% of Zyco LLC's net sales.

6. Flignor, Paul & Orozco, David (2010): Intangible Asset & Intellectual Property Valuation: A Multidisciplinary Perspective.

## 5.4 INTANGIBLE PROPERTY: TRANSFER PRICING METHODOLOGY

Like tangible property, the IRS regulations avail specific method for the transfer pricing of intangible.

### 5.4.1 Comparable Uncontrolled Transaction Method

The CUT method evaluates whether the amount charged for a controlled transfer of intangible property is arm's length by referencing the amount charged in CUTs. If an uncontrolled transaction involves a transfer of the same intangible under the same, or substantially the same, circumstances as a controlled transaction, the results derived from applying the CUT method will generally be the most reliable measure of the arm's-length result.[7] If, however, uncontrolled transactions involving the same intangible under the same circumstances cannot be identified, uncontrolled transactions that involve the transfer of "comparable intangibles under comparable circumstances" may be used to apply the CUT method, but the reliability of the results is reduced.

The use of the CUT method requires that the controlled and uncontrolled transactions involve the same or comparable intangible property.[8] In order for intangibles involved in controlled and uncontrolled transactions to be comparable, "both intangibles must: (i) be used in connection with similar products or processes within the same general industry or market; (ii) have similar profit potential."[9]

In evaluating the comparability of the circumstances of the controlled and uncontrolled transactions, although all of the factors described in section 1.482-1(d)(3) must be considered, specific factors that may be particularly relevant to this method include the following:

- the terms of the transfer, including the exploitation rights granted in the intangible, the exclusive or nonexclusive character of any rights granted, any restrictions on use, or any limitations on the geographic area in which the rights may be exploited;
- the stage of development of the intangible (including, where appropriate, necessary governmental approvals, authorizations, or licenses) in the market in which the intangible is to be used;
- rights to receive updates, revisions, or modifications of the intangible;
- the uniqueness of the property and the period for which it remains unique, including the degree and duration of protection afforded to the property under the laws of the relevant countries;
- the duration of the license, contract, or other agreement, and any termination or renegotiation rights;
- any economic and product liability risks to be assumed by the transferee;

7. Section 1.482-4(c)(2)(ii).
8. Section 1.482-4(c)(2)(iii)(B)(1).
9. Section 1.482-4(c)(2)(iii)(B)(1).

- the existence and extent of any collateral transactions or ongoing business relationships between the transferee and transferor; and
- the functions to be performed by the transferor and transferee, including any ancillary or subsidiary services;
- data and assumptions. The reliability of the results derived from the CUT method is affected by the completeness and accuracy of the data used and the reliability of the assumptions made to apply this method.

### 5.4.2 Comparable Profits Method

The CPM evaluates whether the amount charged in a controlled transaction is arm's length based on objective measures of profitability (PLIs) derived from uncontrolled taxpayers that engage in similar business activities under similar circumstances. The CPM and the determination of an arm's length result is based on the amount of operating profit that the tested party would have earned on related-party transactions if its profit level indicator were equal to that of an uncontrolled comparable (comparable operating profit). Comparable operating profit is calculated by determining a profit level indicator for an uncontrolled comparable and applying the profit level indicator to the financial data related to the tested party's most narrowly identifiable business activity for which data incorporating the controlled transaction is available (relevant business activity). To the extent possible, PLIs should be applied solely to the tested party's financial data that is related to controlled transactions. The tested party's reported operating profit is compared to the comparable operating profits derived from the PLIs of uncontrolled comparables to determine whether the reported operating profit represents an arm's length result. The tested party will be the participant in the controlled transaction whose operating profit attributable to the controlled transactions can be verified using the most reliable data and requiring the fewest and most reliable adjustments, and for which reliable data regarding uncontrolled comparables can be located. Consequently, in most cases the tested party will be the least complex of the controlled taxpayers and will not own valuable intangible property or unique assets that distinguish it from potential uncontrolled comparables. The tested party's operating profit must first be adjusted to reflect all other allocations under section 482, other than adjustments pursuant to this section.

PLIs are ratios that measure relationships between profits and costs incurred or resources employed. A variety of PLIs can be calculated in any given case. Whether use of a particular profit level indicator is appropriate depends upon a number of factors, including the nature of the activities of the tested party, the reliability of the available data with respect to uncontrolled comparables, and the extent to which the profit level indicator is likely to produce a reliable measure of the income that the tested party would have earned had it dealt with controlled taxpayers at arm's length, taking into account all of the facts and circumstances. The PLIs should be derived from a sufficient number of years of data to reasonably measure returns that accrue to uncontrolled comparables. PLIs that may provide a reliable basis for comparing operating profits of the tested party and uncontrolled comparables include the following:

(a) Rate of ROCE. The rate of ROCE is the ratio of operating profit to operating assets. The reliability of this profit level indicator increases as operating assets play a greater role in generating operating profits for both the tested party and the uncontrolled comparable. In addition, reliability under this profit level indicator depends on the extent to which the composition of the tested party's assets is similar to that of the uncontrolled comparable. Finally, difficulties in properly valuing operating assets will diminish the reliability of this profit level indicator.
(b) Financial ratios. Financial ratios measure relationships between profit and costs or sales revenue. Since functional differences generally have a greater effect on the relationship between profit and costs or sales revenue than the relationship between profits and operating assets, financial ratios are more sensitive to functional differences than the rate of ROCE. Therefore, closer functional comparability is normally required under a financial ratio than under the rate of ROCE to achieve a similarly reliable measure of an arm's length result. Financial ratios that may be appropriate include the following:
   - ratio of operating profit to sales; and
   - Ratio of gross profit to operating expenses. Reliability under this profit level indicator also depends on the extent to which the composition of the tested party's operating expenses is similar to that of the uncontrolled comparables.

### 5.4.3 Profit Split Methods

The PSM evaluates whether the allocation of the combined operating profit or loss attributable to one or more controlled transactions is arm's length by reference to the relative value of each controlled taxpayer's contribution to that combined operating profit or loss. The combined operating profit or loss must be derived from the most narrowly identifiable business activity of the controlled taxpayers for which data is available that includes the controlled transactions (relevant business activity). The relative value of each controlled taxpayer's contribution to the success of the relevant business activity must be determined in a manner that reflects the functions performed, risks assumed, and resources employed by each participant in the relevant business activity, consistent with the comparability provisions of section 1.482-1(d)(3).

The regulations also provide two PSMs, under which the relative values of each controlled party's contribution to the combined profit from use of the intangible are used to determine an arm's length "profit split." The arm's length charge for the intangible is the amount required to achieve the appropriate split of the combined profits.

#### *5.4.3.1 Comparable Profit Split Method*

The CPS compares the division of operating profits among the controlled taxpayers to the division of operating profits among uncontrolled taxpayers engaged in similar activities under similar circumstances. The CPS method relies exclusively on external market data to determine the appropriate profit split; thus, the combined operating profits of controlled taxpayers are split based on the split of combined operating profits of uncontrolled taxpayers with similar transactions and activities in the relevant business activity. If there are differences between the controlled and uncontrolled taxpayers that would materially affect the division of operating profit, adjustments must be made according to the provisions of section 1.482-1(d)(2). The degree of consistency between the controlled and uncontrolled taxpayers in accounting practices that materially affect the items that determine the amount and allocation of operating profit affects the reliability of the result. Thus, for example, if differences in inventory and other cost accounting practices would materially affect operating profit, the ability to make reliable adjustments for such differences would affect the reliability of the results. Further, accounting consistency among the participants in the controlled transaction is required to ensure that the items determining the amount and allocation of operating profit are measured on a consistent basis.

#### *5.4.3.2 Residual Profit Split Method*

The RPS method relies on external transactions principally in order to determine the amount appropriately allocable to routine contributions and, in some cases, to determine the split of residual non-routine return amongst the parties. Under this method, the combined operating profit or loss from the relevant business activity is allocated between the controlled taxpayers following the two-step process:

- The first step allocates operating income to each party to the controlled transactions to provide a market return for its routine contributions to the relevant business activity. Routine contributions are contributions of the same or a similar kind to those made by uncontrolled taxpayers involved in similar business activities for which it is possible to identify market returns. Routine contributions ordinarily include contributions of tangible property, services and intangibles that are generally owned by uncontrolled taxpayers engaged in similar activities. A functional analysis is required to identify these contributions according to the functions performed, risks assumed, and resources employed by each of the controlled taxpayers. Market returns for the routine contributions should be determined by reference to the returns achieved by uncontrolled taxpayers engaged in similar activities, consistent with the methods described in sections 1.482-3, 1.482-4, and 1.482-5.
- The residual profit generally should be divided among the controlled taxpayers based upon the relative value of their contributions of intangible property to the relevant business activity that was not accounted for as a routine

contribution. The relative value of the intangible property contributed by each taxpayer may be measured by external market benchmarks that reflect the Fair Market Value (FMV) of such intangible property. Alternatively, the relative value of intangible contributions may be estimated by the capitalized cost of developing the intangibles and all related improvements and updates, less an appropriate amount of amortization based on the useful life of each intangible. Finally, if the intangible development expenditures of the parties are relatively constant over time and the useful life of the intangible property of all parties is approximately the same, the amount of actual expenditures in recent years may be used to estimate the relative value of intangible contributions. If the intangible property contributed by one of the controlled taxpayers is also used in other business activities (such as transactions with other controlled taxpayers), an appropriate allocation of the value of the intangibles must be made among all the business activities in which it is used.

## 5.5 CASE STUDY

The appropriate treatment of intangible transfers has consistently been at the center of transfer pricing disputes and is central to the few opinions issued in recent years.

### 5.5.1 Eli Lilly & Co. v. Commissioner[10]

(a) The case involved IRC section 482 allocation issues between a US pharmaceutical company and its Puerto Rican manufacturing subsidiary. The Eli Lilly case also illustrates the complexity of the adjustment process as Lilly tried to sustain the arm's length nature of its prices by comparing its product to that of a generic product manufactured by an unrelated party and making adjustments for various differences between the two. Among other differences considered by the Court were the uniformity of the content and weight, as well as purity and effectiveness of the product.

(b) Eli Lilly had taken advantage of the tax incentives herein mentioned and had created a subsidiary in Puerto Rico. The parent company had developed two manufacturing intangibles for which afterwards deducted research and development costs. Later, Lilly made a section 351 tax-free transfer of the patents and manufacturing know-how to its subsidiary in Puerto Rico, retaining no rights in these transferred intangibles. The subsidiary manufactured the drugs in Puerto Rico and later sold them to Lilly, meaning that the subsidiary made all the tax-free income while Lilly deducted all expenses; effectively having manipulated transfer prices.

10. Eli Lilly & Co. v. Commissioner, 84 T.C. 996 (1985), affirmed in part and reversed in part, 856 F. 2d 855 (7th Cir. 1988).

(c) The Commissioner argued that the subsidiary's ownership of the intangible should be disregarded and the profits generated by the intangibles should be allocated completely to Lilly. The Court, rejecting this argument, concluded that Lilly in fact was able to do the intangibles transfer because of Code section 351. It determined that the Commissioner's allocation was unreasonable but recognized that it could allocate some of the income to the parent company since the fact that there was no lump-sum payment, royalty, or cost sharing agreement, created a distortion of income between Lilly and the Puerto Rican subsidiary (not making it an arm's length transaction).

(d) It further concluded that a PSM should be used to adequately allocate the income between both (ignoring the fact that regulations stipulated three methods for arm's length pricing).

(e) The Court examined seven adjustments proposed by Lilly that would have increased the price of the generic product, an external transaction from USD 7.55 per unit to USD 12.17 per unit:
   (i) the cost of raw materials furnished at no charge to the generic manufacturer;
   (ii) the tougher credit terms provided by the generic manufacturer;
   (iii) the sample for which the generic manufacturer charged;
   (iv) the rental value of equipment loaned to the generic manufacturer at no cost;
   (v) the quality control performed for the generic manufacturer at no cost;
   (vi) the lower quality of the generic product; and
   (vii) available patents hold by the related manufacturer.

(f) The T.C. analyzed the facts and underlying assumptions to determine the amounts of the allowable adjustments to increase the external CUP from USD 7.55 per unit to USD 9.80 per unit. Lilly could not quantify the value of the differences involving free loaned equipment, quality control, quality ant patents.

In conclusion, Lilly did get allocated some of the profits generated by the intangibles, but the Court came up with its own methods, making no deference to the Commissioner's arguments.

### 5.5.2 The Compaq Computer Corp.[11]

Compaq Computer's purchase price for printed circuit assemblies from its Singapore subsidiary was challenged by the IRS. In this decision, the US T.C. found that Compaq's calculations were consistent with arms-length principles. The relevant fact under the case are summarized as follows:

11. Compaq Computer Corp. v. CIR, T.C Memo. 1999.

- Compaq Computer Corporation is a Delaware corporation with its principal place of business in Houston, Texas. Compaq Computer Corporation and subsidiaries filed consolidated Federal income tax returns for the taxable years ended November 30, 1991, and November 30, 1992.
- Compaq US manufactured Central Processing Units (CPUs) for its PC's at Compaq US in Houston, at Compaq Asia (Pte) Ltd. (Compaq Asia) in Singapore, and at Compaq Computer Manufacturing Ltd. in Scotland. In addition, Compaq US purchased PCAs from Compaq Asia and from various unrelated PCA subcontractors (unrelated subcontractors) that were primarily located in the US.
- In the mid-1980s, Compaq US pursued material cost savings allegedly available in Asian markets in both PC and PCA manufacturing. Specifically, in 1984, petitioner began doing business with Automated Assembly of Singapore (AAS), purchasing through hole PCAs.
- As with Compaq US, the top priority of Compaq Asia was to produce high-quality products. Compaq US developed in-house workmanship standards that specified acceptable and unacceptable quality of PCAs. All manufacturing sites, including Compaq Asia and unrelated subcontractors, were required to comply with these standards.
- Purchases from Compaq Asia satisfied approximately one-half of the PCA needs of Compaq US from 1990 to 1993.
- Compaq US paid what is recognized in the industry as the turnkey price for the PCAs listed above.
- In 1991 and 1992, the transfer prices for Compaq Asia PCAs were set using a cost plus formula, pursuant to section 1.482-2 A(e)(1), Income Tax Regs. Compaq Asia sales to Compaq US during 1991 and 1992 were 101.5 and 88.1 percent of Compaq US standard cost to produce the PCAs, respectively.
- Compaq US purchases from Compaq Asia were nearly identical to purchases from unrelated subcontractors, but there were some differences in the transactions between the parties.
- At some point in time, Compaq abandoned its cost plus method of calculating the arm's-length prices for Compaq Asia PCAs and, at trial, defended the intercompany prices pursuant to the CUP method based on Compaq US regular and substantial purchases of identical or nearly identical PCAs from uncontrolled subcontractors.
- The IRS challenged Compaq's use of unrelated subcontractor transactions from 1990 and 1993 in establishing an arm's-length price under the CUP method. From the IRS viewpoint, using transactions with unrelated subcontractors from 1990 and 1993 was inappropriate and tainted the validity of the CUP.
- The Court found that the CUP method establishes arm's-length prices for PCAs that were sold by Compaq Asia, and a large profit margin does not prevent the use of the CUP method. That the IRS was unable to identify a single actual market participant that sold PCAs at only two-thirds of the prevailing

market price. Thus, the Court held that Compaq had satisfied its burden of proving that the prices in the intercompany transactions were consistent with arm's-length prices.

### 5.5.3 Sundstrand Corporation & Subsidiaries[12]

Sunstrand licensed technology to its Singapore-based subsidiary, SunPac. The US T.C. ruled that the amounts paid by Sunstrand to SunPac did not constitute and arm's-length consideration under section 482, but also that the IRS overstepped its authority in calculating taxable net income. The Court also eliminated interest penalties imposed by the IRS.

The relevant facts of the case are as follows:

- Sundstrand, a US parent company manufactured and sold numerous products for both commercial and military aircraft.
- Sundstrand, US expanded the operation of its wholly owned subsidiary in Singapore ("SunPac") to include the production of certain aircraft engine sub-systems and related spare parts.
- In 1975, Sundstrand, US and SubPac entered into a license agreement whereby Sundstrand, US granted SunPac the right to use certain manufacturing and marketing intangibles in exchange for a reasonable technical assistance.
- Under the agreement, SunPac agreed to pay Sundstrand a 2 percent royalty, later retroactively increased to 5 percent, based on sales.
- The IRS challenged the arm's length character of both the royalty paid and the sales price by Sundstrand.
- The T.C. rejected the IRS argument that Sundstrand, US and SunPac have entered into a contract manufacturing and found that SunPac was a bona fide licensee. The Court also found that Sundstrand, US products covered by the license were unique and had little or no competition. Therefore, the T.C. concluded that the arm's length royalty rate would be at 10 percent rather than the 5 percent agreed upon by the parties.

### 5.5.4 R.T. French v. Commissioner[13]

(a) R. T. French Co. (French or petitioner) is a Delaware corporation engaged in the business of manufacturing and distributing various food products and other merchandise. Its principal business office was in Rochester.

(b) For a many years French has distributed certain instant mashed potato products in granular form that it has manufactured under various processes

12. Sundstrand Corporation & Subsidiaries v. CIR, 96 T.C. 226; 1991.
13. R.T. French v. Commissioner, 60 T.C. 836 (1973).

derived from one invented by Theodore Rendle, an employee of Chivers & Sons Ltd. (Chivers), a British company. Chivers had acquired Rendle's British patent from him, and during World War II it engaged in the United Kingdom (UK) in the first successful effort to develop an instant mashed potato product that was exploited commercially. Chivers applied for a US patent in 1943 and was granted such a patent on August 7, 1945, but never itself produced or marketed the product in this country.

(c) On or about January 1, 1946, French first entered into a license agreement covering a process for the manufacture of an instant mashed potato product in 1946. The licensor under that agreement was a British company known as MPP; it held British and US patents on the process and marketed instant mashed potatoes in Great Britain. In 1946, 51 percent of the shares of stock in MPP was owned by the British firm of Reckitt & Colman Ltd., which itself was jointly owned by two unrelated British companies then controlling 55 percent and 45 percent, respectively, of the outstanding capital stock in petitioner. The remaining 49 percent of MPP's stock was held by yet another independent British firm, Chivers & Sons Ltd.

(d) Under the main part of the agreement, MPP granted to the petitioner an exclusive license to work, use, and exercise the patented process and to sell the product made in accordance therewith within the US, and MPP further agreed "to advise and assist the Licensee in all matters relating to the method of working the said process, improvement of production, and generally regarding the manufacture of cooked potato products" (punctuation supplied). In consideration of MPP's undertakings, the petitioner was to pay MPP a royalty at a rate of 3 percent of petitioner's net sales of potato products manufactured under the patented process.

(e) The 1946 agreement also contained provisions, operative "During the continuance of this Licence," pursuant to which MPP and petitioner were to disclose to the other all "improvements" and "further inventions" related to the process that might in any manner become known to either party.

(f) The only other agreement entered into by MPP authorizing the exploitation of its mashed potato process by another organization was with a wholly unrelated company known as "Produsol," and the terms of that agreement were at least as favorable to MPP as those of its agreement with petitioner. The "Produsol" agreement, executed in 1949, included no exclusive license provisions based on any patent, but rather was one covering "know-how" only

(g) On August 13, 1946, French and Peck Associates entered into a license agreement covering the mutual exchanges of any improvements and further inventions. Various other research projects were undertaken by Chivers in the name of MPP during the 1940s, some of which generated results that were useful to French.

(h) The 1946 agreement was superseded the 1960 agreement, which granted to French "a nonexclusive license under M.P.P.'s information, knowledge, technical data, and know-how" for the manufacture and sale of the same instant mashed potato product that had been the subject of the 1946 agreement and provided for royalties to be paid at rates (2 percent on sales made up to December 31, 1961, and 1 percent on sales made thereafter) that were roughly comparable to those called for by the 1946 agreement, at least under the supplemental provisions that were to become effective in August of 1962. The 1960 agreement further contained reciprocal covenants, similar to those in the earlier agreement, relating to disclosure of "improvements or inventions" in connection with the licensed process.

(i) In addition, French and Peck Associates pursued their studies of the continuous process, and refinements of that process were made from time to time and communicated to the British laboratories.

(j) The Commissioner disallowed none of the deductions claimed by French in respect of the payments made during the taxable years 1948–1962, alleging: (i) that the license agreements were not made at arm's length. French had received additional income of USD 18,671.90 and USD 19,566.18 in 1963 and 1964, respectively, by reason of the free use of its "trademarks, patents, know-how, etc." by its foreign "brother-sister" affiliates.; (ii) that the affiliates' free use of these intangibles represented a "constructive dividend" flowing from petitioner to the common British parent and that petitioner was required to withhold income tax thereon under section 1442 (a) of the Code (as modified by Article VI of the relevant tax treaty.

(k) While French did not now challenge the Commissioner's determination that it received additional income, it does contest the determination that the free use of the intangibles referred to had given rise to "constructive dividends" to the English parent which are subject to "the 5% withholding tax under section 1442(a) of the 1954 Code as modified by Article VI of the United States-United Kingdom Tax Treaty as then in effect."

(l) The T.C., while agreeing that a distribution by a corporation to a "brother-sister" corporation would be regarded as a dividend to the common shareholder only if the distribution was made for the benefit of the shareholder, found that:

  (i) the dividends actually declared and paid by French in each of the years in issue (USD 1,750,000 in each year) were so vastly in excess of the additional amounts that the Commissioner would treat as dividends to French's parent corporation (USD 18,671.90 in 1963 and USD 19,566.18 in 1964);

  (ii) that the free use of petitioner's intangibles represented an attempt by the parent to direct further benefits to itself;

  (iii) there being no dividend, petitioner had no duty to withhold any tax.

### 5.5.5 Ciba-Geigy Corp. v. Commissioner

(1) Ciba-Geigy Corp. (Ardsley) was, a New York corporation and a wholly owned subsidiary of Ciba-Geigy, Ltd. (Geigy-Basle), a Swiss corporation. Geigy-Basle was founded in Basle, Switzerland, in 1758 as a trading company specializing in imported dyestuffs.
(2) By the early 1940s, Geigy-Basle was successfully engaged in the research and development of industrial chemicals, pharmaceuticals, and pesticides.
(3) Geigy-Basle organized petitioner in 1909 to market and sell its products in the US. By 1951, petitioner was engaged in the formulation and sale of agricultural chemical products and pharmaceutical products.
(4) During the late 1950s, Geigy-Basle selected 15 patented triazine compounds, including simazine, atrazine, atratone, and prometone, for commercialization as herbicides.
(5) By agreement dated May 1, 1958, Geigy-Basle granted Ciba-Geigy a nonexclusive license to manufacture and sell simazine in the US. In return, Ciba-Geigy agreed to pay Geigy-Basle a royalty equal to 10 percent of net sales.
(6) In November 1958, petitioner and Geigy-Basle entered into a similar agreement with respect to atrazine. The simazine license further provided that:
    (a) Ardsley (or Ciba-Geigy) granted a reciprocal royalty-free license to Geigy-Basle of Ardsley's improvements on the diaminochloros-triazine patent.
    (b) Ardsley had the right to extend the simazine license to subsidiaries, which would be bound by the terms of the simazine license, but Ardsley would continue to be responsible directly to Geigy-Basle for paying royalties from its own and its subsidiaries' sales of the licensed compositions.
    (c) Ardsley granted Geigy-Basle a royalty-free, nonexclusive, nontransferable license to cover inventions under existing and later-acquired patents and patent applications in all countries which Ardsley owned or acquired during the term of the simazine license.
    (d) Geigy-Basle had the right to extend the royalty-free, nonexclusive, nontransferable license covering inventions to its subsidiaries and licensees as long as the subsidiaries and licensees granted back to Ardsley a royalty-free, nonexclusive license covering their inventions.
    (e) Geigy-Basle granted Ardsley a right to grant nonexclusive licenses under existing patent claims; the stipulated royalty rate was to equal not less than the amount Ardsley was obligated to pay with regard to the manufacture and sale of the licensed composition.
    (f) Geigy-Basle would be entitled to a cross-grant on any improvement patents under which Ardsley licensed its licensees.
    (g) Ardsley would pay Geigy-Basle a royalty of 10 percent of the net sales price (gross sales price minus discounts, returns, allowances, and costs of containers) on any licensed composition sold by Ardsley.

(h) Ardsley would pay Geigy-Basle 90 percent of royalties collected from Ardsley's sub-licensees for sales of the licensed compositions, and
(i) Geigy-Basle would make available to Ardsley all laboratory, technical, and manufacturing data regarding the licensed compositions, and Ardsley would make available to Geigy-Basle all laboratory, technical, and manufacturing data regarding the licensed compositions.

(7) By agreement dated November 1, 1959, Geigy-Basle granted petitioner a nonexclusive license to manufacture and sell atratone and prometone in the US. In return, petitioner agreed to pay Geigy-Basle a royalty equal to 10 percent of net sales.

(8) By agreement dated January 1, 1961, Ciba-Geigy and Geigy-Basle entered into a consolidated license agreement granting Ciba-Geigy an exclusive license to manufacture and sell simazine and atrazine in the US. Ciba-Geigy and Geigy-Basle entered into a similar agreement on January 1, 1962, granting Ciba-Geigy an exclusive license to manufacture and sell atratone and prometone in the US. Both agreements superseded the individual license agreements previously executed, and provided for a royalty of 10 percent.

(9) These replacement triazine licenses provided in pertinent part that:
(a) The license was an exclusive license allowing Ciba-Geigy (or Ardsley) "to make or have made for it and to sell in the United States Licensed Products."
(b) Ardsley was granted permission to extend the license to its subsidiaries and to successive purchasers of the licensed products.
(c) Ardsley granted to Geigy-Basle a royalty-free, nonexclusive license on improvements on the US patent; Geigy-Basle was permitted to extend the nonexclusive license to its subsidiaries or licensees provided that in return they were willing to extend to Ardsley a license on their improvement patents.
(d) Geigy-Basle granted to Ardsley an exclusive right to grant, directly or through others, nonexclusive licenses covering the "licensed products" to make or to have them made for licensees and to sell them in the US; this grant required a royalty payment at a rate of not less than provided otherwise by the replacement triazine license.
(e) Ardsley promised to pay a royalty to Geigy-Basle at a rate of 10 percent of the net sales price (gross sales price minus discounts, returns, and allowances) of the "licensed products" sold.
(f) Ardsley additionally agreed to pay 90 percent of that royalty amount if sub-licensees were involved.
(g) Ardsley and Geigy-Basle promised to make available to one another all laboratory, technical, and manufacturing data without cost.
(h) Geigy-Basle gave Ardsley the right to bring any patent infringement action at the latter's own expense.

(10) From 1958 to 1969, Ciba-Geigy paid royalties of USD 55,813,000 to Geigy-Basle based on net sales of simazine and atrazine in the US. During this

period, Ciba-Geigy earned net profits after royalties of USD 231,215,000 from the sale of simazine and atrazine in the US.

(11) The Commissioner challenged the license agreements alleging: (i) that in 1951 Basle and Ardsley entered into a joint and cooperative research and development effort under which it would have been reasonable and logical for the two companies to share equally the fruits of their research by providing for a geographical division of the market, thus requiring a royalty-free license; and (ii) that under the criteria contained in section 1.482-2(d)(2), Income Tax Regs., a rate of royalty in an amount less than the 10 percent claimed by petitioner would have been arrived at in arm's-length negotiations between unrelated parties.

(12) Ciba-Geigy argued that an unrelated party would have paid a royalty of 15 percent for similar rights under the triazine patents. Petitioner therefore concludes that it is entitled to apply the difference between a royalty of 15 percent and a royalty of 10 percent as a set off against other section 482 allocations which have been settled by the parties.

(13) Ciba-Geigy, first, pointed to the license agreements entered into between Geigy-Basle and Norddeutsche Affinerie of Germany and Orgachemia of Holland as transfers involving the same or similar intangible property under the same or similar circumstances. Secondly, Ciba-Geigy argued that, because the markup on the sale of the active ingredients plus the 5 percent royalty at least equals the 10 percent royalty paid by them, these third-party license agreements confirm the arm's-length nature of the royalty payments in issue.

(14) The Commissioner argued that the license agreements entered into, between Geigy-Basle and Wolfen, were sufficiently similar to the license agreements in issue to establish an arm's-length consideration. In 1959, Wolfen agreed to pay Geigy-Basle a royalty of 6 percent of net sales for the right to manufacture, formulate, and sell simazine in East Germany. In 1962, the parties entered into a similar agreement with respect to atrazine. Further, the Commissioner argued that because prevailing rates for an exclusive license in the agricultural chemistry industry ranged from 3 percent to 6 percent of net sales during the 1950s, a royalty of 10 percent for an agricultural chemical product could not constitute an arm's-length consideration.

(15) The T.C. found that these third-party licenses were not "sufficiently similar transactions" as contemplated by section 1.482-2(d)(2)(ii). Unlike the licenses herein granting Ciba-Geigy the right to manufacture the active ingredients for the triazine herbicides, the license agreements with Norddeutsche Affinerie and Orgachemia required them to purchase the active ingredients for the triazine herbicides from Geigy-Basle.

(16) The T.C. concluded that:

> A royalty of 10 percent constituted an arm's-length consideration for the exclusive right to manufacture and sell the triazine herbicides in the United

States. It also concluded that Ciba-Geigy was not entitled to an additional setoff for royalties in excess of 10 percent.

(17) In the absence of sufficiently similar transaction involving an unrelated party, the Court looked to the relevant factors identified by section 1.482-2(d)(2)(iii), considering the offers of competing transferors or the bids of competing transferees to arrive at the amount of an arm's-length consideration. The T.C. looked at the Du Pont's industrial and chemical department, negotiation with Geigy-Basle on Du Pont's behalf and found that on both occasions, Du Pont offered to pay Geigy-Basle a royalty of 10 to 12.5 percent of net sales for the nonexclusive right to manufacture, formulate, and sell the triazine herbicides in the US.

(18) Although Geigy-Basles rejected Du Pont's offer, the T.C. went on "arbitrarily" to decide that that offer was highly probative of the amount an unrelated party would have paid for the same intangible property under similar circumstances.

we are convinced that Du Pont's offer to pay at least 10 percent for a license under Geigy-Basle's triazine patent was bona fide and therefore established that an unrelated party would have paid a royalty of at least 10 percent for the triazine agreements in issue.

(19) The T.C. rejected that first argument of the Commissioner as to the creation of a joint-venture between Geigy-Basles and Ciba-Geigy, finding that Geigy-Basle was the developer of the US triazine patent; that Geigy-Basle exercised full control over the research and development of the triazine herbicides; that Geigy-Basle was the developer of the US patents for the triazine herbicides; and that Du Pont's willingness to perform these services without compensation was typical of the policies and practices of the agricultural chemical industry.

(20) From its own reconstruction, the T.C. held that the Commissioner's reduction of the royalty from 10 percent to 6 percent paid by petitioner during the years in issue constituted an abuse of discretion, and that respondent had failed to carry his burden of proving that no royalty payment is allowable.

### 5.5.6 Proctor & Gamble

- Procter & Gamble Company ("P&G") is an Ohio corporation whose principal place of business was in Cincinnati, Ohio. P&G was principally engaged in the business of manufacturing and marketing consumer and industrial products.

- Procter & Gamble A.G. (AG) was a Swiss corporation, a wholly owned subsidiary of P&G, engaged in the marketing of petitioner's products, generally in those countries in which petitioner did not have a marketing subsidiary or affiliate.
- P&G and P&G AG entered into a License and Services Agreement ("package fee agreement") under which AG paid royalties to P&G for the nonexclusive use by AG and its subsidiaries of petitioner's patents, trademarks, trade names, knowledge, research, and assistance in the fields of manufacturing, general administration, finance, buying, marketing, and distribution.
- The royalty amounts paid by AG to A&G were based principally on net sales of AG's products by AG and its subsidiaries, and certain other companies in Greece, Spain, Austria, Saudi Arabia, Morocco, Iran, Libya, and Lebanon. During the years in issue, AG executed technical assistance and other service agreements, similar to package fee agreements, with its directly owned active subsidiaries.
- In 1967, A&G made preparations to organize a wholly owned subsidiary in Spain to manufacture and sell its consumer and industrial products in that country. At that time, many laws, decrees, and orders were in effect in Spain regulating foreign investment in Spanish companies and limiting the payment or assignment of credits in pesetas in favor of residents of foreign countries.
- On September 23, 1967, P&G, upon the advice of competent Spanish counsel, submitted an application letter addressed to the "Presidency of the Spanish Government" requesting authorization to organize a Spanish company, Espana. The application stated that Espana would have as its purpose the manufacture and sale of high quality consumer and industrial products, including synthetic detergents, soaps and toiletries, and other cleaning and washing products.
- The Spanish Government approved P&G's application for a 100 percent interest in Espana by a letter dated January 27, 1968. However, the letter expressly provided that Espana could not pay any amounts for royalties or technical assistance. After receipt of the letter, P&G's Spanish counsel advised that the limitation on royalty payments was within the power of the Spanish Government and reflected normal practice. Counsel further advised that there was no realistic possibility of appealing or protesting the decision as long as P&G intended to retain 100 percent ownership of Espana. Consistent with advice of counsel, P&G did not formally appeal the prohibition on royalty payments. At the time of its organization, Espana had several competitors in Spain who likewise could not make royalty payments abroad.
- After a series of requests, Espana was granted the right to increase its capital. However, the granting letter to Espana stated that Espana "will not pay any amount whatsoever in the concept of fees, patents, royalties and/or technical assistance to the investing firm nor to any of its affiliates, unless with the approval of the Administration."

- In 1973, P&G entered into an engineering services contract with Espana in connection with the expansion of an Espana factory in Mataro, Spain. To gain approval to pay P&G for its actual costs under the contract, Espana requested and obtained a clarification from the Spanish Foreign Investments Office that payments for specific services were not intended to fall within the purview of the prohibition against royalty and technical assistance payments.
- In 1974, after satisfying the concerns of the Ministry of Industry that the engineering services P&G would provide Espana could not be provided by a Spanish company, payments under the contract to P&G were approved.
- In 1976, the Spanish Government reversed course by facilitating and promoting foreign investment in the Spanish market.
- In 1977, Espana was again permitted to make payments to P&G for actual costs arising under a second engineering services contract for further expansion of the Mataro plant. Payment was approved when it was reduced from USD 500,000 to USD 148,905. Finally, engineering services payments were approved from Espana to a Belgian affiliate of P&G in October 1977, for a further expansion of the Mataro plant and the construction of a new manufacturing plant in Cordoba, Spain.
- Espana informally approached Spanish officials regarding Espana's payment of a "package fee" again in 1978. At that time, an Espana employee wrote to P&G's affiliate in Belgium and advised that while it was unlikely that Espana could make payments based on a percentage of its sales, it might be possible for Espana to make regular payments to the Belgian affiliate for actual costs associated with research and development and engineering services to the extent that Espana could document receipt and use of the technology.
- Although the officers of P&G, AG, and Espana discussed the payment of royalties with their counsel from the time of Espana's organization through the years in issue, informal discussions with Spanish officials dissuaded a formal appeal and Espana never formally applied for a reversal of the prohibition. Contrary to normal practice, AG did not have any agreement with Espana during the years in issue under which Espana made any payment, or was required to make any payment, to AG for the use of P&G's technology. However, during the years in issue AG paid a royalty to P&G which was based in part on a percentage of Espana's sales; these royalty payments reduced AG's income.
- Consistent with its membership in the European Economic Community, Spain liberalized and streamlined its system of authorization for foreign investments by Decree 1042/1985 of March 29, 1985. In light of these changes, Espana filed an application for removal of the prohibition against royalty payments on October 30, 1986. By letter dated May 7, 1987, Espana's application was approved. Espana's subsequent application for authorization to pay package fees retroactive to July 1, 1987, was likewise approved.
- The IRS issued a notice of deficiency, respondent determined that income should be allocated in the amounts of USD 1,232,653 and USD 1,795,005 for

the years 1978 and 1979 respectively, from Espana to AG, pursuant to section 482, in order to clearly reflect AG's income.

- The IRS primary argument was that Spanish law did not prohibit the payment of royalties by Espana to AG during the years at issue. The Service viewed the prohibition on the payment of royalties from Espana to AG as merely an administrative decision, arbitrarily determined and subject to appellate review which Espana voluntarily waived.
- Moreover, the Service argued that because AG could have received royalty payments from an unrelated Spanish company, and would have demanded royalties if bargaining at arm's length, the transaction cannot withstand the analysis associated with the second prong of section 482.
- P&G did not contest the amount of the allocation made by respondent or the use of 2 percent in calculating that determination, but contended that no allocation from Espana is proper under IRC section 482. More specifically, P&G asserted that because Spanish law prohibited or blocked royalty payments from Espana to AG, it did not improperly utilize its control to shift income, and thus section 482 does not apply.
- The T.C. held that:

> Section 482 simply does not apply where restrictions imposed by law, and not the actions of the controlling interest, serve to distort income among the controlled group. Accordingly, in order to decide whether respondent's allocation is appropriate in the case sub judice, we must determine whether Spanish law prohibited or blocked Espana from making royalty payments to AG.

- The T.C. also added:

> We find that Spanish law prohibited Espana from making royalty payments to AG. Of paramount importance are the express prohibitions respecting royalty payments contained in the original approval letter, issued at the time of Espana's organization, and the several approval letters Espana received between 1970 and 1978 permitting capital increases. Espana was repeatedly admonished by the Spanish Government not to pay "any amount whatsoever in the concept of fees, patents, royalties, and/or technical assistance to the investing firm nor to any of its affiliates, unless with the approval of the Administration." In addition, prior to the years in issue, the Ministry of Industry made clear through its order of December 5, 1973, that it would consider as unfavorable a provision in a technology agreement imposing royalty payments based upon the technology recipient's level of activity, where the recipient is a subsidiary of the assignor and the latter holds more than 50 percent of its capital. A similar policy was stated in Decree 3099/1976. Under the circumstances, it is clear that in order to do business in Spain, petitioner had to play by Spain's rules.

- The T.C. also found that Espana's competitors were also prohibited from making royalty payments to their foreign parents. Because Spanish law prohibited or blocked Espana from paying royalties to AG, it effectively precluded AG from receiving the same.
- The T.C. to conclude that P&G had not utilized its control over AG and Espana so as to improperly shift income. Rather, there has been a deflection of income by operation of Spanish law. Under the circumstances, an allocation under section 482 is unwarranted.

### 5.5.7 Bausch & Lomb v. Commissioner, 92 T.C. 525 (1989)

- Bausch & Lomb Inc. was a New York corporation with principal corporate offices at Rochester, New York. B&L first entered the contact lens business on a national level in May 1971, when B&L began to manufacture and sell "soft" contact lenses throughout the US on a commercial basis.
- During late 1971 and throughout 1972, B&L and its subsidiaries began to market soft contact lenses in various foreign countries in the Western Hemisphere, Europe, and the Pacific Basin region.
- In 1978, B&L was a major participant in the soft contact lens industry, controlling upwards of 50.6 percent of the US market. Between 1978 and 1980, B&L prepared long-range forecasts that predicted increasing demand for soft contact lenses in international markets, particularly in Europe.
- In 1978, B&L began to investigate the possibility of an overseas manufacturing facility to complement its existing plant in Rochester, New York. Responding to various incentives offered by the Industrial Development Authority of the Republic of Ireland ("IDA"), including a tax holiday on all export profits through 1990, B&L determined to establish a manufacturing facility in Waterford, Ireland.
- Accordingly, B&L Ireland was incorporated on February 1, 1980. B&L Ireland agreed, *inter alia*, not to enter into any royalty commitments, except that B&L Ireland could pay royalties to B&L or any subsidiaries in an amount not to exceed 5 percent of B&L Ireland's annual net sales.
- The license agreement entered into by B&L and B&L Ireland, effective January 1, 1981, required B&L Ireland to pay to B&L 5 percent of the net sales proceeds from the sale of any products manufactured by B&L Ireland using any of B&L's patent rights or technology, or marketed under B&L's trademarks.
- The Commissioner's proposed deficiency sought to "reflect an arm's length consideration for the use of [B&L's] intangible assets by B&L Ireland" by limiting B&L Ireland to "a net profit before taxes of 20 percent of sales."
- The Commissioner argued that: (i) B&L would never have agreed to license its spin cast technology which allowed it to produce soft contact lenses for approximately USD 1.50 per lens and then purchase lenses from the licensee

for USD 7.50 per lens.; and (ii) B&L would have been unwilling to pay an independent third party much more than its costs would have been had it chosen to produce the contact lenses itself.

- B&L argued that 5 percent was the proper royalty percentage, but now contend that the 5 percent should be applied to the ARP of B&L and its subsidiaries from the sale of B&L Ireland contact lenses to third parties (contended to be USD 16.74 in 1981 and USD 15.25 in 1982 for domestic sales, and USD 22.43 in 1981 and USD 18.10 in 1982 for foreign sales).
- Having found that the record did not contain a sufficiently similar transaction involving an unrelated party, the T.C. constructed an arm's-length royalty, by looking to the relevant factors identified by section 1.482-2(d)(2)(iii) for guidance.
- The T.C., using its best judgment, found that at arm's length B&L Ireland would have been willing to invest in the lens production facility even if required to share approximately 50 percent of the profits therefrom with B&L as consideration for use of its intangibles, which equated to a royalty rate of 20 percent of net sales.
- Therefore, the T.C. held that:

> A royalty of 20 percent of B&L Ireland's sales price for soft contact lenses constitutes arm's-length consideration for use of B&L's intangibles. At arm's length B&L would thus have received royalties of $1,674,000 and $5,541,000 from B&L Ireland in 1981 and 1982, respectively.

CHAPTER 6

# Cost Sharing Arrangements

## 6.1 INTRODUCTION

On December 16, 2011, the IRS released new final regulations under section 482 (Treasury Regulation section 1.482-7 or the final regulations) governing Cost Sharing Arrangements (CSAs). These regulations supersede temporary regulations (Treasury Regulation section 1.482-7T or the 2009 temporary regulations) that were issued effective January 5, 2009 and were due to expire on December 30, 2011.

The Final Regulations expand the scope of what constitutes a platform contribution.[1] The Regulations state that the grant of make-or-sell rights (e.g., the right to make, replicate, license or sell an item) with respect to an existing resource, capability or right constitutes a platform contribution if the use of the existing item without further development is reasonably anticipated to contribute to the development of a cost-shared intangible. The principles and methods for valuing platform and operating contributions under a CSA may also apply under a best method analysis to valuing similar contributions in connection with transfers of intangibles outside the context of a CSA and to the provision of intercompany services. Both the Temporary and Final Regulations provide that an aggregation approach to valuing transactions in connection with a CSA may be appropriate in order to determine the combined effect of multiple contemporaneous transactions.[2]

## 6.2 COST SHARING ARRANGEMENTS

A cost sharing arrangement is an agreement under which the parties agree to share the costs of development of one or more intangibles in proportion to their shares of

1. PCT refers to any resource, capability or right reasonably anticipated to contribute to the development of cost-shared intangibles.
2. Temporary and Final Regulations Sections 1.482-7T(g)(2)(iv) and 1.482-7(g)(2)(iv).

Reasonably Anticipated Benefits (RABs) from their individual exploitation of the interests in the intangibles assigned to them under the arrangement. A taxpayer may claim that a cost sharing arrangement is a qualified cost sharing arrangement only if the agreement meets these requirements:

(a) All controlled participants commit to, and in fact, engage in Cost Sharing Transactions (CSTs). In CSTs, the controlled participants make payments to each other (CST Payments) as appropriate, so that in each taxable year each controlled participant's IDC share is in proportion to its respective RAB share.

(b) All controlled participants commit to, and in fact, engage in platform contributions transactions. In a Platform Contribution Transaction (PCT), each other controlled participant (PCT Payor) is obligated to, and must in fact, make arm's length payments (PCT Payments) to each controlled participant (PCT Payee) that provides a platform contribution.

I Each controlled participant must receive a non-overlapping interest in the cost-shared intangibles without further obligation to compensate another controlled participant for such interest. Besides the aforementioned, the Treasury Regulations require that the CSA be recorded in a document that is contemporaneous with the formation (and any revision) of the cost sharing arrangement and include:

(i) a list of the arrangement's participants, and any other member of the controlled group that will benefit from the use of intangibles developed under the cost sharing arrangement;
(ii) a description of the scope of the research and development to be undertaken, including the intangible or class of intangibles intended to be developed;
(iii) a description of each participant's interest in any covered intangibles. A covered intangible is any intangible property that is developed as a result of the research and development undertaken under the cost sharing arrangement (intangible development area);
(iv) the duration of the arrangement; and
(v) the conditions under which the arrangement may be modified or terminated and the consequences of such modification or termination, such as the interest that each participant will receive in any covered intangibles.

Section 482 provides that "In the case of any transfer of intangible property… the income with respect to such transfer shall be commensurate with the income attributable to the intangible." Participants in a Qualified Cost Sharing Agreement (QCSA) relinquish exclusive ownership of all exploitation rights in new intangibles they individually develop and agree to share ownership of, and costs associated with, such intangibles.

Example 1

- Corp. A and Corp. B are members of the same controlled group. Corporations A and B execute an agreement to jointly develop vaccine to treat measles and own the exclusive rights to commercially exploit vaccine in their respective territories, which together comprise the whole world.
- The agreement provides that Corp. A and Corp. B will share some, but not all, of the costs for developing the measles vaccine in proportion to RAB share.
- Such agreement is not a CSA because Corporation A and Corporation B have not agreed to share all of the IDCs in proportion to their respective RAB shares.

## 6.3 REASONABLY ANTICIPATED BENEFIT

RABs are measured either on a direct basis, by reference to estimated benefits to be generated by the use of cost-shared intangibles (generally based on additional revenues plus cost savings less any additional costs incurred), or on an indirect basis, by reference to certain measurements that reasonably can be assumed to relate to benefits to be generated. Regardless of whether a direct or indirect basis of measurement is used, adjustments may be required to account for material differences in the activities that controlled participants undertake to exploit their interests in cost-shared intangibles. Other bases for measuring anticipated benefits may in some circumstances be appropriate, but only to the extent that there is expected to be a reasonably identifiable relationship between the basis of measurement used and additional revenue generated or net costs saved by the use of cost-shared intangibles. For example, a division of costs based on employee compensation would be considered unreliable unless there were a relationship between the amount of compensation and the expected additional revenue generated or net costs saved by the controlled participants from using the cost-shared intangibles.

Anticipated benefits are defined as additional income generated or costs saved by the use of covered intangibles.[3] If parties fail to share such costs in proportion with their benefits, the respondent is authorized to make allocations to the extent necessary to make each controlled participant's share of the costs equal to its share of RABs.[4] For purposes of determining RAB shares at any given time, RABs must be estimated over the entire period, past and future, of exploitation of the cost-shared intangibles and must reflect appropriate updates to take into account the most reliable data regarding past and projected future results available at such time. RAB shares determined for a particular purpose shall not be further updated for that purpose based on information not available at the time that determination needed to be made. However, the Commissioner's power to allocate the RAB by using subsequently available information or data is not limited under these regulations.

3. Section 1.482-7(e)(1).
4. Section 1.482-7(a)(2).

Example 1

- Alpha Corp. is a US Pharmaceutical company based in Florida. Alpha Corp. wholly owned Beta Corp. a subsidiary located in Cayman Islands.
- Alpha Corp. and Beta Corp. are actively involved in the search for vaccine to cure Zika, a virus transmitted through mosquito bites. They agree to share equally (50/50%) the R&D costs. They also agree to share equally the proceed from the soon-to-be discovered vaccine.
- The pool of expenses is expected to be around USD 10 million, which include wages for employees directly involved in the research, technician leaders, quality technicians, and test technicians. This pool of expenses also include stock-based compensation granted to all employees involved in the R&D.
- Given the need for such a vaccine, Alpha Corp. and Beta Corp. RABs to be around USD 500 million.
- The CSA agreement between Alpha and its subsidiary ("Beta") would sustain IRS audit only if both the parent and its subsidiary share equally (50/50%) the USD 10 million pool of expenses. However, if it happened that the US Parent bore much expenses that it ought (say 70%), the IRS may argue the commensurate-with-income standard under IRC section 482 and reallocate the proceeds from the vaccine (IP) between Alpha Corp. and Beta Corp.

The reliability of an estimate of RAB shares also depends upon the reliability of projections used in making the estimate. Projections required for this purpose generally include a determination of the time period between the inception of the research and development activities under the CSA and the receipt of benefits, a projection of the time over which benefits will be received, and a projection of the benefits anticipated for each year in which it is anticipated that the cost-shared intangible will generate benefits. A projection of the relevant basis for measuring anticipated benefits may require a projection of the factors that underlie.

## 6.4 THE BUY-IN PAYMENT

When a controlled participant makes pre-existing intangible property available to a qualified cost sharing arrangement, that participant is deemed to have transferred interests in the property to the other participant and the other participant must make a buy-in payment as consideration for the transferred intangibles.[5] The buy-in payment, which can be made in the form of a lump-sum payment, installment payments, or royalties, is the arm's-length charge for the use of the transferred intangibles.[6]

## 6.5 PLATFORM CONTRIBUTION TRANSACTION

A platform contribution is any resource, capability, or right that a controlled participant has developed, maintained, or acquired externally to the intangible development activity (whether prior to or during the course of the CSA) that is reasonably

5. Section 1.482-7(g)(1) and (2).
6. Section 1.482-7(g)(2), (7).

anticipated to contribute to developing cost-shared intangibles. The determination whether a resource, capability, or right is reasonably anticipated to contribute to developing cost-shared intangibles is ongoing and based on the best available information. Therefore, a resource, capability, or right reasonably determined not to be a platform contribution as of an earlier point in time, may be reasonably determined to be a platform contribution at a later point in time. The PCT obligation regarding a resource or capability or right once determined to be a platform contribution does not terminate merely because it may later be determined that such resource or capability or right has not contributed, and no longer is reasonably anticipated to contribute, to developing cost-shared intangibles. However, platform contributions do not include rights in land or depreciable tangible property, and do not include rights in other resources acquired by IDCs.

For purposes of a PCT, the PCT Payee's provision of a platform contribution is presumed to be exclusive. That is, it is presumed that the platform resource, capability, or right is not reasonably anticipated to be committed to any business activities other than the CSA Activity, whether carried out by the controlled participants, other controlled taxpayers, or uncontrolled taxpayers. The controlled participants may rebut the aforementioned presumption to the satisfaction of the Commissioner.

Under a periodic adjustment provision, the IRS may adjust the amount of required PCT Payments if the ratio of (i) the present value of a participant's actual benefits from the CSA to (ii) the present value of the participant's is outside the harbor range. However, the taxpayer may avoid an adjustment by satisfying the requirements of one of four exceptions. Under one of these exceptions, the taxpayer must show that the reduced AERR that would result from certain modifications to the calculation of the taxpayer's divisional profits or losses would not have fallen out of the safe harbor range.

### 6.5.1 Aggregation of Transactions

Like the Temporary Regulations, the Final Regulations provide that an aggregation approach to valuing transactions in connection with a CSA may be appropriate in order to determine the combined effect of multiple contemporaneous transactions.[7]

The preamble of the final regulations provides:

> The combined effect of multiple contributions, potentially including controlled transactions outside of the CSA (for example, make-or-sell licenses, or intangible transfers governed by Code section 367(d)), may need to be evaluated on an aggregate basis, where that approach provides the most reliable measure of an arm's length result.

The Service goes on to add that the arm's length charge for a platform contribution of services of a research team might be converted into a cost-of-services-plus form of payment, provided that, among other conditions, the method and form of payment

7. Temporary and Final Regulations Sections 1.482-7T(g)(2)(iv) and 1.482-7(g)(2)(iv).

treating the platform value of such research team separately from the arm's length charge for any other platform contributions provide the most reliable measures of the arm's length charges.

### 6.5.2 Periodic Adjustments

Section 1.482-7T(i)(6)(A)(3) makes a technical amendment that will have the effect of making a so-called high-end trigger (and periodic adjustments) less likely to occur. More specifically, the amendment provides that a periodic trigger will not be considered to occur if there is no trigger after the PCT Payor's divisional profits or losses are calculated, by taking into account expenses on account of operating cost contributions and routine platform contributions. Profits or losses attributable to operating cost contributions are added to the list of types of profits and losses that should be excluded from the calculation of profit or loss.

### 6.5.3 Form of Payment

Controlled taxpayers have flexibility to choose a form of payment with respect to an arm's length charge, provided that the form of payment be reasonably expected to yield a value consistent with such arm's length charge determined as of the date of the PCT. Thus, a taxpayer must not only determine an arm's length charge correctly under section 1.482-7(g) but also designate a form of payment that is consistent with that arm's length charge determined as of the date of the PCT. This dual concept of the flexibility in selecting the form of payment as well as the obligation to preserve the arm's length charge through determining the form of payment as of the date of the PCT is clarified by a new sentence added to section 1.482-7(h)(2)(i).

## 6.6 BEST METHOD ANALYSIS FOR EVALUATION OF PCT PURSUANT TO CSA

The Final Regulations contain various methods for valuing platform contributions, including the income method. A best method rule applies to the choice of method. That is, the relative reliability of an application of any method depends on the degree of consistency of the analysis with the applicable contractual terms and allocation of risk under the CSA and this section among the controlled participants as of the date of the PCT, unless a change in such terms or allocation has been made in return for arm's length consideration. Accordingly, the relative reliability of an application of a method also depends on the degree of consistency of the analysis with the assumption that, as of the date of the PCT, each controlled participant's aggregate net investment in the CSA Activity (including platform contributions, operating contributions, operating cost contributions, and cost contributions) is reasonably anticipated to earn a rate of return (which might be reflected in a discount rate used in applying a method) appropriate to the riskiness of the controlled participant's CSA Activity over the entire period of such CSA Activity. If the cost-shared intangibles themselves are reasonably anticipated to contribute to developing other intangibles, then the period described in the preceding sentence includes the period, reasonably anticipated as of the date of the PCT, of developing and exploiting such indirectly benefited intangibles.

### 6.6.1 The Comparable Uncontrolled Transaction

The CUT[8] method, and the Comparable Uncontrolled Services Price (CUSP) method[9] may be applied to evaluate whether the amount charged in a PCT is arm's length by reference to the amount charged in a CUT. Although all of the factors entering into a best method analysis described in section 1.482-1(c) and (d) must be considered. Comparability and reliability under this method are particularly dependent on similarity of contractual terms, degree to which allocation of risks is proportional to RABs from exploiting the results of intangible development, similar period of commitment as to the sharing of intangible development risks, and similar scope, uncertainty, and profit potential of the subject intangible development, including a similar allocation of the risks of any existing resources, capabilities, or rights, as well as of the risks of developing other resources, capabilities, or rights that would be reasonably anticipated to contribute to exploitation within the parties' divisions, that is consistent with the actual allocation of risks between the controlled participants as provided in the CSA.

### 6.6.2 The Income Method

The Income Method is specified by Treasury Regulation section 1.482-7(g)(4) for PCTs. In applying the Income Method, cost sharing and the hypothetical licensing alternative should be viewed as closely related, differing primarily in the obligations of the cost sharing participant that is the PCT Payor. The financial projections used to apply the Income Method should be the same for the licensing and the cost sharing alternatives "except for the licensing payments to be made under the licensing alternative and the cost contributions and PCT Payments to be made under the CSA."

The income method's application is generally limited to cases in which only one participant makes non-routine contributions. The income method determines whether a PCT Payment conforms to the arm's length standard by reference to the participant's best realistic alternative to entering into the CSA. The Income Method Regulations provide that, in certain cases, an analysis of the "differential income stream" may be the best method for applying the income method with respect to PCTs. In general, the differential income stream method treats the present value of the PCT as the difference between the undiscounted income stream in a licensing scenario and the undiscounted operating income stream in a cost sharing scenario (before PCT Payments), with such difference being discounted at an appropriate rate.

In addition, the Final Regulations provide that if different discount rates are used under an income method analysis to determine the cost sharing alternative and the

8. Section 1.482-4(c).
9. Section 1.482-9(c).

licensing alternative, the analysis will be more reliable the greater the extent to which the difference between the rates reflects solely the differences in the risk profiles of the two alternatives.

### 6.6.3 The RPS Method

The Residual Profits Split Method (RPSM) determines whether the allocation of combined operating profits or losses attributable to one or more PCTs is arm's length by reference to the relative value of each participant's contribution to that combined operating profit or loss; this allocation is intended to correspond to the division of profit or loss that would result from an arrangement among similarly situated unrelated parties. Under this method, the present value of each participant's residual divisional profit or loss attributable to non-routine contributions (the "non-routine residual divisional profit or loss") is allocated in accordance with the participants' relative non-routine contributions. This present value is set to equal (i) the present value of the stream of the reasonably anticipated residuals over the duration of the development activity of divisional profit or loss, minus (ii) market returns for routine contributions, operating cost contributions, and cost contributions, using an applicable discount rate.

The IRS explains in the Preamble that market returns are not assigned to cost contributions because resources, capabilities, and rights that benefit the development of cost-shared intangibles are treated as platform contributions.

### 6.6.4 The Acquisition Price Method

The acquisition price method as specified in section 1.482-7(g)(5) typically may be considered for determining PCT Payments with respect to platform contributions as a result of asset or stock acquisitions. The acquisition price method applies the CUT method of section 1.482-4(c), or the CUSP method described in section 1.482-9(c), to evaluate whether the amount charged in a PCT, or group of PCTs, is arm's length by reference to the amount charged (the acquisition price) for the stock or asset purchase of an entire organization or portion thereof (the target) in an uncontrolled transaction. The acquisition price method is ordinarily used where substantially all the target's non-routine contributions, as such term is defined in paragraph (j)(1)(i) of this section, made to the PCT Payee's business activities are covered by a PCT or group of PCTs.

The arm's length charge for a PCT or group of PCTs covering resources, capabilities, and rights of the target is equal to the adjusted acquisition price, as divided among the controlled participants according to their respective RAB shares

### 6.6.5 The Market Capitalization Method

The market capitalization method applies the CUT method of section 1.482-4(c), or the CUSP method described in section 1.482-9(c), to evaluate whether the amount charged in a PCT, or group of PCTs, is arm's length by reference to the average market capitalization of a controlled participant (PCT Payee) whose stock is regularly traded on an established securities market. The market capitalization method is ordinarily used where substantially all of the PCT Payee's non-routine contributions to the PCT Payee's business are covered by a PCT or group of PCTs. The arm's length charge for a PCT or group of PCTs covering resources, capabilities, and rights of the PCT Payee is equal to the adjusted average market capitalization, as divided among the controlled participants according to their respective RAB shares.

### 6.6.6 Unspecified Methods

An unspecified method should take into account the general principle that uncontrolled taxpayers evaluate the terms of a transaction by considering the realistic alternatives to that transaction, and only enter into a particular transaction if none of the alternatives is preferable to it. Therefore, in establishing whether a PCT achieved an arm's length result, an unspecified method should provide information on the prices or profits that the controlled participant could have realized by choosing a realistic alternative to the CSA.

## 6.7 COURT CASES

### 6.7.1 The Veritas Software Corporation & Subsidiaries[10]

In Veritas, a US parent company granted its Irish subsidiary the right to use all of its existing technical and marketing intangibles in order to develop software under a CSA. The Irish subsidiary made a buy-in payment that was determined on the basis of what would be charged in a comparable transaction among unrelated parties (the "comparable uncontrolled transaction method"). The IRS argued that the buy-in payment was insufficient because it should have been determined under an income method approach (whereby the buy-in payment is determined on the basis of the foregone income from the most realistic alternative transaction) on an aggregate basis, assuming a perpetual life for the intangible assets and their income stream, as opposed to a license-by-license approach. In particular, the IRS argued that the buy-in payment should compensate the US parent for access to its R&D team, marketing team, distribution channels, customer lists, trademarks, trade names, brand names, and sales agreements. The court, however, (1) rejected the aggregation approach, (2) limited the useful life of the intangibles to the useful life of the actually transferred intangibles and (3) determined that the buy-in payment should be valued using, with some adjustments, the CUT method employed by the taxpayer.

10. Veritas Software Corporations & Subsidiaries, 133 T.C. No. 14 (2009).

The key facts of the case can be summed up as follows:

- Veritas Software Corporation, a US Corporation incorporated in the State of Delaware entered into a cost sharing arrangement with its foreign subsidiary (Veritas Ireland) to develop and manufacture storage management software products.
- Pursuant to the cost sharing arrangement, Veritas Software granted the Irish subsidiary the right to use certain pre-existing intangibles in Europe, the Middle East, Africa, and Asia.
- As consideration for the transfer of pre-existing intangibles, the Irish Subsidiary made a USD 166 million buy-in payment to Veritas US and employed the CUT method to calculate the payment.
- VERITAS US timely filed Federal income tax returns for 2000 and 2001. On its 2000 return Veritas US reported a USD 166 million lump-sum buy-in payment from Veritas Ireland. In response to Veritas Ireland's updated sales figures and forecasts, Veritas US, on December 17, 2002, amended the 2000 return reducing the lump-sum buy-in payment to USD 118 million.
- In a notice of deficiency issued to Veritas Software corporation, the Commissioner of the IRSs employed an income method and determined a requisite buy-in payment of USD 2.5 billion and made an income allocation to Veritas of that amount.
- In an amendment to answer, the Commissioner reduced the allocation from USD 2.5 to USD 1.675 billion. He (the CIR) also determined that the requisite buy-in payment must take into account access to Verita's research and development team, marketing team, distribution channels, customer lists, trademarks, trade names, brand names, and sales agreements.
- Veritas contends that Commissioner's determinations are arbitrary, capricious, and unreasonable, and the CUT method is the best method to calculate the requisite buy-in payment.
- The IRS claims were developed by its expert, Mr. Hatch.
- The T.C. after reviewing all the facts and evidence submitted found, pursuant to the laws and regulations in effect at the time of the challenged CSA, that Mr. Hatch allegations were unsupported, unreliable, and thoroughly unconvincing. He used: (i) wrong useful life for the products at stake, (ii) wrong discount rate and wrong risk-free rate, (iii) did not even know the full products he intended to include in his determination, and (iv) referred to the intangibles at stake as "platform intangibles" rather than "pre-existing intangibles" as under the existing regulations. The T.C. even noted:

> We note that the term "platform contribution intangibles" does not appear in the regulations applicable to the CSA but is set forth in section 1.482-7T, Temporary Income Tax Regs., 74
> Fed. Reg. -2--regulations effective for transactions entered into on or after January 5, 2009. Thus, respondent's litigating position appears to mirror transfer pricing regulations promulgated 10 years after Veritas US and Veritas Ireland signed the CSA.

- Finally, after several concessions by the CIR lead expert, the IRS challenged the use of the CUT method used by Veritas Software as inappropriate. But the T.C. after all considerations held:

> With the aforementioned adjustments, the CUT method is the best method for determining the requisite buy-in payment relating to Veritas Ireland's transfer of intangibles to Veritas US.

### 6.7.2 Xilinx v. Commissioner[11]

- In Xilinx v. Commissioner, the issue was how to determine the costs that must be shared by the participants, consistent with the arm's-length standard, under the regulations in effect for taxable years 1997 through 1999. The T.C. held that cost sharing participants need not include in the pool of costs to be shared any amount for the value of stock options granted to the employees of the participants because unrelated parties do not do so.
- The cost sharing regulations applicable to the years before the court permitted related parties to enter into qualified cost sharing arrangements if the agreement provided that the participant's share of intangible development costs reflects that participant's share of anticipated benefits. In defining the term "intangible development costs," the regulation stated that the term means "all of the costs incurred by that participant related to the intangible development area," and specifically included operating expenses as defined in section 1.482-5(d)(3) of the regulations.
- The regulations did not address the treatment of stock-based compensation. Based on the evidence at trial that unrelated parties dealing at arm's-length do not explicitly account for such costs, the T.C. rejected the government's position as inconsistent with the application of the arm's length standard described in section 1.482-1(b), and held that stock-based compensation was not a cost that must be shared.
- In 2000 and 2002, the IRS issued notices of deficiency relating to 1996–1998 and 1999, respectively, with deficiencies totaling USD 106 million and penalties totaling USD 21 million. The IRS determined that Xilinx should share its ESO costs with XI using spread theory where cost is based on the difference between the stock market price on the exercise date and the actual exercise price. The deficiency and penalties related to 1996 were later released since the stock options were granted before the date of the cost-sharing agreement.
- In May 2009, the Ninth Circuit reversed the T.C., but did not accept the reasoning of the government. On appeal, the government did not appeal the

11. Xilinx, Inc. v. Commissioner, 567 F.3d 482 (9th Cir. 2009).

finding that unrelated parties would not share employee stock option costs in the types of transactions on which the T.C. based its holding.

- The government position was that such transactions were not comparable to cost sharing arrangements, rendering the treatment of stock-based compensation by parties to those transactions irrelevant to application of the arm's-length standard. The government argued that the costs must nevertheless be shared in order to achieve an arm's length result.
- Rejecting that argument, the appellate panel instead agreed with the lower court conclusion that the requirement of the cost sharing regulations to share "all of the costs" was inconsistent with the arm's-length standard and could not be reconciled. Because the cost sharing regulation was the more explicit of the two regulatory provisions. The Ninth Circuit agreed with the government that stock-based compensation is a cost, and therefore must be included in the pool of costs to be shared.
- In March 2010, the Ninth Circuit affirmed the T.C. decision and concluded that the arm's-length standard did not require that stock-based compensation costs of related parties be shared under cost sharing agreements. In reaching this conclusion, the Ninth Circuit examined what it referred to as the "dominant purpose" of the regulation, which it said was to create "parity between taxpayers in uncontrolled transactions and taxpayers in controlled transactions." Thus, it concluded that if Xilinx were required to share its stock option costs, Xilinx would not have had tax parity with an independent taxpayer.

### 6.7.3 Altera Corp. v. Commissioner[12]

(a) Altera Corp. develops, manufactures, markets, and sells Programmable Logic Devices (PLDs) and related hardware, software, and pre-defined design building blocks for use in programming the PLDs (programming tools). Altera US and Altera International entered into concurrent agreements that became effective May 23, 1997: a master technology license agreement (technology license agreement) and a technology research and development cost sharing agreement (R&D cost-sharing agreement).

(b) Under the technology license agreement, Altera US licensed to Altera International the right to use and exploit, everywhere except the US and Canada, all of Altera US's intangible property relating to PLDs and programming tools that existed before the R&D cost sharing agreement (pre-cost sharing intangible property). In exchange for the rights granted under the technology license agreement, Altera International paid royalties to Altera US in each year from 1997 through 2003.

12. Altera Corp. v. Commissioner, T.C., No. 6253-12, 7/27/15).

(c) As of December 31, 2003, Altera International owned a fully paid-up license to use the pre-cost sharing intangible property in its territory.

Under the R&D cost sharing agreement, Altera US and Altera International agreed to pool their respective resources to conduct research and development using the pre-cost sharing intangible property. Under the R&D cost sharing agreement, Altera US and Altera International agreed to share the risks and costs of research and development activities they performed on or after May 23, 1997.

(d) Altera US granted stock options and other stock-based compensation to certain of its employees. Certain of the employees of Altera US who performed research and development activities subject to the R&D cost sharing agreement received stock options or other stock-based compensation. The employees' cash compensation was included in the cost pool under the R&D cost-sharing agreement.

(e) Pursuant to the R&D cost sharing agreement, Altera International made cost sharing payments to Altera US for its 2004-07 taxable years.

(f) Altera, US timely filed its Forms 1120, US Corporation Income Tax Return, for its 2004–2007 taxable years.

(g) The IRS sent notices of deficiency to petitioner with respect to its 2004–2007 taxable years.

(h) The IRS proposed to increase Altera International's cost sharing payments to take into account the stock-based compensation of Altera US, as provided under the 2003 cost sharing regulations, arguing among other that:

  (i) it could make allocations without reference to uncontrolled party conduct;

  (ii) Treasury had authority to issue regulations that modified or even abandoned the arm's-length standard;

  (iii) whether the regulation was a legislative regulation was moot, because Treasury in fact followed notice and comment rulemaking;

  (iv) some propositions require reasoned conclusions because there is scant empirical evidence available;

  (v) he court should defer to Treasury's expertise, citing the Ninth Circuit's deference to the agency expertise of the Bureau of Prisons in Peck v. Thomas; and

  (vi) the regulation should be upheld under the commensurate-with-income principle in section 482.

(i) Altera contended that the final rule lacks a basis in fact because Treasury issued the final rule without any evidence that unrelated parties would ever agree to share stock-based compensation costs.

(j) Altera US petitioned the T.C. under the theory that the 2003 cost sharing regulations were legislative regulations subject to arbitrary-and-capricious review under State Farm and shall comply with section 706(2)(A) of the Advanced Pricing Agreement (APA).

(k) The T.C. stated:

> The commensurate-with-income standard was never intended to supplant the arm's-length standard. Rather, Congress intended for the commensurate-with-income standard to work consistently with the arm's-length standard.

(l) The T.C. found that unrelated parties never share the exercise spread or grant date value of stock-based compensation. Finally, the T.C. concluded that during the years in issue the grant value of stock-based compensation was generally not treated as an expense for tax and financial accounting purposes. Moreover, pursued the T.C., the commensurate-with-income standard, as interpreted by Treasury, cannot provide a sufficient basis for the final rule.
(m) Although both the proposed and the final regulations included the share stock-based compensation costs, the T.C. found the preamble's explanation for Treasury's decision inadequate.

The preamble to the final rule did not rely on Treasury's experience as a party to arm's-length cost sharing agreements, or even on any experience Treasury may have had in examining the arm's-length cost sharing agreements of taxpayers it regulates. Indeed, the preamble to the final rule all but disclaimed Treasury's reliance on any such experience.

## 6.8 THE FUTURE OF THE COST SHARING REGULATIONS

To fully understand the implications of the T.C. decision, a regulatory background history would help assess the T.C. standing:

- Prior to 1986 Act, the regulation addressing cost sharing arrangements was contained in Regulation section 1.482-2(d)(4), which stated:

  > In order for [a cost-sharing] arrangement to qualify as a bona fide arrangement, it must reflect an effort in good faith by the participating members to bear their respective shares of all the costs and risks of development on an arm's-length basis. In order for the sharing of costs and risks to be considered on an arm's length basis, the terms and conditions must be comparable to those which would have been adopted by unrelated parties similarly situated had they entered into such an arrangement.[13]

- In 1988[14] the IRS followed Congress's lead by endorsing the arm's-length nature of cost sharing arrangements as follows:

  > Cost-sharing arrangements have long existed at arm's length between unrelated parties...but the costs to be shared should include all direct and

13. Regulation section 1.482-2(d)(4) (1968).
14. 1988 Study of Intercompany Pricing ("1988 White Paper").

> indirect costs of the research and development undertaken as part of the arrangement. Direct expenses would include expenses for salaries, research materials, and facilities. . . . Indirect costs should include a portion of overall corporate management expense and overall interest expense that is allocated and apportioned to research and development activities in a manner consistent with US expense allocation principles.

- In July 2002, Treasury issued a notice of proposed rulemaking and notice of a public hearing (NPRM) with respect to proposed amendments to the 1995 cost sharing regulations.
- In August 2003 Treasury issued the final rule. The final rule explicitly required parties to QCSAs to share stock-based compensation costs. The final rule provides two methods for measuring the value of stock-based compensation: a default method and an elective method,[15] and the elective method.[16] These final regulations reflect that at arm's length the parties to an arrangement that is based on the sharing of costs to develop intangibles in order to obtain the benefit of an independent right to exploit such intangibles would ensure through bargaining that the arrangement reflected all relevant costs, including all costs of compensating employees for providing services related to the arrangement. Parties dealing at arm's length in such an arrangement based on the sharing of costs and benefits generally would not distinguish between stock-based compensation and other forms of compensation.
- The final regulations provide that stock-based compensation must be taken into account in the context of QCSAs because such a result is consistent with the arm's length standard.
- Finally, the preamble to the final rule states that "[i]t has also been determined that [APA] section 553(b) does not apply to these regulations."
- The T.C. stressed on that "where an agency has articulated no reasoned basis for its decision—where its action is founded on unsupported assertions or unstated inferences—[a court] will not abdicate the judicial duty carefully to 'review the record to ascertain that the agency has made a reasoned decision based on reasonable extrapolations from some reliable evidence.'"
- Several parties have challenged the IRS standing all along the process from the proposed regulations to the final regulations alleging the inexistence of reliable data concerning the cost sharing of stock-based compensation costs. The IRS never addressed the issue.
- The T.C. deliberately overlooked this fact, that Altera itself reported the stock-based compensation as expenses in its accounting books in accordance

15. Under the default method, the costs attributable to stock-based compensation generally are included as intangible development costs upon the exercise of the option and measured by the spread between the option strike price and the price of the underlying stock.
16. Under the elective method, the costs attributable to stock options are taken into account in certain cases in accordance with the "fair value" of the option, as reported for financial accounting purposes either as a charge against income or in footnoted disclosures.

with the Statement of Financial Accounting Standard No. 123. It is a fact that accounting and tax principles often match until and unless the IRC spells out a distinction between them. For, instance, officers' life insurance premium payments and proceeds are deductible from financial accounting purposes, but not for tax returns. The premiums are recognized in the financial statements as business expenses but are not deductible on the income tax return. Another example is this: tax penalties on underpaid taxes and fines resulting from a violation of the law are recognized as expenses on the financial statements but are not deductible expenses on the tax return.

- The case is still pending before the Ninth Circuit Court of Appeals. Regardless of the outcome, the Altera case would extol the playing ground under the APA. The IRS would no longer brush up nor rebut the challenged raised through its actions by making unsupported or unstated inferences, lest its regulations be vacated the courts.

# CHAPTER 7
# Transfer Pricing for Services

## 7.1 INTRODUCTION

The final service regulations require taxpayers to apply the arm's-length standard in establishing compensation amounts for the provision of intercompany services. Similar to other sections of the transfer pricing regulations, taxpayers involved in the provision of intercompany services must adhere to the best method, comparability, and the arm's-length range requirements of Treasury Regulation section 1.482-1.

## 7.2 METHODOLOGY

On 31 July 2009, the IRS and the treasury issued final regulations in connection with controlled service transactions, which supersede Temporary Regulation 1.482-9T. The final regulations recognized the following six methods.

### 7.2.1 The Comparable Uncontrolled Services Price Method

The CUSP method evaluates whether the amount charged in a controlled services transaction is arm's length by reference to the amount charged in a comparable uncontrolled services transaction. Although all of the factors described in section 1.482-1(d)(3) must be considered, similarity of the services rendered, and of the intangible property (if any) used in performing the services, generally will have the greatest effects on comparability under this method. Comparability under this method depends on close similarity with respect to these factors or adjustments to account for any differences. If there are differences between the controlled and uncontrolled transactions that would affect price, adjustments should be made to the price of the uncontrolled transaction according to the comparability provisions of section 1.482-1(d)(2). Factors that may be particularly relevant to application of this method include:

(1) quality of the services rendered;
(2) contractual terms (e.g., scope and terms of warranties or guarantees regarding the services, volume, credit and payment terms, allocation of risks, including any contingent-payment terms and whether costs were incurred without a provision for current reimbursement);
(3) intangible property (if any) used in rendering the services;
(4) geographic market in which the services are rendered or received;
(5) risks borne (e.g., costs incurred to render the services, without provision for current reimbursement);
(6) duration or quantitative measure of services rendered;
(7) collateral transactions or ongoing business relationships between the renderer and the recipient, including arrangement for the provision of tangible property in connection with the services; and
(8) alternatives realistically available to the renderer and the recipient.

### 7.2.2 The Gross Services Margin Method

The Gross Services Margin (GSM) method evaluates whether the amount charged in a controlled services transaction is arm's length by reference to the gross profit margin realized in CUTs. This method ordinarily is used in cases where a controlled taxpayer performs services or functions in connection with an uncontrolled transaction between a member of the controlled group and an uncontrolled taxpayer. This method may be used where a controlled taxpayer renders services (agent services) to another member of the controlled group in connection with a transaction between that other member and an uncontrolled taxpayer. This method also may be used in cases where a controlled taxpayer contracts to provide services to an uncontrolled taxpayer (intermediary function) and another member of the controlled group actually performs a portion of the services provided. The appropriate gross services profit is computed by multiplying the applicable uncontrolled price by the gross services profit margin in CUTs. The determination of the appropriate gross services profit will take into account any functions performed by other members of the controlled group, as well as any other relevant factors described in section 1.482-1(d)(3). The comparable gross services profit margin may be determined by reference to the commission in an uncontrolled transaction, where that commission is stated as a percentage of the price charged in the uncontrolled transaction. The degree of comparability between an uncontrolled transaction and a controlled transaction is determined by applying the comparability provisions of section 1.482-1(d). Comparability under this method is particularly dependent on similarity of services or functions performed, risks borne, intangible property (if any) used in providing the services or functions, and contractual terms, or adjustments to account for the effects of any such differences. If there are material differences between the controlled and uncontrolled transactions that would affect the gross services profit margin, adjustments should be made to the gross services profit margin, according to the comparability provisions of section

1.482-1(d)(2). If there are differences in functions performed, however, the effect on gross services profit of such differences is not necessarily equal to the differences in the amount of related costs. Specific examples of factors that may be particularly relevant to this method include:

(1) contractual terms (e.g., scope and terms of warranties or guarantees regarding the services or function, volume, credit and payment terms, and allocation of risks, including any contingent-payment terms);
(2) intangible property (if any) used in performing the services or function;
(3) geographic market in which the services or function are performed or in which the relevant uncontrolled transaction takes place; and
(4) risks borne, including, if applicable, inventory-type risk.

The degree of consistency in accounting practices between the controlled transaction and the uncontrolled comparables that materially affect the gross services profit margin affects the reliability of the results under this method.

### 7.2.3 The Cost of Services Plus Method

The Cost of Services Plus Method (CSPM) evaluates whether the amount charged in a controlled services transaction is arm's length by reference to the gross services profit mark up realized in CUTs. The CSPM is ordinarily used in cases where the controlled service renderer provides the same or similar services to both controlled and uncontrolled parties. This method is ordinarily not used in cases where the controlled services transaction involves a contingent-payment arrangement, as described in paragraph (i)(2) of this section.

The CSPM measures an arm's length price by adding the appropriate gross service profit. The appropriate gross services profit is computed by multiplying the controlled taxpayer's comparable transactional costs by the gross services profit mark up, expressed as a percentage of the comparable transactional costs earned in CUTs. Comparable transactional costs must be determined on a basis that will facilitate comparison with the CUTs. If possible, the appropriate gross services profit mark up should be derived from CUTs of the same taxpayer participating in the controlled services transaction because similar characteristics are more likely to be found among services provided by the same service provider than among services provided by other service providers. If there are material differences between the controlled and uncontrolled transactions that would affect the gross services profit mark up, adjustments should be made to the gross services profit mark up earned in the CUT according to the provisions of section 1.482-1(d)(2). If there are differences in functions performed, however, the effect on gross services profit of such differences is not necessarily equal to the differences in the amount of related comparable transactional costs. Specific examples of the factors that may be particularly relevant to this method include:

(1) the complexity of the services;
(2) the duration or quantitative measure of services;
(3) contractual terms (e.g., scope and terms of warranties or guarantees provided, volume, credit and payment terms, allocation of risks, including any contingent-payment terms);
(4) economic circumstances; and
(5) risks borne.

The degree of consistency in accounting practices between the controlled transaction and the uncontrolled comparables that materially affect the gross services profit mark up affects the reliability of the results under this method.

### 7.2.4 The Profit Split Method

#### *7.2.4.1 The Comparable Profit Split Method*

The CPM evaluates whether the amount charged in a controlled transaction is arm's length, based on objective measures of profitability (PLIs), derived from uncontrolled taxpayers that engage in similar business activities under similar circumstances.

Where the tested party determined under section 1.482-5(b)(2) is instead the recipient of the controlled services, the rules under this paragraph (f) are not applicable to determine the arm's length result. A profit level indicator that may provide a reliable basis for comparing operating profits of the tested party involved in a controlled services transaction and uncontrolled comparables is the ratio of operating profit to total services costs. Consistency in accounting practices between the relevant business activity of the tested party and the uncontrolled service providers is particularly important in determining the reliability of the results under this method, but less than in applying the CSPM.

Example: Ratio of operating profit to total services costs as the appropriate profit level indicator.

(i) A Country T parent firm, Company A, and its Country Y subsidiary, Company B, both engage in manufacturing as their principal business activity.
Company A also performs certain advertising services for itself and its affiliates. In year 1, Company A renders advertising services to Company B.
(ii) Based on the facts and circumstances, it is determined that the CPM will provide the most reliable measure of an arm's length result.
Company A is selected as the tested party. No data are available for comparable independent manufacturing firms that render advertising services to third parties. Financial data are available, however, for ten independent firms that render similar advertising services as their principal business activity in Country X. The ten firms are determined to be comparable under section 1.482-5(c). Neither Company A nor the comparable companies use valuable intangible property
in rendering the services.

(iii) Based on the available financial data of the comparable companies, it cannot be determined whether these comparable companies report costs for financial accounting purposes in the same manner as the tested party. The publicly available financial data of the comparable companies segregate total services costs into cost of goods sold and sales, general and administrative costs, with no further segmentation of costs provided. Due to the limited information available regarding the cost accounting practices used by the comparable companies, the ratio of operating profits to total services costs is determined to be the most appropriate profit level indicator. This ratio includes total services costs to minimize the effect of any inconsistency in accounting practices between Company A and the comparable companies.

#### *7.2.4.2 The Residual Profit Split Method*

The PSM evaluates whether the allocation of the combined operating profit or loss attributable to one or more controlled transactions is arm's length by reference to the relative value of each controlled taxpayer's contribution to that combined operating profit or loss. The relative value of each controlled taxpayer's contribution is determined in a manner that reflects the functions performed, risks assumed, and resources employed by such controlled taxpayer in the relevant business activity. The residual PSM may not be used where only one controlled taxpayer makes significant non-routine contributions.

Example: Residual profit split.

(i) Company A, a corporation resident in Country X, auctions spare parts by means of an interactive database. Company A maintains a database that lists all spare parts available for auction. Company A developed the software used to run the database. Company A's database is managed by Company A employees in a data center located in Country X, where storage and manipulation of data also take place. Company A has a wholly owned subsidiary, Company B, located in Country Y. Company B performs marketing and advertising activities to promote Company A's interactive database. Company B solicits unrelated companies to auction spare parts on Company A's database, and solicits customers interested in purchasing spare parts online. Company B owns and maintains a computer server in Country Y, where it receives information on spare parts available for auction. Company B has also designed a specialized communications network that connects its data center to Company A's data center in Country X. The communications network allows Company B to enter data from uncontrolled companies on Company A's database located in Country X. Company B's communications network also allows uncontrolled companies to access Company A's interactive database and purchase spare parts. Company B bore the risks and cost of developing this specialized communications network. Company B enters into contracts with uncontrolled companies and provides the companies access to Company A's database through the Company B network.

(ii) Analysis of the facts and circumstances indicates that both Company A and Company B possess valuable intangible property that they use to conduct the spare parts auction business. Company A bore the economic risks of developing and maintaining software and the interactive database. Company B bore the economic risks of developing the necessary technology to transmit information from its server to Company A's data center, and to allow uncontrolled companies to access Company A's database. Company B helped to enhance the value of Company A's trademark and to establish a network of customers in Country Y. In addition, there are no market comparables for the transactions between Company A and Company B to reliably evaluate them separately. Given the facts and circumstances, the Commissioner determines that a RPS method will provide the most reliable measure of an arm's length result.

(iii) Under the RPS method, profits are first allocated based on the routine contributions of each taxpayer. Routine contributions include general sales, marketing or administrative functions performed by Company B for Company A for which it is possible to identify market returns. Any residual profits will be allocated based on the non-routine contributions of each taxpayer. Since both Company A and Company B provided non-routine contributions, the residual profits are allocated based on these contributions.

### 7.2.5 The Services Cost Method

The Services Cost Method (SCM) is intended to provide a practical and administrable means of identifying low-margin services that may be evaluated by reference to total services cost without a mark up. To be eligible for the SCM, a service must be a covered service, the service cannot be an excluded activity, the service cannot be precluded from constituting a covered service by reason of the business judgment rule, and adequate books and records must be maintained with respect to the service.

To determine if the SCM should apply to a particular service (or group of services) performed by a group of employees, the aggregation principle of the Treasury Department and the IRS believe that the interquartile range of the comparable median mark up is an appropriate measure.

### 7.2.6 Unspecified

Consistent with the specified methods, an unspecified method should take into account the general principle that uncontrolled taxpayers evaluate the terms of a transaction by considering the realistic alternatives to that transaction, including economically similar transactions structured as other than services transactions and only enter into a particular transaction if none of the alternatives is preferable to it. In establishing whether a controlled services transaction achieved an arm's length result, an unspecified method should provide information on the prices or profits that the controlled taxpayer could have realized by choosing a realistic alternative to the controlled services transaction (e.g., outsourcing a particular service function, rather than performing the function itself).

Example

(i) Company T, a US corporation, develops computer software programs including a real estate investment program that performs financial analysis of commercial real properties. Companies U, V, and W are owned by Company T. The primary business activity of Companies U, V, and W is commercial real estate development. For business reasons, Company T does not sell the computer program to its customers (on a compact disk or via download from Company T's server through the Internet). Instead, Company T maintains the software program on its own server and allows customers to access the program through the Internet by using a password. The transactions between Company T and Companies U, V, and W are structured as controlled services transactions whereby Companies U, V, and W obtain access via the Internet to Company T's software program for financial analysis. Each year, Company T provides a revised version of the computer program including the most recent data on the commercial real estate market, rendering the old version obsolete.

(ii) In evaluating whether the consideration paid by Companies U, V, and W to Company T was arm's length, the Commissioner may consider, subject to the best method rule of section 1.482-1(c), Company T's alternative of selling the computer program to Companies U, V, and W on a compact disk or via download through the Internet. The Commissioner determines that the controlled services transactions between Company T and Companies U, V, and W are comparable to the transfer of a similar software program on a compact disk or via download through the Internet between uncontrolled parties. Subject to adjustments being made for material differences between the controlled services transactions and the CUTs, the uncontrolled transfers of tangible property may be used to evaluate the arm's length results for the controlled services transactions between Company T and Companies U, V, and W.

## 7.3 COURT CASES

### 7.3.1 US Steel Corp. v. Commissioner Service (CUST)

- United States Steel Corporation was a major vertically integrated producer of steel. It owned iron ore mines in the US and elsewhere.
- In 1947, Steel discovered a vast new source of iron ore in Cerro Bolivar, a remote part of north-eastern Venezuela on the Orinoco River. The transport of Orinoco ore to the Atlantic required the dredging of an extensive channel. Steel proceeded to develop these mines at a cost of approximately USD 200 million. In 1949, Steel formed Orinoco Mining Company ("Orinoco"), a wholly owned Delaware subsidiary, to own and exploit the Cerro Bolivar mines.
- Orinoco began selling ore from its mines in 1953. Initially, the ore purchased by Steel from Orinoco was transported to the US in chartered vessels owned by two independent companies, Universe Tankships, Inc. ("Universe"), and

Joshua Hendy Corp. ("Hendy"). But in December 1953, Steel incorporated another wholly owned subsidiary, Navios, Inc. ("Navios") in Liberia. Navios, with its principal place of business in Nassau, in the Bahamas, was a carrier which did not own any vessels.

- From July 1954 on, Navios, instead of Steel, chartered vessels from Universe, Hendy, and other owners, and Steel paid Navios for the transport of ore from Venezuela to the US. Navios was an active company, having in the period 1954–1960 between 53 and 81 full-time employees.
- Although Steel was by far the largest customer of Navios, Navios sold its transport services to other domestic steel producers (collectively "the independents") and to foreign steel companies. The prices charged by Navios to other domestic ore importers during the relevant period were the same prices charged to Steel, although the rates charged to companies importing ore to countries other than the US were different.
- Orinoco did not sell exclusively to Steel, although its parent was by far its largest customer. Orinoco sold to the independents and to foreign steel companies at the same prices it charged Steel. Orinoco sold ore bound for the US FOB Puerto Ordaz, Venezuela in an attempt to arrive at a fair market price in order to minimize conflict with the Venezuelan taxing authorities, who had the power to revalue, for taxation purposes, the price at which Orinoco sold its ore if they considered that price too low.
- Orinoco was subject to a Venezuelan tax of up to 50 percent on income, and to a US tax of 48 percent on any residue not offset by foreign tax credits. Steel was subject to a US tax of 48 percent of net income. Navios was subject to a 2.5 percent excise tax in Venezuela and no tax in the US. Dividends paid by Navios to Steel, of course, would be taxed at a rate of 48 percent.
- In 1960, Steel found with a wholly owned subsidiary possessing nearly USD 80 million in cash and cash equivalents. Navios paid no dividends to Steel during the period involved in this case. In effect, then, Navios became an offshore tax shelter.
- In the tax years 1957 through 1960, Navios earned approximately USD 391 million in gross revenues, all on the transport of iron ore from Venezuela to various points in the eastern continental US and in Europe. Of this total, revenues from Steel amounted to USD 286 million, or 73 percent of the total; and from independent domestic steel purchasers USD 21 million, or 5 percent of the total.
- Two steel companies, Bethlehem Steel and Eastern Gas and Fuel Associates, used other means of transportation for ore which they purchased from Orinoco. Bethlehem had mines and exported from Venezuela small quantities of ore from the Orinoco area prior to Steel's development of its mines. Bethlehem had earlier set up a transportation system from minehead to the US to which it adhered during the period in question. Eastern Fuel and Gas, a much smaller concern, contracted directly with shipowners, including its own shipowning affiliates.

- During 1957–1960, there was no information publicly available from which a "market price" for the carriage of iron ore by sea could be determined. Unlike the practice in the oil tanker industry, for example, ship charter contract prices for ore carriage were not published.
- The Commissioner determined that Navios had overcharged Steel by 25 percent, and allocated income from Navios to Steel. The Commissioner also argued that the fact that Steel paid the same rates as the independents is itself sufficient evidence that Steel was overcharged, pointing out that some of the Orinoco ore was shipped to Great Britain, but that although the distance from Venezuela to Great Britain is, on the average, 54 percent greater than the distance to the US, the rates charged by Navios were not 54 percent higher than the Venezuela-to-US rates.
- The T.C. reviewed the history of Steel's relations with its subsidiaries Navios and Orinoco and concluded that a section 482 reallocation was justified because Steel had caused Navios to charge rates such that, at all times, the delivered price of Orinoco-origin ore in the US was equivalent of the Lower Lake Erie price.
- In the T.C.'s view, this equivalence served several purposes: (i) it protected Steel's interest in the revenues of its subsidiary, Oliver Mining Co., by insuring that the Lower Lake Erie price was not undercut by cheaper foreign ore; (ii) because Steel could be sure of selling its Orinoco production so long as the delivered US price did not exceed the Lower Lake Erie price, it enabled Steel to earn "extra" profits; (iii) such extra profits were not subject to Venezuelan tax and were sheltered from US tax because they were earned through Navios.
- However, the Court used two alternative means of arriving at what Navios' revenues would have been had it charged a "market" price for its services: (i) the Court extrapolated hypothetical rates for 1957–1960 from what Universe and Hendy charged in their 1954 contracts with Steel, adding adjustments to account for increased costs, risks, and profits. As a check on the accuracy of this historical approach, (ii) Judge Quealy also constructed hypothetical rates based on estimates of what Navios' costs had been in the taxable years in question, adjusting these estimates to allow for risk and profit. He then chose the method which, for each taxable year, would result in the lowest reallocation in favor of the government.
- The Court then held:

> Considering all the relevant facts, the evidence was sufficient to show similar enough transactions with independent buyers to establish that the price Steel paid Navios was an arm's length price....That the amounts Steel paid Navios for ore transport were the same rates paid by other independent purchasers of Orinoco ore.... That the shipments of Orinoco ore to independent American buyers represented a series of transactions substantial in both frequency and volume.

- Further, the T.C. found that the transactions between Navios and Jones & Laughlin, Sharon and Youngstown were "independent" in that Steel had no ownership or control interest in any of these firms and thus was not in a position to influence their decision to deal with Navios.
- Consolidated Return Issue.

### 7.3.2 Stanley Diefenthal v. United States[1]

- Southern Scrap Material Co., Ltd. ("Scrapco") was organized around the turn of the century. Since its inception and until 1965, when Adolph and his wife died, Scrapco was wholly owned by Adolph.
- Scrapco was engaged in the business of purchasing, processing, and selling scrap metal. As the business developed, Scrapco received orders from Japanese steel manufacturers, which required Scrapco to deliver the scrap to a port or ports in Japan.
- In order to fix the cost of each such shipment in advance, Scrapco established an unvarying policy of chartering vessels only on a voyage charter basis, at a set amount for the trip, from the company's headquarters in New Orleans to the port of destination in Japan.
- In the mid-1950s, one of the heirs of Scrapco, Mr. Stanley formed his own domestic corporations, which time-chartered vessels and then in turn voyage-chartered the vessels to Scrapco. Thus Stanley's capital assumed the risk of delayed shipment and profited to the extent the trips were completed without incident.
- In the early 1960s Stanley set up a Panamanian corporation, Fukaya Trading Company, S.A. ("Fukaya") for the purpose of establishing a brokerage agency in Japan to solicit and handle business for Scrapco in return for a commission of 1 percent of sales. Fukaya had an office in Japan and employed three to six employees. It used the trade name of "Southern Scrap Far East, Ltd." It was formed to act as agent for Scrapco in Japan because of unsatisfactory results achieved by independent agents used prior thereto.
- After a while, Stanley liquidated the domestic (New Orleans) corporations which had engaged in the time chartering business, and properly reported any income realized on such liquidations as capital gain. Then he began using Fukaya, under the trade name of Compania Transporte Arroyo (CTA), to handle the time charters previously handled by his domestic corporations.
- The liquidation of domestic corporations had a dual tax advantage: (i) the income from time charters became exempt from US taxation as long as it was retained in the foreign corporate entity; and (ii) because the ship chartering

1. Stanley Diefenthal v. US, 367 F.Supp. 506 (1973).

income accounted for more than 70 percent of Fukaya's total income, the sales income from the brokerage office in Japan was similarly exempt until actually distributed to an American shareholder.

- A problem arose when Japanese officials refused to allow Fukaya, as a foreign corporation, to operate its sales office under an assumed trade name. Accordingly, upon advice of a Japanese consultant, Stanley formed a Panamanian subsidiary of Fukaya, Southern Scrap Far East, Ltd., S.A., and then registered its name in Japan.
- Southern Scrap Far East, Ltd., S.A. was a shell entity which never conducted any business. The Japanese sales activities continued to be on behalf of the parent, Fukaya. The income always went to Fukaya directly and expenses were paid by Fukaya directly.
- Stanley treated the sales income as income of Fukaya in the information returns filed with the US government, but reported the sales income as income of Southern Scrap Far East, Ltd., S.A. on returns filed with the Japanese government.
- At the request of some shipowners, Scrapco, in connection with some but not all of the 1966 charters, issued letters to the shipowners with a performance guarantee clause.
- The Commissioner utilized section 482 to allocate all of the net chartering income from Fukaya to Scrapco for the tax year of 1966. The Commissioner contended that: (i) Fukaya was provided certain services without charge; (ii) the ships were allowed to use Scrapco wharves, rather than having to load in open water, and Scrapco provided fresh water for the journey; (iii) and various employees of Scrapco rendered services for Fukaya without being directly compensated by Fukaya.
- The IRS conceded before trial that the Commissioner erroneously allocated USD 58,033.34 too much income to Scrapco, and that, to that extent, taxpayers had been forced to overpay taxes. However, the government still maintained that it was appropriate to allocate the remaining USD 103,720.19 of the original figure of USD 161,753.53.
- The Court found that Stanley made inquiries of knowledgeable sources, including competitors and ship brokers, including the head of voyage charter operations for Simpson, Spence & Young, to ask for the market rate of a voyage charter for a ship of comparable size from New Orleans to Japan. That only after so determining the current market price for a voyage charter, Stanley would arrange such a charter between CTA and Scrapco at a price which he considered to be slightly below market, in order to be sure that Scrapco and all of its owners were being treated fairly, and also to compensate Scrapco for his time and the time of other Scrapco employees who did work on the charters.
- The Court also found that the possible variation between Fukaya's voyage charter price and market price, as well as the amounts of services rendered Fukaya by Scrapco without any specific compensation, was less than USD

10,000. When compared to the USD 1,138,000 total shipping business between the two companies, the USD 10,000 discrepancy is reasonable.
- Therefore, the Court held:

> Because Scrapco paid no more than an arm's length price to Fukaya, the Commissioner acted unreasonably, arbitrarily, and capriciously in allocating income.

# CHAPTER 8
# The Best Method Rule

## 8.1 INTRODUCTION

The arm's length result of a controlled transaction must be determined under the method that, under the facts and circumstances, provides the most reliable measure of an arm's length result. Thus, there is no strict priority of methods, and no method will invariably be considered to be more reliable than others. An arm's length result may be determined under any method without establishing the inapplicability of another method, but if another method subsequently is shown to produce a more reliable measure of an arm's length result, such other method must be used. Similarly, if two or more applications of a single method provide inconsistent results, the arm's length result must be determined under the application that, under the facts and circumstances, provides the most reliable measure of an arm's length result. The particular method that applies will depend in part on the type of transaction at issue. Whatever method chosen, there is no reference to any referential method, and the taxpayer has to choose among the available methods, the one that provides the most reliable measure of an arm's length result.

Here, the US transfer pricing methodologies differ from the OECD, where the transfer pricing must first seek to comply with the three basic methods, before using the rest of the available methods. However, choosing the appropriate method is not always an easy task when there are not or there are fewer comparables. Therefore, the taxpayer may have to select the best method to determine transfer prices for tax purposes in a variety of situations and contexts. The best method rule requires an analysis of transfer prices under the method that provides the most reliable estimate of arm's length prices under the given circumstances. The singular often used "best method" can be misleading as the best method rule can turn out to be the "best methods," depending on the transaction involved. Tax planners can segregate the transactions, whenever necessary, and apply one best method proper to a particular segment of the transaction, such as in PerkinElmer,[1] where the CUP analysis was coupled with the RP method, and again the CUP method at the last segment of the transaction. The regulations state that the two primary factors to take into account in selecting the best method are:

(1) the degree of comparability between the controlled transactions and any uncontrolled comparables; and
(2) the quality of data and assumptions used in the analysis.

Tax planners may develop the analysis under several methods and still have difficulty deciding which of one or more pricing method is the best. Often, after two methods seeming closed in result, tax planners might seek for a third method as a test. Meanwhile, they have to keep all relevant documents related to the transactions to avoid heavy penalties.

Treasury Regulation section 1.482-8 provides examples of the application of the best method rule.

## 8.2 EXAMPLES OF THE BEST METHOD RULE

In accordance with the best method rule of section 1.482-1(c), a method may be applied in a particular case only if the comparability, quality of data, and reliability of assumptions under that method make it more reliable than any other available measure of the arm's length result. The following examples illustrate the comparative analysis required to apply this rule. As with all of the examples in these regulations, these examples are based on simplified facts, are provided solely for purposes of illustrating the type of analysis required under the relevant rule, and do not provide rules of general application. Thus, conclusions reached in these examples as to the relative reliability of methods are based on the assumed facts of the examples and are not general conclusions concerning the relative reliability of any method.

## 8.3 COURT DETERMINATION OF THE BEST METHOD

When the taxpayer overcomes the Commissioner's presumption of correctness and proves that the deficiencies set forth in the notice of deficiency are arbitrary, capricious, or unreasonable, but fail to prove that alternative allocations it proposes satisfy the arm's-length standard, the Court must determine from the record the proper allocation of income between petitioner and the Service.[2]

1. Perkin-Elner v. CIR, T.C Memo. 1983.
2. Eli Lilly & Co. v. Commissioner, 856 F.2d 855, 860 (7th Cir. 1988) (Lilly II).

Put starkly, where none of the acceptable methods can reasonably be applied under the facts and circumstances of a particular case, the regulations authorize use of any other appropriate method, or variations of such methods, for determining an arm's-length price.[3]

Courts are expected to make their own best estimates as to the appropriate transfer price on the basis of the available record under the principles of Cohan v. Commissioner.[4]

In the Medtronic case,[5] for instance, imperfect comparables served as a base from which the court determined the arm's length consideration for the intangible property involved in the dispute.

### 8.3.1 Sundstrand Corp. v. CIR

- In the Sundstrand case, for example, the Commissioner did not present any evidence to sustain independently the cost plus methodology which he relied upon in the notice of deficiency as the basis for the section 482 allocations. Nor did the Service expert (Dr. Lynk) make any attempt to support the Commissioner's determination on the basis of the cost plus method used by Agent Pierson.
- The Service's determination, using the cost plus method, was premised on SunPac acting as a subcontractor of Sundstrand. However, the Court concluded that such a determination was arbitrary, capricious, and unreasonable. Therefore, the taxpayer carried its burden of proof as to this matter. As Sundstrand could provide an alternative acceptable transfer pricing for the disputed transactions, the Court has no other choice but to look to another appropriate method, or variations of such methods, for determining an arm's-length consideration. Of course, the appropriate method to use would depend on the availability of information regarding comparable companies and what adjustments, if any, would be needed to determine a reasonable arm's-length price.
- After scrutinizing the record, the Court determined that, ideally, different pricing methods should have been used to price the various categories of parts: unfinished parts could have been priced possibly using the cost plus method; finished parts could have been priced separately under possibly the

3. Section 1.482-2(e)(1)(iii).
4. Cohan v. Commissioner, 39 F.2d 540 (2d Cir. 1930).
Cohan Rule is a common law rule whereby taxpayers, when unable to produce records of actual expenditures, may rely on reasonable estimates provided there is some factual basis for it. "Absolute certainty in such matters is usually impossible and is not necessary; the Board should make as close an approximation as it can, bearing heavily if it chooses upon the taxpayer whose inexactitude is of his own making."
5. Medtronic, Inc. and Consolidated Subsidiaries v. CIR (2016), T.C. Memo. 2016-112.

comparable uncontrolled price method or the RPM depending on whether the parts were to be sold to airline customers and overhaul centers or used internally by petitioner.

- Thus, the Court held that for 1977 and 1978 the arm's-length consideration for SunPac parts was the applicable catalog price, less a discount of 20 percent. In arriving at this discount rate the Court relied heavily on certain sales and/or distribution agreements Sundstrand had with unrelated third parties and on certain representations Sundstrand made to the US Customs Service.
- As for the royalty fee, the Court found that the arm's-length consideration for the intangible property involved was 10 percent of the net selling price of the SunPac parts sold.
- Finally, the Court found that Sundstrand had to include in its income USD 1,389,365 and USD 1,289,106, for 1977 and 1978, respectively, for the arm's-length charge for the technical assistance Sundstrand gave to SunPac during those years.

### 8.3.2 Altera Corp. v. Commissioner[6]

In the Altera case, the Court states that Service cannot escape the arm's-length standard by arguing that controlled parties have distinct incentives from unrelated parties. The IRS has argued that the differences in incentives among controlled parties as compared to uncontrolled parties amounted to differences in circumstances, which justified its standing. Rather, the T.C. went on to clarify two legal principles: (i) that the arm's-length standard of Regulation section 1.482-1(b)(1) requires an empirical analysis of what unrelated parties would do under comparable circumstances, and (ii) that the court discussed the challenged regulations under the APA through the lenses of the US Supreme Court's directive to hold Treasury and the IRS to the same reasoned decision-making standard as any other agency.

### 8.3.3 Medtronic, Inc. and Consolidated Subsidiaries v. CIR[7]

The relevant facts of the case are as follows:

(a) Medtronic US and Medtronic Puerto Rico entered into license agreements for the intangible property necessary to manufacture and sell Devices and Leads.

(b) Under the terms of the license agreements, Medtronic Puerto Rico obtained the exclusive right to use, develop, and enjoy the intangible property used in manufacturing Devices for sale to customers in the US and Leads for sale to customers worldwide.

6. Altera Corp. v. Commissioner, 145 T.C. No. 3 (2015).
7. Medtronic, Inc. and Consolidated Subsidiaries v. CIR (2016), T.C. Memo. 2016-112.

(c) Medtronic Puerto Rico agreed to pay an arm's length royalty of 29 percent to Medtronic US on its US net intercompany sales of Devices (20 percent on trade sales) and 15 percent to Medtronic US on its worldwide net intercompany sales of Leads (11 percent on trade sales).
(d) Medtronic Puerto Rico was responsible for, among other things, manufacturing and selling Cardiac Rhythm Disease Management (CRDM) and Neurological ("Neuro") medical device pulse generators ("Devices") and medical therapy delivery devices ("Leads").
(e) In due course of its business, Medtronic Puerto Rico purchased certain component parts used in Devices and Leads from Medtronic, Inc. and licensed the intangible property necessary to manufacture and sell Devices and Leads from Medtronic US, along with the requisite trademarks and trade names.
(f) Medtronic Puerto Rico sold finished Devices and Leads to Medtronic USA, Inc. ("Med USA") primarily for sale in the US.
(g) The IRS disregarded Medtronic's CUT and instead applied the CPM to the Medtronic-MedPR license, with MedPR as the tested party. It did the same with respect to MedPR's sales of spinal screws to a US distribution affiliate. For both transactions, the IRS analysis produced a transfer price that increased the Medtronic group's US income.
(h) Medtronic alleged that the IRS rejection of the CUT method it used and the application/substitution of the CPM was arbitrary and capricious based on a mischaracterization of the tested party's role.
(i) IRS views MedPR as a contract manufacturer, not as an "entrepreneurial, risk-bearing, and functionally autonomous manufacturer" that would, at arm's length, negotiate a lower royalty rate and insist on retaining a larger share of the final price for the goods it manufactures.
(j) The IRS argued that the CPM was the best method to determine the arm's length royalty rates on the intercompany sales of Devices and Leads. From the IRS analysis, the only economically significant function that Medtronic Puerto Rico performed was "assembling" finished products with Medtronic US's significant oversight and help. That the four intercompany transactions, at stake, should have been aggregated.
(k) Further, the IRS contended that Medtronic's use of the CUT method did not meet the standard of section 482 and the regulations thereunder, and that Medtronic's experts' uncontrolled license agreements were not comparable to the Device and Leads Licenses.
(l) Medtronic, on the other side, argued that the Puerto Rico MOU royalty rates on the intercompany sales of Devices and Leads from Medtronic Puerto Rico to Medtronic US were greater than arm's length. That, using the CUT method, the proper arm's length intercompany royalty rates were 29 percent for Devices and 15 percent for Leads. Medtronic maintained that the separate intercompany transactions should be respected and priced individually.

(m) On June 9, 2016, the T.C. rejected the IRS position. The T.C. held that: (1) the "CUT" method used by Medtronic was the best method; (2) the transaction proposed by Medtronic could have been adjusted; and (3) no intangibles were transferred to Medtronic Puerto Rico Operations Co. ("Medtronic Puerto Rico") that could trigger IRC section 367(d).

(n) The Court found that:
  - The IRS-asserted comparables were not performing the same functions and were not manufacturing the same types of products as Medtronic Puerto Rico.
  - The aggregation approach pushed forward by the IRS expert was not the best method and that, therefore, Medtronic had met its burden of showing that the IRS's allocations were arbitrary, capricious, or unreasonable.
  - That the prices charged for the components and finished goods were arm's length and that the trademark royalty was also arm's length.

(o) Concerning the royalty rates contained in the Device and Leads Licenses, the T.C. found that both Medtronic and the IRS have failed to establish the arm's length price: Medtronic had failed to meet its burden of proving that its allocations met the arm's length standard, and the IRS approach to determining comparability was unreasonable.

(p) Thus, based on the unfolded facts of the case, the T.C. determined that the CUT method was the most appropriate method of determining the arm's length royalty rates of the Device and Leads Licenses.

CHAPTER 9
# Functional Analysis

## 9.1 INTRODUCTION

Determining the degree of comparability between controlled and uncontrolled transactions requires a comparison of the functions performed, and associated resources employed, by the taxpayers in each transaction. This comparison is based on a functional analysis that identifies and compares the economically significant activities undertaken, or to be undertaken, by the taxpayers in both controlled and uncontrolled transactions. A functional analysis serves two primary purposes: (i) it provides an overview of the organizational and business structure; (ii) it assists in identifying the various functions performed by each entity within a group.

A functional analysis should also include consideration of the resources that are employed, or to be employed, in conjunction with the activities undertaken, including consideration of the type of assets used, such as plant and equipment, or the use of valuable intangibles. A functional analysis is not a pricing method and does not itself determine the arm's length result for the controlled transaction under review. Functions that may need to be accounted for determining the comparability of two transactions include:

(a) research and development;
(b) product design and engineering;
(c) manufacturing, production, and process engineering;
(d) product fabrication, extraction, and assembly;
(e) purchasing and materials management;
(f) marketing and distribution functions, including inventory management, warranty administration, and advertising activities;
(g) transportation and warehousing; and
(h) managerial, legal, accounting and finance, credit and collection, training, and personnel management services.

## 9.2 FUNCTIONAL ANALYSIS

Whether the company or group has an in-house team of transfer pricing expert or relies upon advisory ("external") transfer pricing experts, the first step within the functional analysis process is to review the taxpayer organizational structure or chart and/or to conduct interviews within the headquarter and the related entities considered.

### 9.2.1 The Review of the Taxpayer Organizational/Business Structure

A description of the taxpayer's organizational structure (including an organization chart) which covers all related parties engaged in transactions is very relevant to the functional analysis. Modern businesses have their own organizational charts which assist "insiders as well as outsiders" understand the different parties, segments of the whole business operations.

Any operating organization should have its own structure in order to operate efficiently. For an organization, the organizational structure is a hierarchy of people and its functions.

The organizational structure of an organization tells you the character of an organization and the values it believes in. Therefore, when you do business with an organization or get into a new job in an organization, it is always a great idea to get to know and understand their organizational structure.

Depending on the organizational values and the nature of the business, organizations tend to adopt one of the following structures for management purposes. Although the organization follows a particular structure, there can be departments and teams following some other organizational structure in exceptional cases. Sometimes, some organizations may follow a combination of the following organizational structures as well.

Following are the types of organizational structures that can be observed in the modern business organizations.

#### *9.2.1.1 Bureaucratic Structure*

Bureaucratic structures maintain strict hierarchies when it comes to people management. There are three types of bureaucratic structures:

(1) Pre-bureaucratic Structure

This type of organizations lacks the standards. Usually this type of structure can be observed in small-scale, start-up companies. Usually the structure is centralized and there is only one key decision maker.

The communication is done in one-on-one conversations. This type of structures is quite helpful for small organizations due to the fact that the founder has the full control over all the decisions and operations.

(2) Bureaucratic Structures

These structures have a certain degree of standardization. When the organizations grow complex and large, bureaucratic structures are required for management. These structures are quite suitable for tall organizations.

(3) Post-bureaucratic Structures

The organizations that follow post-bureaucratic structures still inherit the strict hierarchies but open to more modern ideas and methodologies. They follow techniques such as total quality management (TQM), culture management.

#### *9.2.1.2 Functional Structure*

The organization is divided into segments based on the functions when managing. This allows the organization to enhance the efficiencies of these functional groups (Figure 9.1). As an example, take a software company:

Software engineers will only staff the entire software development department. This way, management of this functional group becomes easy and effective. Functional structures appear to be successful in a large organization that produces high volumes of products at low costs. The low cost can be achieved by such companies due to the efficiencies within functional groups. In addition to such advantages, there can be disadvantages from an organizational perspective if the communication between the functional groups is not effective. In this case, organization may find it difficult to achieve some organizational objectives at the end.

*Figure 9.1 Functional Structure*

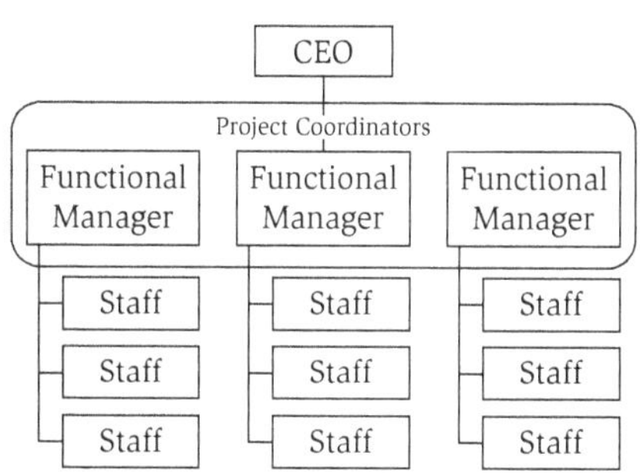


#### *9.2.1.3 Divisional Structure*

These types of organizations divide the functional areas of the organization to divisions. Each division is equipped with its own resources in order to function independently (Figure 9.2). There can be many bases to define divisions.

Divisions can be defined based on the geographical basis, products/services basis, or any other measurement.

As an example, take a company such as General Electrics. It can have microwave division, turbine division, etc., and these divisions have their own marketing teams, finance teams, etc. In that sense, each division can be considered as a micro-company with the main organization.

*Figure 9.2 Divisional Structure*

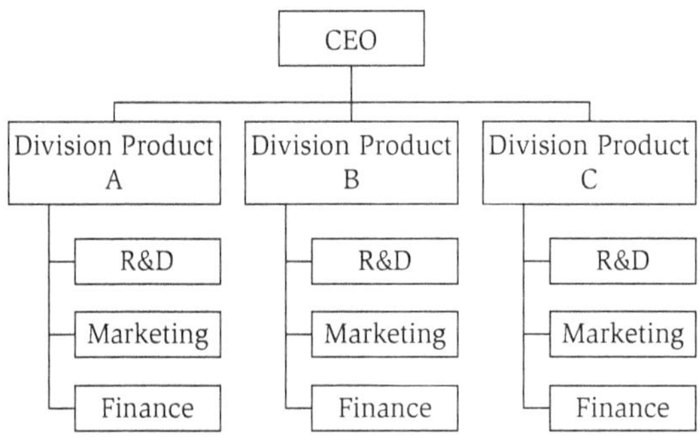


### 9.2.1.4 Matrix Structure

When it comes to matrix structure, the organization places the employees based on the function and the product. The matrix structure gives the best of the both worlds of functional and divisional structures.

In this type of an organization, the company uses teams to complete tasks. The teams are formed based on the functions they belong to (ex: software engineers) and product they are involved in (ex: Project A).

This way, there are many teams in this organization such as software engineers of project A, software engineers of project B, QA engineers of project A (Figure 9.3).

*Figure 9.3 Matrix Structure*

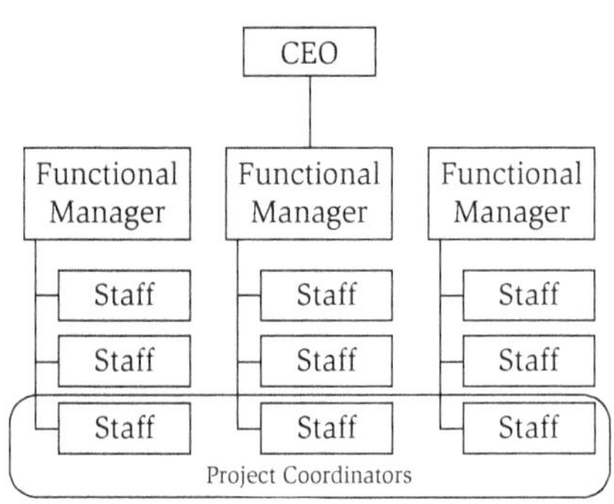

### 9.2.2 Prerequisites Functional Analysis

The understanding of the following elements constitutes the prerequisites in conducting functional analysis:

- the operations of its affiliates (US and foreign);
- the relationship between the taxpayer and its affiliates in other countries;
- the role each entity plays in carrying out the activities of the controlled group;
- the US taxpayer's intangibles

This requires or entails the review of: the taxpayer financial statements (i.e., Form K-10, SEC Filing); articles about the taxpayer from trade publications and other sources; reports published by securities firms; internal publications; minutes of meetings of the board of directors; shareholders' general assembly; e-mails, faxes, and other written correspondence between the US taxpayer and foreign affiliates.

### 9.2.3 The Use of Checklist and Conduct of Interviews

The IRS has prepared a checklist that may be useful for this purpose:

Example 1: Offshore Manufacturing

A foreign subsidiary manufactures apparel for its US parent. The US parent and the foreign subsidiary performed the following functions:

| **Functions Performed** | **Subsidiary** | **Parent** |
|---|---|---|
| a. Product Design | | x |
| b. Product | | x |
| c. Process Engineering | | |
| 1. Small Scale Production | | x |
| 2. Large Scale Production | x | |
| d. Purchasing | | |
| 1. Selection of Materials and Trimmings | | x |
| 2. Purchase of Materials and Trimmings from Unrelated Vendors | | x |
| e. Inventory Control | x | |
| f. Production Scheduling | x | |
| g. Apparel Production | | |
| 1. Marking | x | |
| 2. Spreading | x | |
| 3. Cutting | x | |
| 4. Sewing | x | |
| 5. Packaging | x | |
| h. Quality Control | x | |
| i. Distribution | | |

| | | |
|---|---|---|
| 1. Sales of Finished Product to US Parent | X | |
| 2. Resales of Finished Product under Brand Name to Authorized Dealers and Distributors | | X |
| 3. Resales of Finished Product under Private Labels to Major Retail Chains | | X |
| j. Marketing | | X |
| k. Advertising | | X |
| l. Warranty Administration | | X |
| m. Accounting & Finance | X | X |
| n. Data Processing | X | X |
| o. Engineering | X | X |
| p. Human Resources | X | X |

Example 2: Offshore Manufacturing and Distribution

A US parent established both a manufacturing branch and a distribution subsidiary in a foreign country. The branch and subsidiary share the same facility. The branch sells its output of personal care products to the subsidiary. The US parent, the branch, and the subsidiary perform the following functions:

| **Functions Performed** | **US Parent** | **Foreign Branch** | **Foreign Subsidiary** |
|---|---|---|---|
| a. Developed Formula for Product | x | | |
| b. Owns US Patent | x | | |
| c. Owns Foreign Country Patent | x | | |
| d. Manufactures Personal Care Product | | x | |
| e. Transfers Product Title to the Subsidiary When Subsidiary Pulls Product to Fill Shopping Orders | | x | |
| f. Owns US Tradename | x | | |
| g. Owns Foreign Country Tradename | x | | |
| h. Establishes Marketing Strategy | | | x |
| i. Implements Marketing Plan | | | x |
| j. Sells Product to Unrelated Parties | | | x |
| k. Reimburses Subsidiary for All Budgeted Advertising, Promotion, and Market Research Expenses | | x | |

## 9.3 FUNCTIONAL ANALYSIS

A functional analysis involves tracing the flow of products and services within the organization. Delivering products to a market generally involves various stages. Performing a functional analysis involves more than a review of the books and records. It involves active interaction with the taxpayer, which shall go beyond the tax department and include operational personnel. Very often, the tax department generally lacks the knowledge needed to complete a functional analysis. A functional analysis identifies the economically significant activities performed in connection with the transaction. An economically significant activity is one that, at arm's length, materially affects the following:

- the price charged in a transaction; and
- the profits earned from a transaction

A functional analysis involves determining the following:

- what functions were performed by the transacting parties concerning the transaction?
- who performed the functions?
- when were the functions performed?
- where were the functions performed?
- how were the functions performed?
- why were the functions performed?
- what intangibles were employed in the performance of functions?
- how were intangibles employed in the performance of functions?
- why was the transaction structured the way it was?

### 9.3.1 Functional Analysis for Both the CUP/CUT and CUST

For both CUP, CUT, and CUST the functional analysis shall focus on the characteristics of the product, the intangible or the service, the contractual terms, the size or volume of the transactions and any other relevant factors that could affect the price between an unrelated seller or buyer.[1] Comparability of the products or services is of particular essence to the application of CUP, since product/service qualities and characteristics are central in the determination of prices.

For the RPM, functional analysis shall concentrate on the functions performed, assets utilized, and risks borne. Likewise, for the CP, functional analysis shall focus on the functions performed, the assets used, and the risks borne in order to determine the appropriate mark-up range.

1. Amerkhil, Valerie (2006): Functional Analysis and Choosing the Best Method, ESC, 12-9.

### 9.3.2 Functional Analysis for Cost Sharing

In cost sharing functional analysis, the taxpayer must assess the risks associated with the cost sharing and licensing alternatives and conduct functional analysis of resources, capabilities, and rights made available to the CSA and the expected cost shared intangibles.

### 9.3.3 Functional Analysis for Profit Split

Under the PSM, two separate analyses must be conducted: (i) residual analysis; and (ii) contribution analysis. Under the residual analysis, a routine profit is first provided for each of the parties for the routine functions performed in the controlled transaction. Under the contribution analysis, an analysis of the contribution by each party to the controlled transaction is carried out and valued accordingly.

### 9.3.4 Functional Analysis for TNMM/CPM

It is also important to consider functions performed in determining the degree of comparability between the tested party and an uncontrolled taxpayer. The degree of functional comparability required to obtain a reliable result under the CPM, however, is generally less than that required under the resale price or CPs. For example, because differences in functions performed often are reflected in operating expenses, taxpayers performing different functions may have very different gross profit margins but earn similar levels of operating profit.

## 9.4 DEVELOPING TRANSFER PRICING POLICY IN A FIRM

The implementation of transfer pricing is a juggernaut task which goes far beyond the tax function. Effective implementation of transfer pricing requires considerable coordination among operations, finance, and tax. A multinational seeking to improve its transfer pricing strategy may consider establishing a cross-functional committee with a mandate to govern and manage intercompany processes. That is, a holistic view of the MNE transfer pricing, accounting, legal, and finance departments is necessary to establish a connection between its business and operational models.

MNEs should know where their high-value functions such as R&D, licensing, business development, manufacturing, and marketing are located as well as the risks borne by each affiliates in order to define an efficient transfer pricing policy (Figure 9.4).

*Figure 9.4 Firm Transfer Pricing Policy*

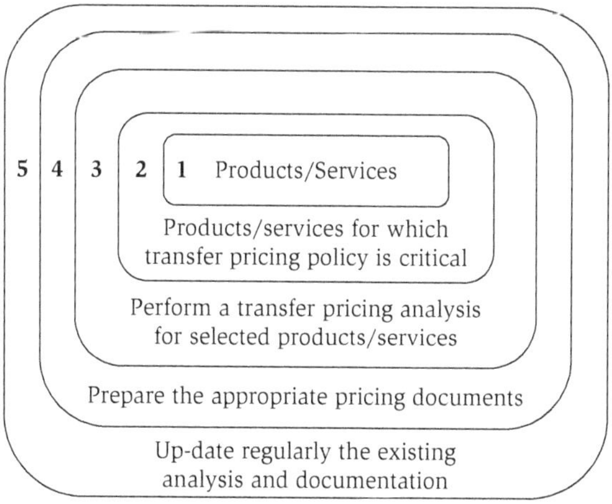


The first step in the design of any MNE consists of: (i) identifying the relevant business context, (ii) the design of the transfer pricing system, (iii) the documentation of the transfer pricing, and (iv) the management of transfer pri.

(i) Identify the Business Context

This step provides the assessment of the MNE within the industry in which it operates. In practice, the firm must provide and collect the key macroeconomic data relevant to its industry, the description of the industry features and prospects (i.e., markets forecasts). This step also includes a comprehensive Porter Five industry analysis: (a) the level of competition in the industry, (b) the potential of new entrants into the industry, (c) the power of suppliers, (d) the power of customers, and the threat of substitutes products or services. Finally this step provides a broad functional analysis of the key activities performed by each entity within the MNE, the assets used and the risks borne.

(ii) Designing a Transfer Pricing System

At this stage, the MNE must determine the appropriate return for each related entity identified. The MNE must also align its transfer pricing system with its business model, strategy, and objectives. The choice of the transfer pricing method as well as the economic analysis are conducted at this level.

(iii) Documenting the Transfer Pricing Method(s)

Once the transfer pricing is well-identified, the MNE must collect all needed information and documents to support the aforementioned transfer pricing policy. This is followed by an economic analysis to test the soundness of the policy and methods selected to ensure that the MNE prices or results are within appropriate ranges (i.e., operating profit margins are often a vital metric).

The MNE result ranges need to be compared with its competitor(s) within the same industry and with the industry average ranges in order to comply with the arm's length requirement of transfer pricing.

(iv) Managing the Transfer Pricing Model

The transfer pricing model designs by an MNE is not fixed. Rather, the overall framework needs to be constantly updated based on the changes in the relevant factors, the premises upon which the system was built (i.e., industry change, firm policies, strategy and objectives).

# CHAPTER 10
# Documentation and Penalties

## 10.1 INTRODUCTION

A penalty for understatements of tax attributable to a transfer pricing issue applies, unless the taxpayer maintains and provides to the IRS upon request contemporaneous documentation supporting the taxpayer's pricing methodology. Even if a taxpayer's understatement does not meet the threshold for application of the transfer pricing penalty, the understatements may nonetheless be subject to the accuracy-related penalty on one of the other grounds enumerated in section 6662(b).

I.R.C. section 6662(a) imposes a 20 percent addition-to-tax penalty on the portion of the underpayment of tax attributable to the accuracy-related penalties. Under certain circumstances, including gross valuations misstatements, the accuracy-related penalty can be increased to 40 percent.[1]

Under the general rules of section 6662, a penalty applies to the portion of any underpayment that is attributable to: (1) negligence, (2) any substantial understatement of income tax, (3) any substantial valuation misstatement, (4) any substantial overstatement of pension liabilities, or (5) any substantial estate or gift tax valuation understatement. If the correct income tax liability exceeds that reported by the taxpayer by the greater of 10 percent of the correct tax or USD 5,000 (or, in the case of corporations, by the lesser of: (a) 10 percent of the correct tax (or USD 10,000 if greater) or (b) USD 10 million), then a substantial understatement exists and a penalty may be imposed equal to 20 percent of the underpayment of tax attributable to the understatement. In most cases, a penalty may be avoided if a taxpayer establishes that he had reasonable cause and acted in good faith.

1. IRC section 6662(h).

In contrast, if the threshold for applicability of the transfer pricing penalty is met, then reasonable cause sufficient to avoid a transfer pricing penalty requires compliance with the contemporaneous documentation requirements. The threshold may be met in one of two ways:

(1) The price for any property or services (or for the use of property) claimed on a tax return is 200 percent or more (or 50 percent or less) than the correct price (referred to as a "transactional penalty").

Example

- Man Corp. manufactures wigs to be sold worldwide. In 2014, the unit price of a wig was determined at USD 6 (COGS), and the sale price at USD 12,00.
- Man Corp. has sold 1 million wigs and reported USD 12 million of net income.
- In 2015, the IRS issued a notice of deficiency to Man Corp. under IRC section 482. The IRS determined the unit price sale at USD 25. Therefore, the Service allocation and adjustment increased Man Corp.'s net income by USD 13 million.
- The 20% transactional penalty will be due because the adjustment under IRC section 482 is greater than the amount Man Corp. claimed on its tax return.

(2) The net section 482 adjustment for the taxable year exceeds the lesser of: (a) USD 5 million, or (b) 10 percent of the taxpayer's gross receipts (referred to as a "net adjustment penalty").

Example

- Man Corp. manufactures wigs to be sold worldwide. In 2015, the unit price of a wig was determined at USD 6 (COGS), and the sale price at USD 12 per unit.
- Man Corp. has sold 10 million wigs and reported USD 120 million of net income.
- In 2015, the IRS issued a notice of deficiency to Man Corp. under section 482. The IRS determined the unit price sale at USD 15. Therefore, the Service allocation and adjustment increased Man Corp.'s net income by USD 30 million.
- Because IRC section adjustment is greater than the threshold of USD 5 million, the 20% penalty (the net income adjustment) is due.

## 10.2 IRC SECTION 6662 EXCEPTIONS

Section 6662 imposes a 20 percent addition to tax on the amount of the underpayment due to negligence or disregard of rules or regulations. For purposes 6662(a), negligence includes any failure to make a reasonable attempt to comply with the provisions of the IRC, and disregard includes any careless, reckless, or intentional disregard. Negligence has also been defined as a "lack of due care or failure to do what a reasonable and ordinarily prudent person would do under the circumstances."[2] The taxpayer bears the burden to prove that his failure to file a tax return was due to a reasonable cause.

But not every tax underpayment is subject to section 6662's penalties. A taxpayer who had "a reasonable cause" for the underpayment, and acted in good faith with respect to that portion, has a valid defense. Whether a taxpayer had reasonable cause depends on all of the pertinent facts and circumstances of a particular case, with the most important factor being the taxpayer's effort to assess his proper tax liability.

A common means of demonstrating reasonable cause is to show reliance on the advice of a competent and independent professional advisor. However, relying on a professional will not always get a taxpayer off the hook. To constitute reasonable cause, the reliance must have been reasonable in light of the circumstances. At a minimum, the taxpayer must show that the advice was: (1) based on all relevant facts and circumstances, meaning the taxpayer must not withhold pertinent information, and (2) not based on unreasonable factual or legal assumptions, including those the taxpayer knows or has reason to know are untrue. Other relevant considerations are the taxpayer's education, sophistication, business experience, and purposes for entering the questioned transaction. A taxpayer is not reasonable, however, in relying on an adviser burdened with an inherent conflict of interest about which the taxpayer knew or should have known.

There are two principal exceptions pursuant to which a taxpayer may avoid a penalty. Both require contemporaneous documentation be maintained and provided to the IRS within 30 days of a request and apply to both the transactional and the net adjustment penalties, depending whether the taxpayer uses a specified or an unspecified transfer pricing method(s).

- The taxpayer uses a specified method under section 482 regulations: Under the first exception, if the taxpayer uses a specified method, the taxpayer must show that the method chosen was reasonable.
- The taxpayer uses an unspecified method: Under the second exception, if a taxpayer uses an unspecified method, the taxpayer must establish that: (a) none of the specified methods was likely to clearly reflect income, and (b) the pricing method used by the taxpayer was likely to produce a price that would clearly reflect income.

With respect to the transactional penalty, the exceptions apply on a transaction-by-transaction basis. Exceptions to the net adjustment penalty operate by excluding from the net section 482 adjustment the portion of the adjustment that satisfies one of the exceptions. If a single transaction is part of a net section 482 adjustment, then the rules for the net adjustment penalty apply to that transaction. For purposes of both exceptions, the regulations provide a nonexclusive list of specific factors to be considered in determining whether the taxpayer's selection of its method was reasonable. The regulations identify principal documents that must be maintained, regardless of the type of method used by the taxpayer. The documents must be adequate to

2. Neely v. Commissioner, 85 T.C. 934, 947 (1985).

accurately and completely describe the analysis conducted by the taxpayer. In addition, background documents must also be available, although need not be provided within 30 days in response to a request for principal documents, but may be subject of a subsequent request within the discretion of the IRS.

To prevent the imposition of penalties, taxpayers are required to maintain contemporaneous and detailed records of their transfer pricing transactions.

Pursuant to section 6662(e) a penalty is imposed on any underpayment attributable to a substantial valuation misstatement pertaining to either a transaction between persons described in section 482 (the transactional penalty) or a net section 482 transfer price adjustment (the net adjustment penalty). The penalty is equal to 20 percent of the underpayment of tax attributable to that substantial valuation misstatement.

## 10.3 SUBSTANTIAL VALUATION MISSTATEMENT

Pursuant to section 6662(h) the penalty is increased to 40 percent of the underpayment in the case of a gross valuation misstatement with respect to either penalty. There is a substantial valuation misstatement if a net section 482 adjustment is greater than the lesser of USD 5 million or 10 percent of gross receipts. By definition, an understatement of income tax is substantial if it exceeds the greater of USD 5,000 or 10 percent of the tax required to be shown on the return. Pursuant to sectiol491(c), the Commissioner bears the burden of producing sufficient evidence showing that the imposition of the penalty is appropriate in any given case.

Further, Treasury Regulation section 1.6662-5(g), provides that when an asset's true value or adjusted basis is zero, "the value or adjusted basis claimed . . . is considered to be 400 percent or more of the correct amount," so that the resulting valuation misstatement is automatically deemed gross and subject to the 40 percent penalty.[3]

Example

- In 2014, Man Corp. sold 200,000 Techcool devices, which includes valuable proprietary technology protected under several patents.
- Man Corp. reported USD 800,000 of net income from the transactions.
- In 2015, the IRS issued a notice of deficiency under section 482. The Service determined that the price per Techcool device should have been USD 41.
- Therefore, the Service allocation and adjustment increases Man Corp.'s net income by USD 6.2 million.
- Because the two threshold conditions (transaction and net income) are met, and the adjustment relates to valuation misstatement, the penalty would be increased to 40% under IRC section 6662(h).

3. United states v. Woods, US SCt, 571 US, 2013.

## 10.4 SUBSTANTIAL AND GROSS VALUATION AND THE NOLs

Treasury Regulation 1.6662-6(e) sets forth special rules for carry-backs and carryovers:

> If there is a substantial or gross valuation misstatement for a taxable year that gives rise to a loss, deduction or credit that is carried to another taxable year, the transactional penalty and the net adjustment penalty will be imposed on any resulting underpayment of tax in that other taxable year. In determining whether there is a substantial or gross valuation misstatement for a taxable year, no amount carried from another taxable year shall be included. The character and penalty rate of the misstatement are determined in the year the misstatement is made, not in any other year in which the misstatement gives rise to an underpayment of tax.

## 10.5 EXCEPTION FROM THE ADJUSTMENT CALCULATION

I.I. 6664(c) sets forth the reasonable cause exception applicable to penalties asserted under I.R.C. sections 6662 and 6663. In general, I.R.C. section 6664(c) provides that no penalty will be imposed on any portion of underpayment of tax if the taxpayer had reasonable cause and acted in good faith with respect to that portion of the underpayment. The determination of whether a taxpayer acted with reasonable cause and in good faith is made on a case-by-case basis, taking into account all pertinent facts and circumstances. Generally, the most important factor is the extent of the taxpayer's effort to assess the taxpayer's proper tax liability. Courts have frequently held that reasonable cause would be established when a taxpayer shows that he reasonably relied on the advice of an accountant or tax attorney... even when such advice turned out to have been mistaken.[4]

### 10.5.1 Exception for Transactional Penalty

Treasury Regulation 1.6662-6(b)(3) provides, with minor modification, that the transactional penalty will not be imposed on any portion of an underpayment with respect to which the requirements of Treasury Regulation 1.6664-4 are met. That is, the taxpayer must show that there was reasonable cause for, and he/she acted in good faith with respect to, such portion.[5]

### 10.5.2 Exception for Net Adjustment Penalty

I.R.C. 6662(e)(3)(B) rules require that the taxpayer maintains contemporaneous documentation to show adherence and compliance with the arm's length standard. The rules differ depending on whether the taxpayer used a pricing methodology specified in the I.R.C or an unspecified method.

4. Boyle, 469 US 241, 250 (1985).
5. Treas. Reg. 1.6664-4(a).

## 10.6 EXCLUSION FOR THE ADJUSTMENT

When reasonable cause and good faith exception requirements are met with regard to specific adjustments made pursuant to I.R.C. section 482, those amounts are not subject to a penalty. The threshold amounts must be satisfied by any adjustments that have not met the reasonable cause and good faith exception requirements.

## 10.7 TRANSFER PRICING DOCUMENTATION

A taxpayer is not required to prepare and submit transfer pricing documentation. Producing the documentation is a voluntary decision made by the taxpayer. The regulations serve to encourage taxpayers to prepare contemporaneous transfer pricing documentation through the use of the penalty. Taxpayers are free to produce or not produce documentation based upon their risk-based assessment or cost/benefit analysis. If the documentation is not provided within 30 days, it may not satisfy the reasonable cause and good faith exception requirements depending upon the length of and reason for the delay.

- The Principal Documents

The principal documents should accurately and completely describe the basic transfer pricing analysis conducted by the taxpayer. The documentation must include the following 10 items:

(1) overview of the business;
(2) description of the organizational structure of all related parties engaged in transactions potentially relevant under I.R.C. section 482;
(3) documentation explicitly required by the regulations under I.R.C. section 482;
(4) description of the transfer pricing method selected and explanation of why it was selected;
(5) description of the methods that were considered and explanation of why they were not selected;
(6) description of the controlled transactions;
(7) description of the comparables that were used;
(8) explanation of the economic analysis and projections relied upon in developing the method;
(9) description of any relevant data that is obtained after the end of the tax year and before filing a tax return, and which would help determine if a specified method was selected and applied in a reasonable manner;
(10) index of the principal and background documents and a description of the record keeping system used for cataloguing and accessing those documents.

## 10.8 TRANSFER PRICING ADJUSTMENTS AND SETTLEMENT

The IRS has three years from the date of the tax return to make transfer pricing adjustment under IRC section 482. However, the three-year period is extended to six years if the taxpayer has omitted gross income in excess of 25 percent of its reported gross income. Finally, the Service can make adjustment anytime if the taxpayer has filed a fraudulent return or failed to file its tax return.

## 10.9 LITIGATION OF TRANSFER PRICING CONTROVERSIES

The bulk of IRC section 482 disputes are resolved in the course of the IRS examination, or based on consideration by Appeals. Thus, very few disputes involving transfer pricing result in issuance of a statutory notice of deficiency, which is the legal demand for payment of additional tax. The issuance of such a notice gives rise to jurisdiction for filing by the taxpayer of a petition in US T.C., or for payment of tax and filing of a claim for refund in US District Court or the US Court of Federal Claims. In the case of petitions in T.C., the IRS Counsel from the specific division that issued the notice generally defends the case in T.C.. District Court and Court of Federal Claims refund actions are defended by attorneys of the Department of Justice, Tax Division.

Transfer pricing litigation is very resource intensive,[6] given that it usually involves a large factual record, submission of expert testimony on specialized matters, and economic and other analysis needed to support the IRS adjustment under the applicable standard of review. Substantial work generally must be performed in addition to the development and analysis done in the IRS examination. The precedential value of a decision involving section 482 may be quite limited, due to the highly factual nature of most disputes. Nonetheless, the IRS devotes substantial resources to litigation in this area. Cases defended by the IRS Office of Chief Counsel fall into three basic categories:[7] (1) general litigation, (2) notice cases, and (3) designated cases. All of these cases involve similar resources on the part of LMSB Counsel, but notice cases and designated cases involve coordinated issues or other matters and call for more extensive involvement by Associate Offices of IRS Chief Counsel, generally ACC(I).

## 10.10 CASE STUDY

### 10.10.1 DHL v. Commissioner[8]

- DHL is a worldwide overnight package delivery company that was formed in the US before expanding into international services.

---

6. US Congress (2007): Report to the Congress on Earnings Stripping, Transfer Pricing and U.S. Income Tax Treaties, p. 45.
7. *Idem*.
8. DHL v. Commissioner, 76 TCM. 122 (1998).

- In 1972, DHL Corporation ("DHL") was split along geographic lines to comply with certification requirements of the US Civil Aeronautics Board.
- In 1979, after the split, DHL continued to operate the US courier and package delivery business, while the foreign business was operated by Document Handling Limited, International (DHLI), a Hong Kong sister corporation of DHL.
- In the 1980s, DHL faced with serious cash flow issues hired Bain and Company to assist in returning the company to profitability.
- Following a failed attempt to merge with UPS, DHL and DHLI began negotiations with a group of foreign investors that included Japan Air Lines, Nissho Iwai, and Lufthansa. In 1990, the foreign investors acquired a 2.5 percent interest in DHL, a 12.5 percent interest in DHLI, and an option to purchase an additional 45 percent interest in DHLI. This option was exercised in 1992, and it brought the new investors' collective ownership of DHLI to 57.5 percent.
- During the due diligence activity, a proposal was made for DHLI to purchase the DHL trademark as a vehicle for capitalizing DHL.
- With respect to the value of the DHL trademark, DHL contended that the USD 20 million value set in connection with the acquisition by the foreign investors (and confirmed by Bain) was determinative, but that, in any event, the USD 50 million value originally placed on the trademark by the foreign investors represented a maximum value.
- The Service contended, however, that the trademark had a value of USD 300 million. After reviewing expert testimony proffered by DHL and by the Service, the court ultimately determined that the value of the trademark was USD 100 million.
- The T.C. imposed accuracy-related penalties on some, but not all, of the foregoing transfer pricing adjustments under IRC section 6662 totaling USD 163 million.
- Under IRC section 6662, a taxpayer that has adequate documentation showing that it made a reasonable attempt to comply with section 482 will not be subject to a penalty event, though the size of the IRS adjustment may allow the imposition of a penalty.
- The court upheld the Service's assertion of the 40 percent penalty on the adjustment to the value of the DHL trademark on the ground that the price set by DHL constituted a "gross valuation misstatement."
- The T.C. decision states that:

> it was not reasonable for [DHL] to rely on (or more properly hide behind) the Bain appraisal or comfort letter. If the parties to the transaction had given the valuation to an independent valuation entity before any values being placed on the trade mark by the parties and/or not advised the evaluator of a value, it might have been reasonable for petitioners to rely on such an appraisal. As this trial has again demonstrated, parties can find experts who will advance and support values that favour the position of the person or entity that hired them.

### 10.10.2 Xilinx and Subsidiaries v. Commissioner[9]

- Xilinx Inc. entered into a cost sharing agreement to develop intangibles with its foreign subsidiary (Xiling Ireland). Each party was required to pay a percentage of the total research and development costs based on its respective anticipated benefits from the intangibles.
- Xilinx Inc. issued stock options to its employees performing research and development. In determining the allocation of costs pursuant to the agreement, Xilinx Inc. did not include in research and development costs any amount related to the issuance of stock options to, or exercise of stock options by, its employees.
- The CIR determined deficiencies in the amounts of USD 24,653,660, USD 25,930,531, USD 27,857,516, and USD 27,243,975 and triggered section 6662(a) accuracy-related penalties in the amounts of USD 4,935,813, USD 5,189,389, USD 5,573,412, and USD 5,448,795 relating to Xilinx' 1996, 1997, 1998, and 1999 Federal income taxes, respectively.
- The IRS contended that Xilinx Inc. paid its employees ESOs in exchange for research and development services, and such services contributed to Xilinx Inc.'s development of intangibles.
- The T.C. held that the express language in section 1.482-1(a)(1), states that the arm's-length standard applies to section 1.482-7 for purposes of determining appropriate cost allocations. However, because unrelated parties would not share the spread or the grant date value, the Service imposition of such a requirement was inconsistent with section 1.482-1. Put more starkly, the regulations applicable to the years in issue did not authorize the Service to require taxpayers to share the spread or the grant date value relating to ESOs. Accordingly, the T.C. held that the Service allocations were arbitrary and capricious; that Xilinx' allocations met the arm's-length standard mandated by section 1.482-1, and Xilinx and subsidiaries were not liable for the section 6662(a) penalties.

9. Xilinx Inc. and Subsidiaries v. Commissioner, 125 T.C. No. 4 (2013).

# Chapter 11
# Advance Pricing and Mutual Agreement

## 11.1 INTRODUCTION

To reduce uncertainty related to cross-border transactions among affiliates and avoid multiple taxation, MNCs are entering into advance pricing agreement with various tax authorities.

An APA is an agreement between a taxpayer and the IRS that determines the acceptable transfer pricing methodology for covered transactions in the years subject to the agreement. The procedures for obtaining an APA were first published in 1991 and are now found in Revenue Procedure 2015-41.

In February 2012, the former APA Program was moved from the Office of Chief Counsel to the Office of Transfer Pricing Operations (TPA), Large Business and International Division of the IRS (TPO) and combined with the United States Competent Authority (USCA) staff responsible for transfer pricing cases, thereby forming the Advance Pricing and Mutual Agreement (APMA) Program.[1] The APMA Program is comprised of 55 team leaders, 26 economists, and 10 senior managers organized in 10 groups (7 team leader groups and 3 economist groups). The team leader groups are organized by country with each group having responsibility for multiple countries. Because of the large volume of cases with certain treaty partners, some countries are the responsibility of more than one group.[2]

APMA's APA program provides a voluntary process whereby the IRS and taxpayers may resolve transfer pricing issues and issues for which transfer pricing principles may be relevant in a principled and cooperative manner on a prospective basis. APMA is committed to conducting the APA process in a manner that is fair, timely, and consistent with principles of sound tax administration. The APA process increases the efficiency of tax administration by encouraging taxpayers to come

1. IRS Announcement and Report Concerning Advance Pricing Agreements-, March 27, 2014, p. 2.
2. *Idem.*, p. 2.

forward and present all the facts necessary for a proper evaluation of their coverable issues and to work towards a resolution of such issues in a spirit of openness and cooperation. The voluntary and prospective nature of the APA process lessens the burden of compliance by giving taxpayers greater certainty regarding their covered issues and promotes the principled resolution of these issues by allowing for their discussion and resolution in advance before the consequences of such resolution are fully known to either taxpayers or the IRS.[3] Revenue Procedure 2015-41 raises the general user fee to USD 60,000 and USD 30,000 for small business' APA. However, the renewal fee is kept to USD 35,000.

## 11.2 ADVANTAGES AND DISADVANTAGES OF APA

An APA provides certainty with respect to transfer pricing issues that might otherwise give rise to long, time-consuming disputes with the IRS or one or more foreign tax authorities. Another advantage of APAs is their availability of special rollback procedures, through which the agreed transfer pricing methodology of an APA can be applied to resolve other transfer disputes pricing involving the same transactions in prior open tax years, including issues under examination. Finally, bilateral and multilateral APAs can be particularly relevant in their ability to resolve transfer pricing issues in both US and abroad. However, APA bears some disadvantages as well: (i) the initial upfront cost of an APA is higher; (ii) APA procedure is time consuming and lengthy; (iii) an APA request may lead the IRS or foreign tax authority to uncover or raise issues that otherwise would not be raised during the context of an examination.

## 11.3 TYPES OF APAs

### 11.3.1 Individual APAs

Where the APA process does not involve or require agreement with a tax treaty partner or involves a country with which US does not have a taxation treaty, the arrangement between the taxpayer and the IRS is referred to as a unilateral APA. A unilateral APA is concluded between the IRS and a taxpayer under the Commissioner's power of general administration of the income tax legislation and the taxpayer and IRS agree in writing to be bound by the terms of the APA. This does not guarantee the agreement of the tax treaty partner(s) and does not depend on that agreement or require it to be sought.

### 11.3.2 Bilateral APAs

A bilateral APA is an arrangement between the IRS and a tax treaty partner concerning the transfer pricing of international related-party dealings. It is concluded under the

3. IRS Proposed Revision of procedures for Advance Pricing Agreements, Notice 2013-79, p. 13.

Mutual Agreement Procedure (MAP) Article of the relevant taxation treaty. Each treaty partner confirms the terms of the APA in writing through a letter or similar document with their resident taxpayer and agrees to be bound by them. A bilateral APA therefore provides certainty for taxpayers that acting consistently with it will avoid double taxation.

### 11.3.3 Multilateral APAs

A multilateral APA is an arrangement between the relevant taxpayers, the IRS and more than one tax treaty partner and binds all its parties.

## 11.4 GENERAL REQUIREMENTS FOR INITIATING AND CONTINUING THE APA PROCESS

To initiate the APA process, the taxpayer must: (i) meet the pre-filing requirements; (ii) submit a complete APA request, and (iii) pay the fees.

The taxpayer shall meet with APMA in a pre-filing conference prior to filing the APA request. For the same reason, APMA invites, and in some cases requires, the taxpayer to submit a pre-filing memorandum prior to filing the APA request. However, the pre-filing requirements do not apply to APA requests that are eligible for the small case APA user fee. A taxpayer that seeks to file such an APA request may submit the small case APA user fee together with a complete APA request or may contact APMA. A taxpayer that wishes to hold a pre-filing conference with APMA must submit its request as part of a pre-filing memorandum filed with the APMA. Whenever, the pre-filing is mandatory, a pre-filing memorandum must be filed if: (a) the taxpayer wishes to file a unilateral APA request to cover an issue that is eligible for coverage by a bilateral or multilateral APA; (b) the taxpayer seeks permission to file an abbreviated APA request; or (c) the covered issue(s) proposed by the taxpayer will, or could reasonably be expected to, involve any of the following:

- the license or other transfer of intangibles in connection with, or the development of intangibles under, an intangible development arrangement;
- any arrangement that qualifies as a global trading arrangement; or
- unincorporated branches, pass-through entities, hybrid entities, or entities disregarded for US tax purposes.

A taxpayer may voluntarily submit a pre-filing memorandum in cases other than when the pre-filing was not mandatory. APMA recommends that a pre-filing memorandum be submitted for APA requests that may present novel or complex substantive or procedural issues. Optional pre-filing memoranda may be submitted on an anonymous basis. APMA generally recommends, however, that optional pre-filing memoranda be provided on a named basis so as to facilitate a more informed understanding of the procedural and substantive issues that may arise during the APA process.

### 11.4.1 Contents of Pre-filing Memorandum

A pre-filing memorandum must have a length and content appropriate to the size and complexity of the covered issue(s) proposed by the taxpayer. The pre-filing memorandum must have a length and content appropriate to the substantive or procedural issues the taxpayer wishes to raise with APMA. The memorandum must also do the following:

(a) include a "penalties of perjury" statement modeled on the statement set forth in the appendix (unless the memorandum is submitted on an anonymous basis);
(b) state whether the taxpayer seeks a pre-filing conference and, if so, the issues the taxpayer wishlto discuss;
(c) propose at least three possible dates for a pre-filing conference, whether or not the taxpayer seeks a pre-filing conference, in case APMA requires a pre-filing conference;
(d) include covered issue diagrams if the pre-filing memorandum is required
(e) if the pre-filing memorandum is submitted pursuant to section 3.02(4)(b), it must: (i) present the taxpayer's arguments that the applicable law, facts and circumstances, economic conditions, and other factors surrounding its proposed covered issue(s) and method(s) for the proposed APA years are substantially the same as those surrounding the current APA or surrounding the MAP resolution in the MAP case; (ii) specify any information, documents, or other materials the taxpayer proposes to omit from its APA request; and (iii) discuss the taxpayer's arguments that the information, documents, or other materials the taxpayer proposes to omit from its APA request are not necessary for APMA's evaluation of the APA request;
(f) list the name and contact information for the taxpayer's point of contact and, unless the pre-filing memorandum is submitted on an anonymous basis, provide Form 2848 authorizing the point of contact to represent the taxpayer in connection with the APA request or Form 8821 authorizing the point of contact to inspect or receive confidential tax information about the taxpayer in connection with the APA request; and
(g) identify all open pre-APA years of the taxpayer and which of such years, if any, are under examination by the IRS.

Two printed copies and one electronic copy of the pre-filing memorandum must be submitted to APMA at the address provided. APMA will notify the taxpayer whether it will accept or decline the taxpayer's request to hold a pre-filing conference. The taxpayer will also be notified if a pre-filing conference is required, even if the taxpayer did not request a conference. If a pre-filing conference is held, it will address procedural and substantive issues pertinent to the APA request. During the conference, the taxpayer should be prepared to discuss the relevant facts and circumstances surrounding the issue(s), method(s), and terms and conditions it proposes to cover in the APA.

If APMA declines the taxpayer's request for a pre-filing conference or decides that no pre-filing conference is required, APMA will direct the taxpayer as how to proceed with its APA request.

### 11.4.2 Time for Filing

An APA request must be duly filed by the applicable deadline depending on the type of the APA:

- Unilateral APA Request

The taxpayer must file a complete unilateral APA request no later than the due date prescribed by the statute (including extensions) for filing its Federal income tax return (or, if the taxpayer receives an extension to file its Federal income tax return, a date no later than the actual filing date of the return) ("return due date") for the first proposed APA year.

- Bilateral and Multilateral APA Request

Unless otherwise provided, a complete bilateral or multilateral APA request must be filed no later than the earlier of: (i) the return due date for the first proposed APA year, and (ii) within 60 days after the bilateral or multilateral APA request regarding the same proposed covered issue(s) and APA years has been filed with a foreign competent authority.

It should be noted that any information submitted by a taxpayer in connection with its APA request must be true, correct, and complete. All documents in or described in the APA request must be explained in sufficient detail to make their contents readily understandable. Such an explanation might include, for example, definitions of terms used, explanations of the goal and flow of calculations, the sources of data, and the identity of a document's creator and the purpose for which it was created.

### 11.4.3 The Submission of a Complete APA Request

The submission of a complete APA request, updated and supplemented will be a factor taken into account in determining whether the taxpayer has met the documentation requirements of Treasury Regulation §1.6662-6(d)(2)(iii) for the proposed APA years. Submission of a complete APA request does not, in itself, suspend examination or enforcement proceedings. Although APMA will coordinate within the IRS to minimize duplicative requests in conducting its due diligence, the taxpayer remains obligated to respond to information document requests issued, and according to deadlines set, by other IRS offices in any examination or enforcement proceedings. Although the appropriate APA term will be determined on a case-by-case basis, a request for an APA should propose an APA term of at least five years, unless the taxpayer states a compelling reason for a shorter term. Additionally, it is in the interest of sound tax administration for APMA to seek to have at least three prospective taxable years remaining in the APA term upon the execution of an APA (in the case of a unilateral

APA) or upon the execution of a MAP resolution (in the case of a bilateral or multilateral APA). If the APA team determines that it needs additional information to analyze the APA request, the taxpayer will be asked, and thereby required, to provide such information. The taxpayer must respond similarly to requests made by a foreign competent authority, as applicable.

After the APA request is filed, any material errors or any material omissions in the APA request or in supplemental submissions must be promptly corrected or remedied. The taxpayer must also submit any information or documents discovered or created during the APA process that are, or reasonably may be, relevant to the APA request. The taxpayer must notify APMA of all material changes and updates to information previously submitted in connection with the APA request. Any financial data produced in connection with the APA request during the APA process must be updated annually or on a schedule that is mutually acceptable to the taxpayer and to APMA. In addition, the APA request must be supplemented with a demonstration of the application of the proposed covered method(s) to the actual financial results of the applicable members of the proposed covered group for each taxable year completed while the APA request is pending. Such a supplemental submission must be provided within 180 days of the close of the taxable year. APMA may, at its discretion, grant an extension or modify these requirements if the taxpayer provides written notification before the date the supplemental submission would otherwise be due.

The taxpayer may withdraw its APA request at any time before it executes the APA. APMA generally will not refund user fees if the taxpayer withdraws its APA request after APMA has begun its due diligence.

The taxpayer must supplement its APA request and provide updated information. Further, throughout the APA process, the taxpayer and the IRS will execute consent agreement(s) as necessary to extend the period of limitations for assessment of tax for each proposed APA year and for each proposed APA rollback year. The taxpayer will be instructed as to the type of consent to execute, viz., general or restricted, and the duration of the extension for each proposed APA year and each proposed APA rollback year.

## 11.5 THE APA PROCESS: FORMATION OF APA TEAM, OPENING CONFERENCE, CASE PLAN, AND TAXPAYER REVIEW

### 11.5.1 Formation of APA Team

Once APMA has determined that the APA request is complete and that it will continue with the APA process, the APA team leader will contact the taxpayer to set a date for an opening conference or, depending on the nature of the proposed covered issue(s) and method(s) and other aspects of the APA request, inform the taxpayer that an opening conference may be unnecessary before the APA team moves forward with its analysis. If the opening conference is held, the taxpayer may be asked to respond to questions from the APA team about the APA request by a given date before the opening conference or at the opening conference itself. The APA team leader may postpone the opening conference if the responses are not provided by the date set or agreed to by the APA team leader.

### 11.5.2 Opening Conference

The primary purpose of an opening conference is to give the taxpayer an opportunity to acquaint the APA team with the APA request and the issue(s), method(s), and terms and conditions the taxpayer is proposing to be covered by the APA. The meeting may also include a more detailed discussion of particular aspects of the taxpayer's proposals. Accordingly, the taxpayer should be prepared to discuss the APA request in detail and respond as fully as possible to questions about its proposals.

The opening conference will also cover general procedural issues, including whether a case plan is appropriate and, if so, when it may be useful in the APA process for a case plan to be implemented, in light of the due diligence and analysis the APA team expects to undertake in the APA process. If feasible in light of the scope and complexity of the proposed APA, the APA team may also provide an estimate of the time it will take to complete its evaluation of the APA request. Whether this estimate holds true in any given case will primarily depend upon a variety of factors: the quality of the APA request; the extent of the taxpayer's cooperation with the APA team, including the completeness and timeliness of its responses to information requests and other due diligence inquiries during the APA process; and, in the case of bilateral or multilateral APAs, the speed with which the foreign competent authority is able to be prepared to discuss the case with the APA team. Accordingly, any timetable discussed or set forth in a case plan is only an estimate and is subject to revision and extension. For a bilateral or multilateral APA request, APMA will consider requests from, and may invite or require, the taxpayer to make presentations jointly to the US and foreign competent authorities during the APA process. APMA will consult with the foreign competent authority as to its interest in joint presentations and notify the taxpayer accordingly.

At the conclusion of the APA team's due diligence and evaluation of a bilateral or multilateral APA request, the APA team leader will provide to the taxpayer a memorandum conveying the substance of the APA team's views on the proposed APA. The memorandum will have a length, content, and format appropriate to the size and complexity of the proposed covered issue(s) and method(s) and other relevant facts and circumstances surrounding the case. The taxpayer will be invited to respond to the memorandum by a deadline set by the APA team leader.

### 11.5.3 Case Plan

In the case of a unilateral APA, the APA team and taxpayer will proceed to finalize an APA after the APA team has completed its due diligence and evaluation of the APA request. In the case of a bilateral or a multilateral APA, the APA team and the taxpayer will proceed to finalize an APA after a MAP resolution has been reached in the case.

### 11.5.4 Taxpayer Review

The APA will enter into force as of the date it is executed by APMA and the taxpayer and become effective on that specific date. In the case of an APA that includes a member of a consolidated group other than the common parent (as defined in Treasury Regulation §1.1502-1), the common parent must also sign the APA as provided in Treasury Regulation §1.1502-77. The person signing the APA must be an authorized officer of the taxpayer, have personal knowledge of the APA's covered issue(s), covered method(s), and terms and conditions, perform duties not limited to obtaining letter rulings or determination letters from the IRS or entering into APAs, and have authorization to sign the taxpayer's income tax return pursuant to section 6062 of the Code. The person signing for any non-corporate taxpayer must be an individual having personal knowledge of the APA's covered issue(s), covered method(s), and terms and conditions, and have authorization to sign the taxpayer's income tax return pursuant to sections 6061 or 6063 of the Code, as applicable.

## 11.6 APA ROLLBACKS AND COORDINATION WITH REVENUE PROCEDURE 2014-XX

Under Revenue Procedure 2014-XX, APMA may propose that a taxpayer pursues ACAP to extend a MAP resolution in its MAP case to one or more ACAP years. APMA may also affirmatively seek of its own accord to roll forward a MAP resolution in a MAP case to the taxpayer's ACAP years where it is feasible, practicable, and in the interest of sound tax administration to do so. APMA may also discuss with the taxpayer the possibility of extending the MAP resolution into APA years. A request to extend a MAP resolution into APA years may be made either by filing a complete APA request or by filing an abbreviated APA request. A taxpayer must file a complete APA request unless it has obtained APMA's permission to file an abbreviated APA request. APMA will grant permission to file an abbreviated APA request only if: (i) the taxpayer satisfies the pre-filing requirements set forth, and (ii) the applicable law, facts and circumstances, economic conditions, and other relevant factors surrounding the taxpayer's proposed APA years and proposed APA rollback years are reasonably expected to be substantially the same as such factors surrounding its MAP years or its MAP and ACAP years covered by the MAP resolution. If either of these requirements is not satisfied, the taxpayer must file a complete APA request and otherwise comply with all other provisions of this revenue procedure.

A taxpayer that seeks to file an abbreviated APA request to extend a MAP resolution in a MAP case to APA years must submit a pre-filing memorandum. Among the other required items, the pre-filing memorandum must: (i) present the taxpayer's arguments that the applicable law, facts and circumstances, economic conditions, and other factors surrounding its proposed covered issue(s) and method(s) for the proposed APA years and any proposed APA rollback years are substantially the same as those surrounding the MAP resolution in the MAP case; (ii) specify any information, documents, or other materials the taxpayer proposes to omit in its submission; and (iii) discuss the taxpayer's arguments that the information, documents, or other materials the taxpayer proposes to omit from its APA request are not necessary for APMA's evaluation of the APA request.

APMA will determine whether to hold a pre-filing conference after reviewing the pre-filing memorandum. APMA may determine that no pre-filing conference is required and that an abbreviated APA request will be acceptable. In that event, APMA will provide the taxpayer with instructions on preparing the request. If APMA determines that a pre-filing conference is required, the taxpayer will be expected to discuss the arguments presented in its pre-filing memorandum. If APMA decides to accept an abbreviated APA request after the pre-filing conference, it will provide the taxpayer with instructions on preparing the abbreviated APA request. If APMA decides that it will not accept an abbreviated APA request, the taxpayer will be instructed to file a complete APA request.

### 11.6.1 APA Rollbacks

A taxpayer may request an APA rollback to cover one or more of its pre-APA years. An APA rollback request should be included in the taxpayer's APA request. APMA may consider a later request for an APA rollback only if the APA rollback request is submitted in writing within three months after the APA request is filed, unless APMA agrees otherwise.

Whether included in the APA request or in a subsequent written request, the APA rollback request must include the same information for the pre-APA years that is required to be submitted for the APA years proposed by the taxpayer. After coordinating and collaborating with other offices within the IRS, APMA will inform the taxpayer whether its APA rollback request has been accepted.

Regardless of whether the taxpayer pursues an APA rollback request, APMA reserves the right to coordinate with applicable IRS offices to pursue an APA rollback to any or all of the taxpayer's open pre-APA years. In general, APMA will consider taking such action where there is sufficient similarity in relevant facts and circumstances across the taxpayer's APA and pre-APA years. APMA will inform the taxpayer in writing, either before the APA process begins or at any time during the APA process, whether it will pursue an APA rollback and the pre-APA years it will seek to cover. If the taxpayer refuses to accept an APA rollback, APMA may decline to initiate the APA process or suspend or terminate the process if it has already begun.

An APA rollback request submitted in connection with a bilateral or multilateral APA request, and involving a taxable year under the jurisdiction of IRS Appeals, will be deemed to constitute a request for SAP review, provided that an affirmative statement requesting SAP review is included in the APA request or in the subsequent written APA rollback request.

## 11.7 LEGAL EFFECTS OF AN APA

An APA is a binding agreement between the taxpayer and the IRS. If the taxpayer complies with the APA's terms and conditions, the IRS will not contest the application of the covered method(s) to the covered issue(s) of the APA except as provided in this revenue procedure. The taxpayer remains otherwise subject to US income tax laws and applicable US income tax treaties. An APA will have no legal effect except with respect to the taxpayer, taxable years, and issues to which the APA specifically relates.

Unless provided otherwise by written agreement or regulations, the IRS and the taxpayer may not introduce the APA or non-factual oral and written representations made in conjunction with the APA request as evidence in any judicial or administrative proceeding regarding any tax year, issue, or person not covered by the APA. This paragraph does not preclude the IRS and the taxpayer from agreeing to roll back the APA covered method(s), or the IRS's use of any non-factual material otherwise discoverable or obtained other than in the APA process merely because the parties considered the same or similar material in the APA process.

Unless provided otherwise by written agreement or regulations, the IRS and the taxpayer may not introduce a proposed, cancelled, or revoked APA, or any non-factual oral or written representations or submissions made during the APA process, as an admission by the other party, in any judicial or administrative proceeding regarding any taxable year of the requested APA term. This paragraph does not preclude the IRS's use of any non-factual material otherwise discoverable or obtained other than in the APA process merely because APMA and the taxpayer considered the same or similar material in the APA process.

## 11.8 ADMINISTRATION OF APA

An APA annual report must be filed for each APA year. The report must demonstrate the taxpayer's compliance with the APA terms and conditions, including the amount of any APA primary adjustment for a given APA year. The report must also include all other items required by the APA and disclose any pending or contemplated requests to renew, modify, or cancel the APA. In addition, the report must identify and correct any materially false, incorrect, or incomplete information submitted during the APA process that the taxpayer discovers during the APA year.

The taxpayer must file two printed copies and one electronic copy of the annual report before the later of: (i) the 15th day of the 12th month following the close of the APA year, and (ii) 90 days after the effective date of the APA. APMA may agree to alternative filing dates if requested by the taxpayer. The taxpayer must file all three copies of the annual report with APMA at the address set forth in the appendix. For bilateral and multilateral APAs, APMA may require the taxpayer to simultaneously file a copy of the annual report with the applicable foreign competent authority.

The taxpayer will be notified if it is necessary to clarify or complete the information submitted in the annual report. The taxpayer must supply the additional information by the date specified in the notice.

Any request the taxpayer receives to clarify or complete information in an annual report is not an examination or the commencement of an examination of the taxpayer for purposes of section 7605(b) of the Code or any other provision of the Code. The taxpayer must amend its annual report within 45 days after becoming aware of any incomplete or incorrect information or any incorrect application of the covered method(s) presented in the report. APMA may, at its discretion, grant an extension to submit the annual report if the taxpayer provides written notification of its request before the due date and explains the circumstances necessitating the extension.

The annual report must contain the following declarations, as applicable:

- Under penalties of perjury, I declare that I have examined this annual report including accompanying documents, and, to the best of my knowledge and belief, this annual report contains all the relevant facts relating to the annual reporting requirements pursuant to the APA, and such facts are true, correct, and complete.
- The taxpayer must sign the declaration according to the instructions in the appendix regarding perjury statements. Failure to file a timely, complete, or accurate annual report may be grounds for cancelling or revoking the APA.

## 11.9 REVOKING AN APA

APMA may revoke an APA due to fraud or malfeasance (as defined in section 7121 of the Code), or disregard (as defined in sections 6662(b)(1) and (c) of the Code) by the taxpayer in connection with the APA, including, but not limited to, fraud, malfeasance, or disregard involving: (i) material facts in the request or subsequent submissions (including an annual report) or (ii) lack of good faith compliance with the APA terms and conditions.

APMA may cancel an APA due to the taxpayer's misrepresentation, mistake with respect to a material fact, failure to state a material fact, failure to file a timely annual report, or lack of good faith in compliance with the APA terms and conditions.

Unless the parties agree to revise the APA, APMA will cancel an APA in the event of a failure of a critical assumption or a material change in governing case law, statute, regulation, or applicable treaty.

For purposes of this section 7.06(1) and (2), APMA will consider facts material if, for example, knowledge of the facts could reasonably have resulted in an APA with significantly different terms and conditions. With respect to annual reports, APMA will consider facts material if, for example, knowledge of the facts would have resulted in: (a) a materially different allocation of income, deductions, or credits than those reported in the annual report, or (b) the failure to meet a critical assumption.

APMA may waive cancellation if the taxpayer can show good faith and reasonable cause and agrees to make all adjustments proposed to correct for the misrepresentation, mistake regarding a material fact, failure to state a material fact, or noncompliance. If APMA revokes an APA, the revocation relates back to the first day of the first APA year. The IRS may:

- determine deficiencies in income taxes and additions thereto;
- deny relief under Revenue Procedure 99-32;
- allow the taxpayer relief under Revenue Procedure 99-32, but determine the interest on any account receivable established under section 4.01 of Revenue Procedure 99-32 without mutual agreement or correlative relief;
- revoke the APA as an "egregious case" under Revenue Rulings 80-231, 1980-2 C.B. 219, to deny the taxpayer a foreign tax credit; and
- deny a request for relief submitted to its review.

APMA's cancellation of an APA generally is effective as of the beginning of the taxable year in which the critical assumption failed or the beginning of the year to which the misrepresentation, mistake regarding a material fact, failure to state a material fact, or noncompliance relates. If, however, the cancellation results from a change in case law, statute, regulation, US income tax treaty, or coordination agreement, the cancellation generally is effective at the beginning of the year that contains the effective date of the change in case law, statute, regulation, US income tax treaty, or coordination agreement. For periods following the effective date of the cancellation, the APA has no further force and effect with respect to the IRS and the taxpayer for US income tax purposes. APMA will seek to coordinate any action concerning the cancellation of a bilateral or multilateral APA with the foreign competent authority.

## 11.10 RENEWING THE APA

A request to renew a current APA may be made either by filing a complete APA request or by filing an abbreviated APA request. A taxpayer must file a complete APA request unless it has obtained APMA's permission to file an abbreviated APA request. APMA will grant permission to file an abbreviated APA request only if:

- the taxpayer satisfies the pre-filing requirements set forth in section 3 and detailed in section 8; and
- the applicable law, facts and circumstances, economic conditions, and other relevant factors surrounding the covered issue(s), covered method(s), and terms and conditions of the current APA are reasonably expected to be substantially the same as those in the proposed renewal APA years. If either of these requirements is not satisfied, the taxpayer must file a complete APA request and otherwise comply with all other provisions of this revenue procedure. Taxpayers are encouraged to file a request to renew a current APA nine months before the expiration of the final APA year.

A taxpayer that seeks to file an abbreviated APA request to renew an APA must submit a pre-filing memorandum. Among the other required items, the pre-filing memorandum must:

- present the taxpayer's arguments that the applicable law, facts and circumstances, economic conditions, and other factors surrounding its proposed

covered issue(s) and method(s) for the proposed APA years are substantially the same as those surrounding the current APA;
- specify any information, documents, or other materials the taxpayer proposes to omit from its submission; and
- discuss the taxpayer's arguments that the information, documents, or other materials the taxpayer proposes to omit from its APA request are not necessary for APMA's evaluation of the APA request.

APMA will determine whether to hold a pre-filing conference after reviewing the pre-filing memorandum. APMA may determine that no pre-filing conference is required and that an abbreviated APA request will be acceptable. In that event, APMA will provide the taxpayer with instructions on preparing the abbreviated APA request. If APMA determines that a pre-filing conference is required, the taxpayer will be expected to discuss the arguments presented in its pre-filing memorandum. If after the pre-filing conference APMA decides that an abbreviated APA request is acceptable, it will provide the taxpayer with instructions on preparing the request. If APMA decides that it will not accept an abbreviated APA request, the taxpayer will be instructed to file a complete APA request.

## 11.11 APA DISCLOSURE

### 11.11.1 Confidentiality

An APA, any background information relating to an APA, and the taxpayer's APA request and any supplementary materials submitted in conjunction with the APA request are return information and are confidential.[4]

### 11.11.2 Written Determinations

An APA, background information related to the APA, an APA request, and supplementary materials submitted in conjunction with the APA request are not "written determinations" and are not open to public inspection. *See* section 6110 of the Code.

### 11.11.3 Statutory Report

The Secretary must prepare an annual report for public disclosure. *See* section 521(b) of the Ticket to Work and Work Incentives Improvement Act of 1999, Pub. L. 106-170, 113 Stat. 1860, 1925. That report includes specifically designated information concerning all APAs, in a form that does not identify taxpayers, their trade secrets, or proprietary or confidential business or financial information.

4. IRC sections 6103, 6105, 894, and 7852(d).

### 11.11.4 Exchange of Information

APAs, annual reports, and factual information contained in APA requests are subject to exchange of information under US income tax treaties or US income Tax Information Exchange Agreements (TIEAs) in accordance with the terms of such treaties and agreements (including terms regarding relevancy, confidentiality, and the protection of trade secrets). In cases in which the exchange of information would be discretionary, information may be exchanged to the extent consistent with sound tax administration and the practices of the relevant foreign competent authority.

## 11.12 APA TRANSACTIONS COVERED IN 2014

Twenty-three percent of the transactions covered in APAs executed in 2014 involved the sale of tangible goods and 18 percent involved the provision of services. Although more than 75 percent of covered transactions involve tangible goods and services transactions, the IRS also has successfully completed numerous APAs involving transfers of intangibles.[5]

## 11.13 APA TYPES OF TESTED PARTIES, FUNCTIONS, AND RISKS

The tested parties of the APAs executed in 2014 fell primarily into one of two categories. Combined, these two types of tested parties represent over 50 percent of the total. No other single type of entity represents greater than 10 percent of the total.

More than 60 percent of the tested parties in the APAs executed in 2014 involved distribution or related functions, e.g., marketing and product support.[6]

The risks borne by the tested parties were primarily business risks (e.g., market risk and general business risk). A small percentage of the tested parties bore other risks such as product liability or research and development risk.[7]

## 11.14 TRANSFER PRICING METHODS USED IN APAs

The primary transfer pricing method used for transfers of both tangible and intangible property in APAs executed in 2014 was the Comparable Profits Method/Transactional Net Margin Method (CPM/TNMM).

In controlled transactions using the CPM/TNMM, the Operating Margin was the most common PLI used to benchmark results for transfers of tangible and intangible property. Per the applicable regulations, Operating Margin is defined as the ratio of operating profits to sales. The Berry ratio, defined as the ratio of gross profit to

5. *Idem.*, p. 9.
6. *Idem.*, pp. 8–9.
7. *Idem.*, p. 10.

operating expenses, was applied as the profit level indicator in 6 percent of the controlled transactions that used the CPM/TNMM. Each other profit level indicator accounted for a smaller share.

For services transactions, the majority of cases applied the SCM or the CPM/TNMM. The SCM evaluates the amount charged for certain services with reference to the total services costs.[8] When the CPM/TNMM is used to benchmark services transactions, the Berry ratio continues to be the most frequently used PLI.

## 11.15 RANGES, TARGETS, AND ADJUSTMENT MECHANISMS

Almost 70 percent of the transactions covered in APAs executed in 2014 target an interquartile range as described in Treasury Regulation §1.482-1(e)(2)(iii)(C). Where the transaction involves a royalty payment for the use of intangible property, both points and ranges have been used. In some cases where the covered transaction is the payment of a royalty based solely on external royalty agreements, a secondary method (e.g., a test of the post-royalty operating margin) has been imposed. The testing periods of the APAs executed in 2014 included either:

- a single year;
- the term of the APA not including any rollback years; or
- the term of the APA including rollback years.[9]

## 11.16 CRITICAL ASSUMPTIONS

Under §11.03(2) of Revenue Procedure 2006-9, the IRS may require the taxpayer to show compliance with all the critical assumptions included in the APA. If the taxpayer's results violate the critical assumption, then the taxpayer is required to report to the IRS the event or events creating the violation. Pursuant to §11.06(3) of Revenue Procedure 2006-9, when a critical assumption is violated, the APMA Director may agree to modify the APA. However, if there is no agreement to modify the APA, then the APA may be cancelled.

## 11.17 CONCLUSION

Although the APA is praised as a good step moving forward, it still resents some lingering issues: (i) completing the APA process is costly and time consuming;[10] and (ii) APAs are not published and in the absence of comparables are not subject to any standards. That may open door to lobbying efforts at the expense of the Treasury or the taxpayers.

8. *Idem.*, p. 11.
9. *Idem.*, p. 13.
10. Avi-Yonah, Reuven (2009): The Rise and Fall of Arm's Length: A Study in the Evolution of US International Taxation.

CHAPTER 12

# Transfer Pricing and Base Erosion and Profit Shifting

## 12.1 INTRODUCTION

The erosion of the corporate tax base caused by the shifting of profits into tax havens is not just a US tax problem. Base Erosion and Profit Shifting (BEPS) opportunities impair the ability of countries to achieve their tax policy goals, effectively undermining their sovereignty.[1] The phenomenon is by no means limited to US multinational corporations as 74 percent of the Fortune Global 500 companies are non-US-headquartered companies. A recent Congressional Research Service study in the US reported that BEPS activities are estimated to reduce US corporate tax revenue by USD 10–USD 60 billion annually.[2]

In July 2013 and September 16, 2014, the Organisation for Economic Co-operation and Development (OECD) released action plans to better assist governments in their efforts to combat BEPS within the international tax system, and particularly in the field of transfer pricing.

In October 2015, the OECD released a series of action steps that the organization and G20 countries have agreed upon.

The US Treasury Department and IRS have actively joined the ongoing OECD effort to develop better international principles for taxing multinational corporations, by requiring multinationals to disclose their business operations and tax payments on a CbC basis, stop improper transfers of profits to tax havens, and stop avoiding taxation

1. Saint-Amans, Pascal (July 22, 2013): Testimony of the Director, Centre for Tax Policy and Administration, Organization for Economic Co-operation and Development (OECD) Before the United States Senate Committee on Finance, p. 6.
2. Saint-Amans, Pascal (July 22, 2013): Testimony of the Director, Centre for Tax Policy and Administration, Organization for Economic Co-operation and Development (OECD) Before the United States Senate Committee on Finance, p. 3.

in the countries in which they have a substantial business presence.[3] In June 2014, the European Commission opened three investigations to assess whether tax authorities in Ireland, the Netherlands and Luxembourg complied with EU rules on state aid regarding their dealings with three companies—Apple, Starbucks, and Fiat Finance and Trade. Under EU rules, tax authorities must not allow companies to pay less tax than they should. Tax advantages are regarded by the EU as state aid and subject to strict controls.

## 12.2 BEPS SHORTCOMINGS

Under the OECD BEPS package released in 2015, the purpose of Actions 8–10 is to assure that transfer pricing outcomes are in line with value creation.[4]

Despite the great optimism of the BEPS, the project[5] only addresses artificial profit shifting, not tax competition, and it only applies to the OECD and G20, not to the many source countries outside these two organizations.[6] Thus, it is likely that multinationals can avoid BEPS by sourcing income in countries that are not subject to it. Further, the BEPS package, particularly Actions 8–10 do not depart from the old principle of separately independent entity, while considering the relationship among entities forming an MNE. This leads some experts such as Professor Avi-Yonah to argue that "Actions 8-10 made transfer pricing rules more sophisticated and complex, so as to authorize tax authorities to re-characterize the related-party transactions within the MNE group."[7]

## 12.3 THE TRANSFER PRICING SCHEMES

US corporations are creating opportunities to erode their taxable basis through aggressive transfer pricing gimmicks, allocation of debts among affiliated entities, abusive anti-deferral techniques, allocation of income, transactions deprived of any business purposes, and other improper income shifting. US Multinational firms engage in both "real income shifting"[8] and "artificial income shifting,"[9] by choosing the

3. United States Senate- Permanent Subcommittee on Investigations (April 1, 2014): Caterpillar's offshore tax strategy, p. 7.
4. Avi-Yonah, Reuven (2016): Evaluating BEPS, NYU Tax Policy Colloquium, p. 16.
5. "Base erosion and profit shifting affects all countries, not only economically, but also as a matter of trust. BEPS is depriving countries of precious resources to jump-start growth, tackle the effects of the global economic crisis and create more and better opportunities for all. But beyond this, BEPS has been also eroding the trust of citizens in the fairness of tax systems worldwide. The measures we are presenting today represent the most fundamental changes to international tax rules in almost a century: they will put an end to double non-taxation, facilitate a better alignment of taxation with economic activity and value creation, and when fully implemented, these measures will render BEPS-inspired tax planning structures ineffective."
6. Avi-Yonah, Reuven (2016): Evaluating BEPS, NYU Tax Policy Colloquium, p. 5.
7. Avi-Yonah, Reuven (2016): Evaluating BEPS, NYU Tax Policy Colloquium, p. 16.
8. Real income shifting refers to income that is shifted in a manner that results in both explicit and implicit tax consequences.
9. Artificial income shifting refers to income that is shifted to avoid explicit taxes without incurring the implicit taxes generally associated with a reduction in explicit taxes.

country in which to locate manufacturing facilities, research and development activities, service centers, or the country in which to incur debt payable to unrelated parties. Further, they engage in artificial income shifting through intercompany transfer pricing for sales of goods, intercompany charges for services provided, intercompany royalties for the use of IP, intercompany rentals for the use of tangible property, and/or interest charged on intercompany debt.[10]

### 12.3.1 The Caterpillar Swiss Tax Strategy

- Caterpillar US was engaged in several restructuring from the late 1980s to the 2000s. The US parent company reorganized as Caterpillar Inc. in the State of Delaware, and Caterpillar has currently 30 business segments organized into seven types. From 2008 through 2012, Caterpillar exported more than USD 82 billion in products from the US.
- In 2011, exports from the US made up USD 19.4 billion or about one-third of its USD 60 billion in consolidated sales. While most sales now occur outside the US, most of Caterpillar's machines and parts are still built in the US. In 2012, about 70 percent of finished Caterpillar replacement parts sold offshore were manufactured in the US.[11]
- Although its major operations have always been in the US, Caterpillar has also had a small continuous presence in Geneva-Switzerland for four decades through COSA (Caterpillar Overseas), which was one of the Caterpillar's several offshore marketing companies.
- In 1999, Caterpillar's external auditor, PricewaterhouseCoopers (PwC), and tax consultant approached the management of Caterpillar and offered to assist the company to reduce its overall tax exposure.
- As part of the PwC "skilled tax strategies," COSA was liquidated to give birth to CSARL (Caterpillar SARL). PwC designed a Swiss tax strategy to direct the lion's share of Caterpillar's non-US purchased finished replacement parts (PFRP) profits away from the US to Switzerland, where Caterpillar had negotiated an effective tax rate of 4 percent–6 percent lower even than the Swiss federal statutory rate of 8.5 percent.[12]
- PwC proposed deferring or avoiding that tax by "removing Caterpillar Inc. from the chain of title passage for purchased finished parts (from US or foreign

10. Atwood, T.J. (2013): Are Worldwide Tax Systems Disadvantageous for Residents Firms Compared with Territorial Tax Systems?, Florida Tax Law Review, p. 8.
11. United States Senate—Permanent Subcommittee on Investigations (April 1, 2014): Caterpillar's Offshore Tax Strategy, p. 21.
12. United States Senate—Permanent Subcommittee on Investigations (April 1, 2014): Caterpillar's Offshore Tax Strategy, p. 41.

sources) sold to foreign marketers," and replacing the US parent with a new Swiss entity as the direct purchaser of the third party manufactured replacement parts.[13]

- Prior to the creation of CSARL in 1999, Caterpillar Inc., the US parent corporation, bought the PFRPs needed for Caterpillar machines directly from the third-party suppliers that manufactured the parts for the company.[14]
- Also, Caterpillar was the initial buyer of its third party manufactured replacement parts, and if the replacement parts were to be sold in Europe, Africa, or the Middle East (EAME region), Caterpillar typically sold the parts to its affiliated marketing company, Caterpillar Overseas S.A. (COSA), which was incorporated in Switzerland. COSA, in turn, sold the parts to Caterpillar's independent foreign dealers in the EAME region. Caterpillar's standard practice was to compensate the internal Business Divisions involved with the sales of its non-US parts. Its practice was to assign a routine profit to the divisions that performed routine business services and the residual profits—sometimes called "entrepreneurial" profits—to the divisions that contributed directly to the creation of those residual profits.

  As part of the devised tax strategy, CSARL was formed and assigned the role of "global purchaser" of caterpillar's finished parts in various licensing agreements. According to PwC, that designation resulted in two key changes: (i) Caterpillar Inc., the US parent corporation, was removed from the non-US parts supply chain, and replaced with CSARL, which became the nominal "global purchaser" of PFRP parts,[15] and (ii) CSARL entered into "tolling agreements" with Caterpillar's two main European manufacturing operations in France and Belgium.[16]

  CSARL as a nominal global purchaser entered into several licensing and servicing agreement with related entities and paid minimal royalties to Caterpillar US, the parent company. Further, the "tax strategy" included the construction of a virtual parts inventory, the invoices alteration. All of these were poorly taught with reckless disregard to the basic tax concepts such as business purposes, and economic substance doctrines, the assignment of income, the ALP, the clear ownership of inventories, the definition of intangibles.
- Parts profits reported by CSARL over that eight-year period totaled about USD 8 billion, while the royalty payments paid by CSARL to Caterpillar totaled about USD 1 billion. The data also showed that CSARL retained 84 percent–91 percent of the parts profits each year, leading to an overall eight-year average

13. United States Senate—Permanent Subcommittee on Investigations (April 1, 2014): Caterpillar's Offshore Tax Strategy, p. 43.
14. United States Senate—Permanent Subcommittee on Investigations (April 1, 2014): Caterpillar's Offshore Tax Strategy, p. 46.
15. United States Senate—Permanent Subcommittee on Investigations (April 1, 2014): Caterpillar's Offshore Tax Strategy, p. 50.
16. United States Senate—Permanent Subcommittee on Investigations (April 1, 2014): Caterpillar's Offshore Tax Strategy, p. 51.

of 86 percent. This data confirmed that, overall, Caterpillar obtained 15 percent or less of the non-US parts profits, while CSARL obtained 85 percent or more.[17] As of the end of 2013, Caterpillar's offshore cash assets totaled USD 17 billion, giving the company the 33rd largest offshore amount of 1,000 corporations reviewed by the US Senate Committee.[18]

### *12.3.1.1 Transfer Pricing Out the ALP*

For a transfer between related parties of valuable assets, such as licensing rights, to be valid under the tax code, the transfer must meet an arm's-length standard, including compensating the transferring party as though the transfer were a sale to an unrelated third party.

Caterpillar US explained its transfer pricing policies and practice as follows:

> The fact that a company may have structured its transaction flows one way for some period of time does not prevent the company from structuring its transactions flows in a different way later. Of course there must be compensation for any property transferred and services performed in connection with a restructuring, as there was in Caterpillar's case, but changing a supply chain structure is not, in and of itself, a taxable event.[19]

Subsequent to the tax scheme with the CSARL transaction, Caterpillar gave a significant portion of the profits from its non-US finished replacement parts business to CSARL in exchange for a licensing fee. While Caterpillar contended that the aggregated royalty rate was the more appropriate rate to consider, since that rate contained in the final license agreement which covered both parts and machines, it is notable that the Swiss tax strategy that led to the licensing agreement targeted only the company's non-US parts profits, without mentioning machines. In any event, both profit splits have resulted in lopsided profits allocations in favor of CSARL over Caterpillar. Additional facts also supported the non-arm's length character of the transaction clothes in several licensing and servicing agreements:

(i) Caterpillar continued to perform key functions supporting the non-US sales of Caterpillar branded parts, including much of the parts design, parts forecasting, inventory management, parts ordering, supplier oversight, quality control, parts pricing, and parts storage and delivery. It did so for cost plus a 5 percent mark up, which produced only limited income for the US parent.[20]

---

17. United States Senate—Permanent Subcommittee on Investigations (April 1, 2014): Caterpillar's Offshore Tax Strategy, p. 56.
18. United States Senate—Permanent Subcommittee on Investigations (April 1, 2014): Caterpillar's Offshore Tax Strategy, p. 62.
19. United States Senate—Permanent Subcommittee on Investigations (April 1, 2014): Caterpillar's Offshore Tax Strategy, p. 94.
20. United States Senate—Permanent Subcommittee on Investigations (April 1, 2014): Caterpillar's Offshore Tax Strategy, p. 81.

(ii) It defies logic that Caterpillar would have entered into a licensing transaction with an unrelated party in which it gave away 69 percent, 85 percent, or more of its business profits on an annual basis in exchange for a 31 percent, 15 percent, or smaller share of the profits, while continuing to perform core functions to support those profits and continuing to bear the ultimate economic risk. Caterpillar only engaged in the CSARL transaction, because the profits sent to Switzerland went to CSARL, a related party, and enjoyed a low Swiss tax rate of 4 percent. In addition, CSARL's profits were included in Caterpillar's consolidated financial statements, so that CSARL's financial success contributed directly to Caterpillar's positive results.

(iii) CSARL paid nothing to Caterpillar Inc. to compensate the company for the decades Caterpillar spent developing its parts business before turning it over to CSARL, including developing a third-party supplier base, designing a large selection of proprietary parts, and creating a world class logistics system to store and deliver those parts anywhere in the world within 24 hours. Nor did CSARL compensate Caterpillar Inc. for the right to the future profit streams associated with the non-US parts business—billions of dollars in parts "annuities" that would last as long as Caterpillar's durable machines. In fact, CSARL made no "buy-in" or other payment or provided any super royalty to compensate Caterpillar Inc. for the business it had built or for the future profits that would be generated. Instead, CSARL paid Caterpillar Inc. only an annual royalty equal to 15 percent or less of the profits produced by the non-US parts business each year plus a service fee for performing key parts functions on a cost plus 5 percent basis. It is hard to understand how Caterpillar would ever have entered into such an arrangement with an unrelated party.

### 12.3.2 Apple Tax Abusive Structure

Apple skillful transfer pricing manipulation was achieved through a structure known as "Double Irish with a Dutch Sandwich."

- Apple set up two entities in Ireland through which it was able to funnel two-thirds of its pre-tax worldwide income: Apple Operations Europe and Apple Sales International (ASI).
- Apple Operations International (AOI), created in 1980, has no employees or physical presence, and whose operations are managed and controlled out of the US.[21] AOI has no declared tax residency anywhere in the world and, as a consequence, has not paid corporate income tax to any national government for the past five years.

21. Under Irish law, if the Irish subsidiary is controlled by managers elsewhere, the entity is not considered as an Irish entity and its profits are not subject to taxation anywhere.

- Apple entered into two separate tax rulings with the Irish revenue by which Apple has to compute its profits by reference to a percentage of each's cost, referred to as "cost plus method."
- Apple then set up another subsidiary in the Netherlands. As the Irish treaties make some inter-European transfers tax-free, Apple avoided taxes by routing the profits derived made by Apple Operation Europe and Apple Sale International in its Dutch subsidiary.
- The remaining profits are transferred directly to Cayman Islands or Bermuda.
- Despite receiving USD 30 billion in earnings and profits during the period 2009 through 2011 as the key holding company for Apple's extensive offshore corporate structure, AOI has no declared tax residency anywhere in the world and, as a consequence, has not paid corporate income tax to any national government for the past five years.
- On another hand, ASI has acquired certain economic rights to Apple's IP. Apple Inc. has used those rights of ASI to shift billions in profits away from the US to Ireland, where it pays an agreed upon corporate tax rate of 2 percent.

Apple has USD 145 billion in cash, cash equivalents and marketable securities, of which USD 102 billion is "offshore." Apple has used offshore entities, arrangements, and transactions to transfer its assets and profits offshore and minimize its corporate tax liabilities.[22]

Facing stern criticisms from the EU Commission, the Irish government has amended its corporate laws by closing the non-dual residency enjoyed by several MNCs. Irish Finance Minister Michael Noonan addressed the "Double Irish" during the presentation of his 2015 budget. Under the new rules, no companies would be allowed to use the "Double Irish" after the entry of the 2015 law into application. However, those already engaging in the tax avoidance scheme have a five-year window until 2020 to adjust their structures.

In 2014, the European Commission opened a formal probe into Apple's tax arrangements with Ireland under the prohibition of state aid under which national tax authorities are barred from giving benefits to some companies while the benefits are unavailable to others.

### *12.3.2.1 EU Aid under Article 107*

The role of EU state aid control is to ensure Member States do not give selected companies a better tax treatment than others, via tax rulings or otherwise. More specifically, profits must be allocated between companies in a corporate group, and between different parts of the same company, in a way that reflects economic reality.

22. US Senate Committee—Permanent Subcommittee on Investigations—Apple Inc, Memorandum, p. 5.

This means that the allocation should be in line with arrangements that take place under commercial conditions between independent businesses (so-called arm's length principle).

#### *12.3.2.2 EU Commission Decision*

On August 30, 2016, the European Commission has concluded that the two tax rulings issued by Ireland to Apple had substantially and artificially lowered the tax paid by Apple in Ireland since 1991. The tax rulings issued by Ireland endorsed an artificial internal allocation of profits within ASI and Apple Operations Europe, which has no factual or economic justification.

The tax treatment granted to Apple in Ireland enabled Apple to avoid taxation on almost all profits generated by sales of Apple products in the entire EU Single Market. Most sales profits of ASI were allocated to its "head office" when this "head office" had no operating capacity to handle and manage the distribution business or any other substantive business for that matter. Only the Irish branch of ASI had the capacity to generate any income from trading. Therefore, the sales profits of ASI should have been recorded with the Irish branch and taxed there.

The Commission concluded that the tax rulings issued by Ireland endorsed an artificial allocation of ASI and Apple Operations Europe's sales profits to their "head offices," where they were not taxed. As a result, the tax rulings enabled Apple to pay substantially less tax than other companies, which is illegal under EU state aid rules.

In particular, Ireland must allocate to each branch all profits from sales previously indirectly allocated to the "head office" of ASI and Apple Operations Europe, respectively, and apply the normal corporation tax in Ireland on these reallocated profits.

This selective tax treatment of Apple in Ireland is illegal under EU state aid rules, because it gives Apple a significant advantage over other businesses that are subject to the same national taxation rules. Ireland must now recover the unpaid taxes in Ireland from Apple for the years 2003–2014 of up to EUR 13 billion, plus interest. However, the amount of unpaid taxes to be recovered by the Irish authorities would be reduced if other countries were to require Apple to pay more taxes on the profits recorded by ASI and Apple Operations Europe for this period (Figure 12.1).

Finally, all Commission decisions are subject to scrutiny by EU courts. If a Member State decides to appeal a Commission decision, it must still recover the illegal state aid but could, for example, place the recovered amount in an escrow account pending the outcome of the EU court procedures.

*Figure 12.1 Apple's Offshore Organizational Structure*

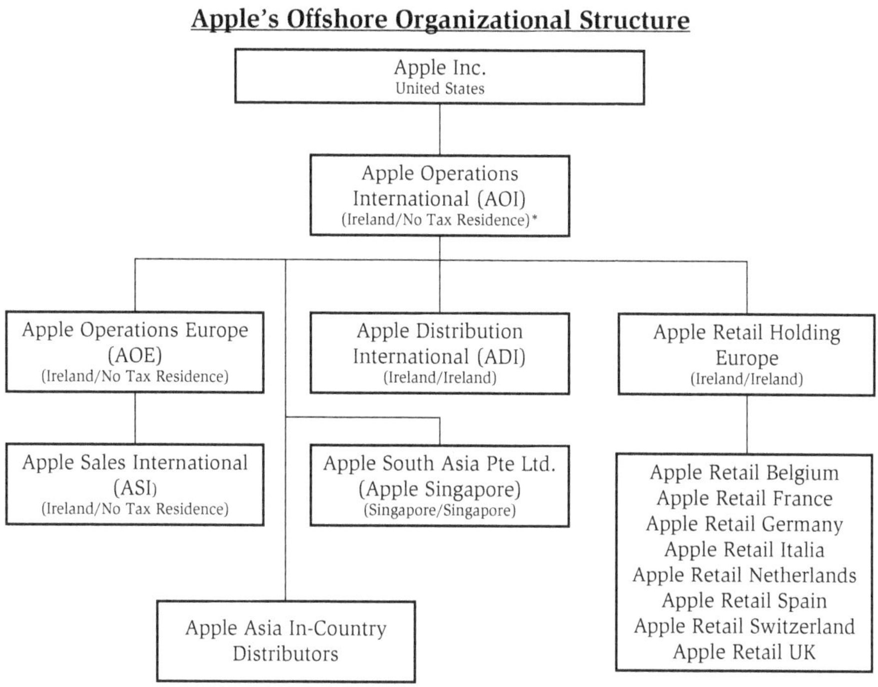


Prepared by the Permanent Subcommittee on Investigations, May 2013.
*Source*: Materials received from Apple Inc.
* Listed countries indicate country of incorporation and country of tax residence, respectively.

### *12.3.2.3 US Senate Committee Investigation on Apple Cost Sharing Agreement*

Apple's transfer of the economic rights to its IP to Ireland has no apparent commercial benefit apart from its tax effects.

Apple Inc.'s Irish affiliates have also helped Apple avoid US taxes in another way, through utilization of a cost sharing agreement and related transfer pricing practices. Three key offshore affiliates in this effort are ASI, its parent AOE, and Apple Distributions International (ADI), each of which holds a second or third tier position in Apple's offshore structure in Ireland. All three companies are incorporated and located in Ireland, and share the same mailing address. Another key second-tier player is Apple South Asia Pte. Ltd., a company incorporated and located in Singapore (Apple Singapore). These offshore affiliates enable Apple Inc. to keep the lion's share of its worldwide sales revenues out of the US and instead shift that sales income to Ireland, where Apple enjoys an unusually low tax rate and affiliates allegedly with no tax residency (Figure 12.2).[23]

In the agreement, Apple Inc. and ASI agree to share in the development of Apple's products and to divide the resulting IP economic rights. To calculate their respective costs, Apple Inc. first pools the costs of Apple's worldwide research and development efforts. Apple Inc. and ASI then each pay a portion of the pooled costs based upon the portion of product sales that occur in their respective regions. For instance, in 2011, roughly 40 percent of Apple's worldwide sales occurred in the Americas, with the remaining 60 percent occurring offshore. That same year, Apple's worldwide research and development costs totaled USD 2.4 billion.[24] Apple Inc. and ASI contributed to these shared expenses based on each entity's percentage of worldwide sales. Apple Inc. paid 40 percent or USD 1.0 billion, while ASI paid the remaining 60 percent or USD 1.4 billion.

The cost sharing agreement that Apple has signed with ASI and AOE is a key component of Apple's ability to lower its US taxes. Several aspects of the cost share agreement and Apple's research and development (R&D) and sales practices suggest that the agreement functions primarily as a conduit to shift profits offshore to avoid US taxes. First, the bulk of Apple's R&D efforts, the source of the intangible value of its products, is conducted in the US, yet under the cost sharing agreement a disproportionate amount of the resulting profits remain outside of the US. Second, the transfer of IP rights to Ireland via the cost sharing agreement appears to play no role in the way Apple conducts its commercial operations. Finally, the cost sharing agreement does not in reality shift any risks or benefits away from Apple, the multinational corporation; it only shifts the location of the tax liability for Apple's profits.[25]

23. US Senate Committee—Permanent Subcommittee on Investigations—Apple Inc, Memorandum, p. 25.
24. US Senate Committee—Permanent Subcommittee on Investigations—Apple Inc, Memorandum, p. 26.
25. US Senate Committee—Permanent Subcommittee on Investigations—Apple Inc, Memorandum, p. 28.

*Figure 12.2 Apple's Offshore Distribution Structure*

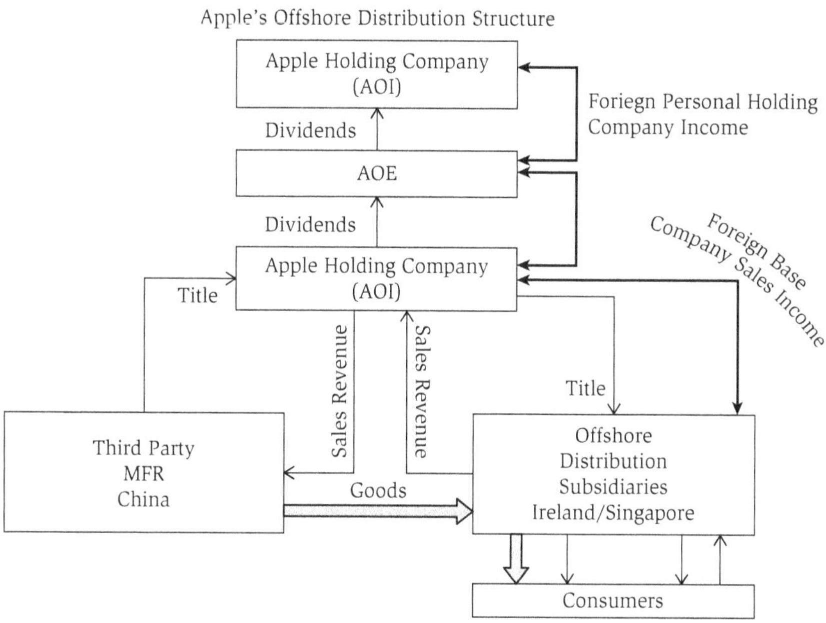


*Source*: Prepared by the Permanent Subcommittee on Investigations, May 2013.

### 12.3.3 Microsoft Tax Abusive Structure

From 2009 to 2011, Microsoft shifted, through aggressive tax planning USD 21 billion offshore, almost half of its US retail sales revenue, saving up to USD 4.5 billion in taxes on goods sold in the US.

Microsoft achieved its BEPS through aggressive transfer pricing with several of its subsidiaries overseas.

#### *12.3.3.1 Microsoft Transfer Pricing*

Microsoft began establishing a complex web of interrelated foreign entities to facilitate international sales and reduce US and foreign tax. It established three regional operating centers in low-tax jurisdictions: Ireland, Singapore, and Puerto Rico. Microsoft Ireland is responsible for retail sales in Europe, the Middle East and Africa; Singapore is responsible for retail sales in Asia; and Puerto Rico is responsible for retail sales in North and South America, including the US. In 2011, over USD 7.8 billion out of a total research budget of USD 9.1 billion was spent on research and development in the US Microsoft received USD 200 million in US tax credits for conducting this research in the US. To transfer IP rights from the US group to foreign subsidiaries, Microsoft and the regional operating centers engage in a worldwide cost sharing agreement. The participating entities each pay a portion of the research and development cost based on the entity's portion of global revenues.

Microsoft Corporation has used aggressive transfer pricing transactions to shift its IP, a mobile asset, to subsidiaries in Puerto Rico, Ireland, and Singapore, which are low or no tax jurisdictions, in part to avoid or reduce its US taxes on the profits generated by assets sold by its offshore entities. From 2009 to 2011, by transferring certain rights to its IP to a Puerto Rican subsidiary, Microsoft was able to shift offshore nearly USD 21 billion, or almost half of its US retail sales net revenue, saving up to USD 4.5 billion in taxes on goods sold in the US, or just over USD 4 million in US taxes each day (Figure 12.3).[26]

*Figure 12.3 Microsoft Intellectual Property Payment*

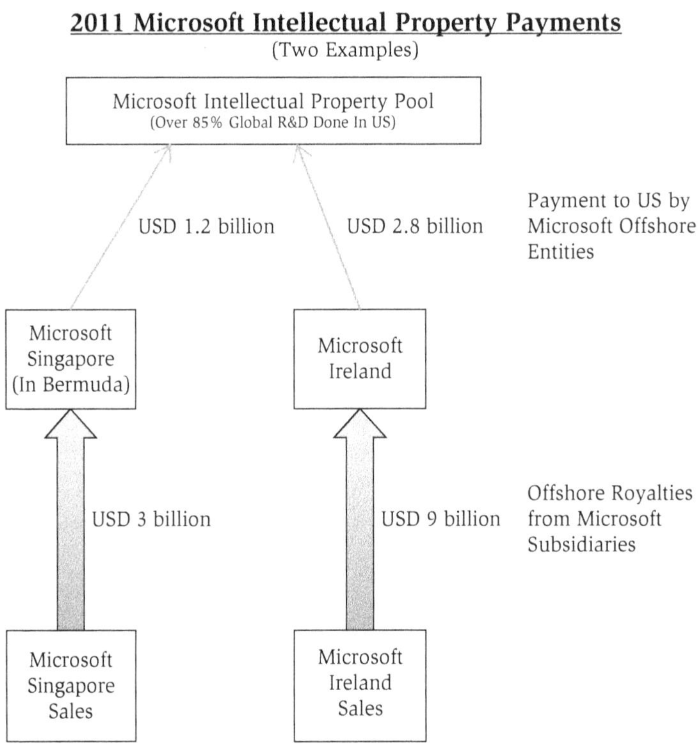


*Source*: Permanent Subcommittee on Investigation, In: Statement of Senator Carl Levin (D-Mich) Before U.S. Senate Permanent Subcommittee on Investigations on Offshore Profit Shifting and the U.S. Tax Code, September 20, 2012.

26. United States Senate Permanent Subcommittee on Investigation—Microsoft, (September 20, 2012).

The hearing featured a case study involving Microsoft's shifting of IP rights for software developed in America, and the earnings that flow from them, to divisions in lower-tax Puerto Rico, Ireland, and Singapore. One witness, Professor Stephen Shay of Harvard Law School, pointed out that in 2011 these three units enjoyed an average effective tax rate of just 4 percent and managed to book USD 15.4 billion of pre-tax profit—55 percent of Microsoft's worldwide total. Their 1,914 employees generated an eyebrow-raising USD 8 million of profit each, compared with USD 312,000 each for the 88,000 working with the rest of Microsoft. Whether or not this apportionment of profits complies with transfer pricing rules, it is "not consistent with a common sense understanding of where the locus of Microsoft's economic activity...is occurring," said Professor Shay. The claim that fair transfer prices were paid is "just not credible given the bottom-line outcome," he added.

In 2011, the Senate investigators asserted, Microsoft's parent company was paid USD 4 billion by Ireland and Singapore for rights that the two subsidiaries used to generate three times that amount in royalty payments from other bits of the group. Under one cost sharing agreement, they said, head office sold Puerto Rico certain rights then repurchased them straight afterwards for a lot more, a money maneuver that saved the group USD 4 billion in tax over three years. A Microsoft man who was grilled at the hearing said the staffers' sums ignored hefty, regular "buy-in" payments that the foreign subsidiaries have to make to the parent.

### 12.3.4 Starbucks[27]

The Commission found that Starbucks' coffee roasting company, established in the Netherlands, was paying an unjustifiably high royalty (for coffee roasting "know-how") to a UK Starbucks entity that was not liable to pay corporate tax in the UK or in the Netherlands. Meanwhile, the Netherlands Entity was also purchasing coffee beans from a Swiss Starbucks entity at an inflated price. The high royalty paid to the UK entity, coupled with the high prices paid to the Swiss entity, reduced the taxable base for the Netherlands Entity. The Commission held that the tax ruling issued by the Netherlands authority, endorsing Starbucks' arrangement, constituted illegal state aid (Figure 12.4).

The relevant facts of the case can be summed up as follows:

- Starbucks Manufacturing BV (SMBV) is the only wholly controlled Starbucks group entity outside of the US which roasts coffee. SMBV roasts, packages, and stores coffee beans, and performs related functions, such as acting as an intermediary distribution company for non-coffee items like Starbucks cups and napkins.
- On April 28, 2008, SMBV concluded an advance pricing agreement with the Dutch tax administration. The SMBV APA was binding for 10 years, from October 1, 2007 to December 31, 2017.

27. SA.38374 (2014/C ex 2014/NN) implemented by the Netherlands to Starbucks, Commission Decision of 21.10.2015.

- The SMBV APA was concluded on the basis of Article 8b(1) of the Dutch Corporation Tax Act 1969.
- The APA applied a mark up of 9 percent–12 percent of SMBV's operating expense to determine SMBV's arm's length remuneration for provision of roasting services and associated supply chain activities. Profits generated by SMBV in excess of that were transferred to Alki LP, a related UK limited partnership, as a tax deductible royalty for the license of IP needed to roast coffee beans.
- The Dutch tax administration accepted that the remuneration determined by Starbucks' tax advisor in the transfer pricing report for the functions performed by SMBV in the Netherlands (including risk assumed and assets used) constitutes an arm's length remuneration. Further, the APA provided that the royalty payment was deductible for corporate income tax purposes but not subject to Dutch withholding tax.
- SMBV set up in the Netherlands entered into various agreements that set out the contractual divisions of the roles and responsibilities of SMBV and its counterparties. The three agreements relevant for this decision are the Roasting Agreement between SMBV and Alki LP, the Green Coffee Purchase Agreement between SMBV and SCTC, and the Supply Agreement between SMBV and the Shops.
- On August 1, 2006, Starbucks Corporation and Alki LP entered into a cost sharing agreement, which determined the direct rights of Alki LP to license and sublicense to third parties the right to: (i) operate Starbucks stores, (ii) operate, and (iii) manufacture and/or distribute products using the Trademarks and Technology and Know-How.
- Under the CSA, Alki LP paid to Starbucks Corporation a royalty, service fees for services provided by Starbucks Corporation, and cost sharing payments for the development of certain intangible assets. The royalty payments consist of: (i) a buy-in royalty allocated to the trademark and business format IP and a (ii) permanent royalty allocated to the coffee knowledge IP.
- The taxable profits of SMBV in the Netherlands, which were determined based on the SMBV APA in reference to the operating expense of the company, were reduced by a royalty paid to Alki LP.
- According to the transfer pricing report submitted by Starbucks advisor, the TNMM was selected by the tax advisor to estimate an arm's length remuneration due to SMBV over other transfer pricing methods, because, in the specific set of Starbucks' circumstances, the net margin was less affected by transactional differences and functional differences, as in the case with measures employed in standard traditional methods.
- In applying the TNMM to SMBV's roasting activities, the tax advisor considered the relevant base for the net profit indicator to be the costs of the services rendered by SMBV, in line with the CP, which was considered an appropriate methodology for supply chain and manufacturing services. However, the mark up was only applied to those costs where, according to the tax advisor,

SMBV added value. The transfer pricing report listed those costs as main operating costs, such as cost of personnel and depreciation, excluding COGS.

- The Commission decided to initiate the formal investigation procedure because it took the preliminary view that the SMBV APA, which accepted the remuneration proposed by Starbucks' tax advisor for the functions performed by SMBV in the Netherlands, concluded by the Dutch tax administration in 2008 appeared to constitute state aid within the meaning of Article 107(1) of the Treaty that is incompatible with the internal market.
- To compare the value of the royalty payment to royalty levels observed on the market set in terms of percentage of turnover, the Commission calculated the amount of the royalty paid by SMBV to Alki LP as a percentage of the sales of roasted coffee by SMBV to the Shops each year. According to those calculations, the royalty payment varies between 1 percent–10 percent and 30 percent–40 percent of SMBV's revenues from sales of coffee over the life of the SMBV APA, confirming the Commission's doubts about the fluctuation of the royalty.
- The Commission considered that a comparison to CUTs using the CUP method, in particular the IP licensing arrangements in several roasting and manufacturing and distribution agreements Starbucks had concluded with third parties, demonstrated that the arm's length value of the royalty paid by SMBV to Alki LP for the roasting IP should be zero. In other words, no royalty should be due for that IP in that specific relationship, since SMBV did not derive any benefit from the use of the roasting IP licensed from Alki LP.
- The Commission observed, first, that the characteristics of the property transferred under the roasting IP arrangement between Alki LP and SMBV was identical to the property transferred in the transactions between Starbucks and the third parties in the roasting agreements listed in Recitals (148) to (150). Both sets of transactions consisted of roasting technology, coffee blends and roasting curves.
- Starbucks assumed more functions vis-à-vis the third parties than Alki LP vis-à-vis SMBV.
- The Commission rejected the claims that any effective risk transfer takes place from SMBV to Alki LP through contractual arrangements. Therefore, any component of the royalty meant to compensate for an entrepreneurial risk transfer cannot be justified. The level of the royalty payment was not justified by the amounts Alki LP pays for technology to Starbucks US under the Cost Sharing Agreement.
- The payments from Alki LP to Starbuck US under the CSA did not appear to be set at arm's length. In particular, regarding the acquisition of the IP relating to business format and brand, Alki LP paid in aggregate EUR [30–40] million for the acquisition of this IP, as of 2005, while that IP was sold by Alki LP for EUR 1–1.5 billion in 2014. That difference in value indicated that that arrangement did not reflect an arm's length remuneration for the IP; the payments under the

permanent royalty could therefore be seen as compensating for the sale of the brand in the same transaction for a value that was too low.

- Since the transfer pricing report failed to examine or analyze whether the price charged for the green coffee beans by SCTC to SMBV was at arm's length, the methodology proposed in that report to determine SMBV's taxable profits departed from a methodology that lead to a reliable approximation of a market-based outcome in line with the ALP. Since the application of that methodology leads to a lowering of SMBV's tax liability under the general Dutch corporate income tax system as compared to non-integrated companies whose taxable profits is determined by the market, the SMBV APA, by accepting that methodology, should be considered to confer a selective advantage on SMBV for the purposes of Article 107(1) of the Treaty.
- The Commission concluded that the SMBV APA concluded by the Dutch tax administration grants SMBV and the Starbucks group a selective advantage which is imputable to the Netherlands, financed through State resources and which distorts or threatens to distort competition and is liable to affect intra-EU trade. The SMBV APA therefore constitutes state aid within the meaning of Article 107(1) of the Treaty.

*Figure 12.4 Starbucks Structure in the Netherlands*

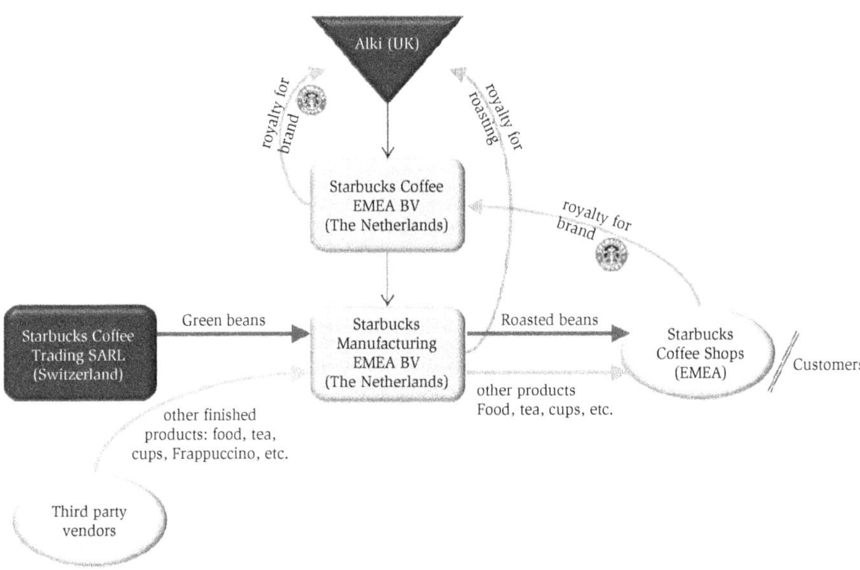

### 12.3.5 The Amazon Case[28]

- Amazon was incorporated in 1994 and operates as an online retailer. It operates 13 global websites, including amazon.com and five European websites. Amazon has divided its operations into two segments: North America and International (Figure 12.5).
- Amazon EU is a Luxembourg commercial company ("Amazon EU Sarl" or "LuxOpCo"), functions as the head office of Amazon for Europe. and is the principal operator of the retail and business services offered through Amazon's European websites. In addition, Amazon EU Sarl performs treasury management functions and holds (directly or indirectly) the other European Amazon subsidiaries that perform merchandising, sales support, and marketing functions. Furthermore, according to the information provided by Amazon to the UK House of Commons Committee of Public Accounts, Amazon EU Sarl owns the inventory, earns the profits associated with the selling of products to end customers, and bears the risk of any loss.
- In 2013, the net turnover of the LuxOpCo amounted to EUR 13,612,449,784.
- Amazon Europe Technologies Holding SCS (hereinafter "Lux SCS"), a Luxembourg limited liability partnership (société en commandite simple) that holds all the shares in Amazon EU Sarl, licenses the Amazon group's "IP" to Amazon EU Sarl to operate the European websites in return for a tax deductible royalty payment (the "License Fee").
- The entities of the Amazon group that are liable to corporate income tax in Luxembourg are Amazon EU Sarl, Amazon Media EU Sarl, Amazon Luxembourg Sarl, Amazon Services Europe Sarl, FinLux Sarl, and Amazon Payments SCA. These companies form a fiscal unity14 in which Amazon EU Sarl operates as the parent of the unity. Outside of the fiscal unity, the Amazon group has two other companies in Luxembourg, Amazon Euasia Sarl and Amazon Europe Core Sarl. Both companies are wholly owned by Amazon Europe Technologies Holding SCS, a limited liability partnership registered in Luxembourg.
- On October 23, 2003, Amazon EU Sarl requested the acceptance of the Luxembourgish tax authorities of the pricing arrangement between Lux SCS and Amazon EU Sarl.
- On October 31, 2003, the tax advisor of Amazon on behalf of Amazon requested the approval of the Luxembourgish tax authorities of the legal structure of Amazon for Luxembourg corporate income tax purposes.
- According to the requests, "LuxOpCo" would function as the principle operator of the retail and business services offered through Amazon's European websites.

28. EU Commission v. Luxembourg; State Aid SA. 38944 (2014/C).

- The retail business includes a range of products, including electronics, computers, books, and outdoor living items. Amazon purchases these products from vendors and fulfills them either through its fulfillment centers or through outsourced fulfillment providers.
- Amazon's business service consists of Amazon's Merchants@, Marketplace, Auctions, and zShops programs. Each of these programs allows third-party individuals and businesses to sell new, used, or collectible products or services through Amazon's websites.
- LuxOpCo was to operate all European websites, through which it was to offer retail products and third-party vendor services, primarily to customers located in Europe. It was anticipated at the moment of the ruling request that Amazon's existing affiliated entities located in Germany, the UK and France would provide various support services with respect to the EU websites by performing customer referral, merchandising and sales support functions, marketing and advertising in order to attract end users, and fulfillment services for the retail business.
- The IP held by Lux SCS is used in the operation of the EU websites by LuxOpCo according to the ruling request. However, the ruling request does not contain any information about the IP itself and what the IP rights consist of.
- On November 6, 2003 the Luxembourgish tax authorities granted the two requests to Amazon.

*Figure 12.5 Amazon Structure in Luxembourg*

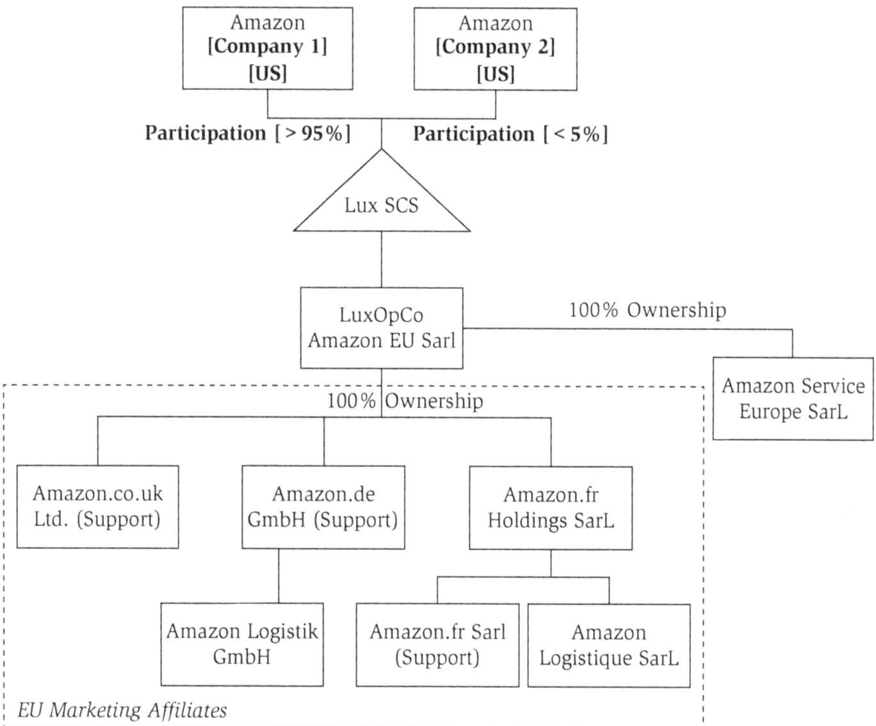


(a) The Transfer Pricing Agreement

- According to the ruling request, Lux SCS would obtain the right, in the context of the reorganization of the Amazon group, to exploit intangibles owned and developed in the US in exchange for a buy-in license and a cost sharing agreement. Although not determined at the time of the ruling request, the terms and conditions of those agreements would be, according to Amazon's tax advisor, at arm's length. Lux SCS would consequently license the Amazon group's IP rights to LuxOpCo.
- Amazon indicated that it presented an economic analysis of functions and risks that LuxOpCo was anticipated to undertake.
- According to Amazon economic analysis, Amazon alleged that it has developed a specific transfer pricing arrangement, under which the license fee that LuxOpCo will be required to pay to Lux SCS for the use of the Amazon group's IP (the License Fee) would be established.
- The License Fee was approved by the contested tax ruling.

- The License Fee would be computed each year and would be equal to a percentage of all revenue (the "Royalty Rate") received by LuxOpCo in connection with its operation of the European websites.
- Lux SCS is a société en commandite simple,[29] a Luxembourg limited liability partnership ("SCS"). An SCS is considered to be a transparent entity for Luxembourgish tax purposes. That means that all the royalties received from the licensing agreement and interest received from intragroup loans by Lux SCS will in principle not be taxed in Luxembourg but in the country of residence of the partners in Lux SCS to whom the profits of Lux SCS are allocated on a yearly basis.

(b) The Permanent Establishment Concerns

- In addition to the transfer pricing arrangement, Amazon also requested confirmation from the Luxembourgish tax authorities that neither the partners of Lux SCS nor Lux SCS itself will have any tangible presence in Luxembourg (offices, employees, etc.) so that in the absence of a fixed place of business, Lux SCS will not be deemed to operate through a Permanent Establishment (PE) in Luxembourg, nor will the partners in Lux SCS be regarded as having a PE in Luxembourg.

(c) The EU Commission Challenge

- The contested tax ruling concerns a transfer pricing arrangement which determines *inter alia* the royalty payments (License Fee) owed by LuxOpCo to Lux SCS for the use of IP rights.
- According to the Commission, an approval of a transfer pricing arrangement which does not reflect a market outcome and which favors a particular undertaking must be considered as prima facie selective, the selective treatment deriving from a deviation or misapplication of the ALP, as set out in the OECD Model Tax Convention and the OECD Guidelines, and incorporated in national law pursuant to Article 164 LIR.
- According to the EU Commission, Amazon has a financial incentive to exaggerate the amount of the royalty when applying the transfer pricing arrangement approved in the contested tax ruling. This is because the royalty is deducted from the taxable profit of LuxOpCo in Luxembourg and paid to Lux SCS, which is a transparent entity from the perspective of Luxembourgish tax law. If the royalty is exaggerated, it would unduly reduce the tax paid by Amazon in Luxembourg by shifting profits to an untaxed entity from the perspective of corporate taxation.

29. A Limited Partnership.

- The Luxembourgish authorities state that an analysis was conducted for the purposes of the transfer pricing arrangement based on agreements between Amazon and non-related third parties, from which it would result that the same or substantially the same IP was made available to third parties. On the basis of that analysis, an arm's length royalty was determined and expressed as a percentage of the sales of LuxOpCo.
- The Luxembourgish authorities further explain that, in parallel, the PSM was applied to analyze the functions and risks of LuxOpCo and Lux SCS. Luxembourg claims that LuxOpCo is the entity with the functions and risks which are most obvious. The functions of LuxOpCo were compared to determine an appropriate level of remuneration. The residual profits would be then attributed to Lux SCS in the form of a royalty.
- During the course of its investigation, the Commission found that: "Luxembourg did not submit to the Commission any transfer pricing report prepared by Amazon in support of the transfer pricing arrangement in the ruling request approved by the contested tax ruling, although it was requested to do so."[30]
- The Commission goes on to add: "in the absence of a transfer pricing report, the Commission has doubts whether the Luxembourgish tax authorities properly confirmed by the contested tax ruling that the transfer pricing arrangement presented in Amazon's ruling request reflected what a prudent independent operator acting under normal market conditions would have accepted."
- Further, the method proposed by Amazon's tax advisor in the ruling request and accepted by the Luxembourgish tax authorities in the contested tax ruling does not seem to correspond to any of the methods listed in the OECD guidelines.
- According to paragraph 6.16 of the OECD Guidelines "a royalty would ordinarily be a recurrent payment based on the user's output, sales, or in some rare circumstances, profits." Instead here, the royalty payment approved by the contested tax ruling is not related to output, sales, or profit. Although the royalty rate is expressed as a percentage of all revenues, the royalty payment is only presented and not calculated in the form of a royalty rate over revenue.
- Instead of calculating an arm's length value for the royalty itself, the pricing method accepted by the contested tax ruling proceeds to calculate, out of the entire European profit earned by LuxOpCo through the EU websites, the profit that is attributable to other functions, that is, the functions performed by LuxOpCo.
- Rather than being expressed as a percentage of revenues, the royalty should be calculated based on revenues.

30. EU Commission v. Luxembourg, State Aid SA. 38944 (2014/C), paragraph 63.

- For the purpose of a transfer pricing analysis and in particular for the purpose of determining whether LuxOpCo performs less complex functions than Lux SCS, a more extensive functions and risk analysis would be required, which is not contained in the ruling request.
- The ruling request also does not contain information about the ownership of inventories, which is contained in the UK House of Commons Committee of Public Accounts, and which is relevant for the assessment of the risks of LuxOpCo.
- The IP for which Lux SCS is remunerated is not described in the ruling request or by the Luxembourgish authorities. It is therefore impossible to conclude on that basis that Lux SCS performs more complex functions than LuxOpCo.
- Although Lux SCS is said to retain all risks associated with the ownership of that IP45, the risks of holding an existing IP are not specified and appear limited, in particular, compared to all the entrepreneurial risks assumed by LuxOpCo.
- If LuxOpCo's remuneration is established on that basis, it would seem to be based on the TNMM. According to the TNMM method, an arm's length remuneration is obtained from a comparison of net profit indicators between independent and associated companies as a means to estimate the profits that one or each of the associated companies could have earned had they dealt solely with independent companies, and therefore the payment those companies would have demanded at arm's length to compensate them for using their resources in the intragroup transaction.
- Therefore, the Commission is of the opinion that the Amazon ruling does not comply with the ALP. To the extent the Luxembourgish authorities have deviated from the ALP as regards the contested tax ruling, the measure should also be considered selective.

The Commission considered that the contested tax ruling appears to result in a reduction of charges that should normally be borne by the entity concerned in the course of its business and should therefore be considered as operating aid.

## 12.4 TRANSFER PRICING DOCUMENTATION AND CBC REPORTING

The OECD Report released in October 2015 describes a three-tiered standardized approach to transfer pricing documentation, which consists of: (i) a master file containing standardized information relevant for all MNE group members; (ii) a local file referring specifically to material transactions of the local taxpayer; and (iii) a CbC Report containing certain information relating to the global allocation of the MNE group's income and taxes paid together with certain indicators of the location of economic activity within the MNE group.

MNE groups with annual consolidated group revenue in the immediately preceding fiscal year of approximately EUR 750 million (USD 800 million) are required to file the CbC reporting. The OECD recommends that the first CbC Reports be required to be filed for MNE fiscal years beginning on or after January 1, 2016. Countries participating in the OECD/G20 BEPS[31] Project agree that they will not require filing of a CbC Report based on the new template for MNE fiscal years beginning prior to January 1, 2016. MNE groups are required to file the CbC Report each year.

Beside the aforementioned exemptions, no special industry exemptions are provided, nor any general exemption for investment funds, and no exemption for non-corporate entities or non-public corporate entities is provided.

### 12.4.1 Master File

The master file provides an overview of the MNE group business. Put differently, the master file provides tax administrations with high-level information regarding the global business operations and transfer pricing policies of the MNE group's transfer pricing practices.[32] The master file information provides a blueprint of the multinational group and contains relevant information in five categories: (i) organizational structure; (ii) description of the business or businesses; (iii) intangibles; (iv) intercompany financial activities; and (v) financial and tax positions.

### 12.4.2 Local File

The local file provides detailed information relating to specific intercompany transactions. It is aimed to identify material related-party transactions, the amounts involved in those transactions, and the company's analysis of the transfer pricing determinations made with regard to those transactions.

### 12.4.3 Specific Conditions

The OECD 2015 report contains specific conditions underpinning the obtaining and the use of the CbC Report, such as: (i) confidentiality; (ii) consistency, and (iii) appropriate use.

#### *12.4.3.1 Confidentiality*

The country tax administration shall use the CbC report for purposes of assessing high-level transfer pricing risks and other BEPS-related risks in country, including assessing the risk of noncompliance by members of the MNE group with applicable transfer pricing rules, and where appropriate for economic and statistical analysis. Transfer pricing adjustments by the country tax administration will not be based on the CbC Report.[33] The country tax administration is also required to preserve the

31. It should be noted that the US is heavily involved in the BEPS discussion.
32. US Joint Committee on Taxation (2015): Background, Summary, and Implications of the OECD/G20 Base Erosion and Profit Shifting Project, p. 30.
33. OECD (2015): Model Legislation Related to Country-by-Country Reporting, Article 6(1).

confidentiality of the information contained in the CbC report at least to the same extent that would apply if such information were provided to it under the provisions of the Multilateral Convention on Mutual Administrative Assistance in Tax Matters.[34]

#### *12.4.3.2 Consistency*

Unless one of the two aforementioned exemptions applies, countries participating in the OECD/G20 shall use their best efforts to adopt a legal requirement that MNE groups' ultimate parent entities resident in their jurisdiction prepare and file the CbC Report.

#### *12.4.3.3 Appropriate Use*

Countries participating in the OECD/G20 BEPS should use appropriately the information in the CbC Report template in accordance with paragraph 25 of the September Report. Put differently, they commit to use the CbC Report for assessing high-level transfer pricing risk, and under no circumstances use the CbC Report for assessing other BEPS-related risks. To that end, countries participating shall not propose adjustments to the income of any taxpayer on the basis of an income allocation formula based on the data from the CbC Report. Moreover, they commit that if such adjustments based on CbC Report data are made by the local tax administration of the jurisdiction, the jurisdiction's competent authority will promptly concede the adjustment in any relevant competent authority proceeding.

### 12.4.4 Country-by-Country Report

The CbC Report requires aggregate tax jurisdiction-wide information relating to the global allocation of the income, the taxes paid, and certain indicators of the location of economic activity among tax jurisdictions in which the MNE group operates. The annual CbC Report provides, for each jurisdiction in which the MNE does business, the amount of revenue, profit before income tax, income tax paid and accrued, the number of employees, stated capital, retained earnings, and tangible assets. It also requires the large MNEs to identify each entity within the group doing business in a particular tax jurisdiction and to provide an indication of the business activities each entity engaged in.

## 12.5 US REGULATIONS FOR CBC REPORTING

On June 26, 2016, the IRS released the final regulation concerning the application of the CbC reporting by certain US persons that are the ultimate parent entities of an MNE

34. OECD (2015): Model Legislation Related to Country-by-Country Reporting, Article 6(2).

group.[35] Under the Final Regulations, ultimate parent entities of a US MNE group with annual revenue of USD 850 million or more for the immediately preceding accounting period must file Form 8975, "Country-by-Country Report," containing information, on a CbC basis, related to the US MNE group's income and taxes paid, as well as other relevant indicators of the US MNE group economic activity.

The final Regulations require filing only by MNE groups with a US ultimate parent entity. An ultimate parent entity of a US MNE group is defined as a US business entity that owns, directly or indirectly:

(a) a sufficient interest in one or more other business entities, at least one of which is organized or tax resident outside the US, such that the US business entity must:
  (i) consolidate the accounts of the other business entities with its own accounts for financial reporting purposes under US generally accepted accounting principles (GAAP); or
  (ii) would be required to consolidate accounts if equity interests in the US business entity were publicly traded on a US securities exchange.[36]

The definition of an ultimate parent entity of a US MNE also encompasses a US business that is not owned directly or indirectly by another business entity that:

- consolidates the accounts of such US business entity with its own accounts under GAAP in the other business entity's tax jurisdiction of residence; or
- would be so required if equity interests in the other business entity were traded on a public securities exchange in its tax jurisdiction of residence.

For purposes of these final regulations, a business entity is: (i) any entity recognized for federal tax purposes that is not properly classified as a trust under section 301.7701-4; (ii) any entity with a single owner that may be disregarded as an entity separate from its owner under section 301.7701-3; and (iii) a PE that prepares financial statements separate from those of its owner for financial reporting, regulatory, tax reporting, or internal management control purposes. However, a business entity does not include: (i) any grantor trust within the meaning of IRC section 671, and (ii) a decedent's estate or a bankruptcy estate under IRC section 1398.

Under the final regulations, a US business is defined as business entity that is organized or has its tax jurisdiction of residence in the US. However, an election is allowed to foreign insurance companies that elect to be treated as domestic corporations under section 953(d) to claim the US business status. With respect to a US MNE group, a constituent entity is defined as any separate business entity of such US MNE group. However, a foreign corporation or foreign partnership for which the ultimate parent entity is not required to furnish information under section 6038(a) or any PE of such foreign corporation or foreign partnership are not deemed constituent entities.

---

35. TD 9773.
36. Treas. Reg. Section 1.6038-4(b)(1)(i) and (ii).

### 12.5.1 Tax Jurisdiction of Residence

A business entity is considered a resident in a tax jurisdiction if, under the laws of that tax jurisdiction, the business entity is liable to tax therein based on place of management, place of organization, or another similar criterion. Conversely, a business entity will not be considered a resident in a tax jurisdiction if the business entity is liable to tax in such tax jurisdiction only by reason of a tax imposed by reference to gross amounts of income without any reduction for expenses, provided such tax applies only with respect to income from sources in such tax jurisdiction or capital situated in such tax jurisdiction:[37]

- if a business entity is resident in more than one tax jurisdiction, then the applicable income tax convention rules, if any, would apply to determine the business entity's tax jurisdiction of residence.
- If a business entity is resident in more than one tax jurisdiction and no applicable income tax convention exists between those tax jurisdictions, or if the applicable income tax convention provides that the determination of residence is based on a determination by the competent authorities of the relevant tax jurisdictions and no such determination has been made, the business entity's tax jurisdiction of residence is the tax jurisdiction of the business entity's place of effective management determined in accordance with Article 4 of the OECD Model Tax Convention on Income and on Capital 2014 or as provided by Form 8975.

### 12.5.2 Stateless Entities

A business entity that is fiscally transparent in the jurisdiction where it is organized and that does not have a PE in that or another tax jurisdiction will not have a tax jurisdiction of residence. The income and other items of all stateless entities must be aggregated and reported on a separate row of Form 8975. The owner of a transparent, "stateless" entity is required to include its share of the revenues and profits of the stateless entity in the row for the tax jurisdiction of residence of the stateless entity's owner, unless the revenues and profits of the stateless entity belong to a PE of that stateless entity.

#### *12.5.2.1 Corporation Organized in Tax Heaven*

A corporation that is organized or managed in a tax jurisdiction that does not impose an income tax on corporations will be treated as resident in that tax jurisdiction, unless such corporation is treated as resident in another tax jurisdiction under another provision of this section.

37. Treas. Reg. Section 1.6038-4(b)(8).

### 12.5.3 Permanent Establishment

The tax jurisdiction of residence of a PE is the jurisdiction in which the PE is located.

Finally, it should be noted that a business entity does not have a tax jurisdiction of residence, then the tax jurisdiction of residence is the business entity's country of organization.

### 12.5.4 The Reporting Period

The reporting period covered by Form 8975 is the period of the ultimate parent entity's applicable financial statement prepared for the 12-month period that ends with or within the ultimate parent entity's taxable year. If the ultimate parent entity does not prepare an annual applicable financial statement, then the reporting period covered by Form 8975 is the 12-month period that ends on the last day of the ultimate parent entity's taxable year.[38]

### 12.5.5 Contents of Return

#### *12.5.5.1 Constituent Entity Information*

The return on Form 8975 must contain the following information with respect to each constituent entity of the US MNE group, and in such form or manner, as Form 8975 prescribes:

- the complete legal name of the constituent entity;
- the tax jurisdiction, if any, in which the constituent entity is resident for tax purposes;
- the tax jurisdiction in which the constituent entity is organized or incorporated (if different from the tax jurisdiction of residence);
- the Tax Identification Number (TIN), if any, used for the constituent entity by the tax administration of the constituent entity's tax jurisdiction of residence; and
- the main business activity or activities of the constituent entity.

#### *12.5.5.2 Tax Jurisdiction of Residence Information*

The return on Form 8975 must contain the following information with respect to each tax jurisdiction in which one or more constituent entities of a US MNE group is resident, presented as an aggregate of the information for the constituent entities resident in each tax jurisdiction, and in such form or manner, as Form 8975 prescribes:

38. Treas. Reg. Section 1.6038-4(c).

- revenues generated from transactions with other constituent entities;
- revenues not generated from transactions with other constituent entities;
- profit or loss before income tax;
- total income tax paid on a cash basis to all tax jurisdictions, and any taxes withheld on payments received by the constituent entities;
- total accrued tax expense recorded on taxable profits or losses, reflecting only operations in the relevant annual period and excluding deferred taxes or provisions for uncertain tax liabilities;
- stated capital, except that the stated capital of a PE must be reported in the tax jurisdiction of residence of the legal entity of which it is a PE unless there is a defined capital requirement in the PE tax jurisdiction for regulatory purposes;
- total accumulated earnings, except that accumulated earnings of a PE must be reported by the legal entity of which it is a PE;
- total number of employees on a full-time equivalent basis; and
- net book value of tangible assets, which, for purposes of this section, does not include cash or cash equivalents, intangibles, or financial assets.

### 12.5.6 Time, Manner, and Record of Filing

Returns on Form 8975 must be filed with the ultimate parent entity's income tax return for the taxable year, in or with which the reporting period ends, on or before the due date (including extensions) for filing that person's income tax return or as otherwise prescribed by Form 8975.

The US person filing Form 8975 as an ultimate parent entity of a US MNE group must maintain records to support the information provided on Form 8975. However, the US person is not required to create and maintain records that reconcile the amounts provided on Form 8975 with the tax returns of any tax jurisdiction or applicable financial statements.

### 12.5.7 Public Disclosure of CbC Reports

The final regulations do not require public release of CbC Reports by the IRS. Such a standing is criticized by some experts and politicians alike. On June 7, 2016, four Democratic US Senators wrote the Treasury Secretary pleading for the release of CbC Reports by the IRS. Likewise, Professor Avi-Yonah strongly argued for the release of all transfer pricing documents to the public and civil society organizations:[39]

> The relevant stakeholders and the public need to have access to the MNEs' transfer pricing documentation. The reason is very simple, BEPS could hurt other taxpayers and stakeholders in relevant jurisdictions.

39. Avi-Yonah, Reuven (2016): Evaluating BEPS, NYU Tax Policy Colloquium, p. 18.

## 12.6 COMPETENT AUTHORITY AGREEMENTS

### 12.6.1 The OECD Multilateral Competent Authority Agreement

Chapter III of the Convention authorizes the exchange of information for tax purposes, including the exchange of information on an automatic basis and allows the competent authorities of the Jurisdictions to agree on the scope and modalities of such automatic exchanges:

> Pursuant to the provisions of Articles 6, 21 and 22 of the Convention, each Competent Authority will annually exchange on an automatic basis the CbC Report received from each Reporting Entity that is resident for tax purposes in its jurisdiction with all such other Competent Authorities of Jurisdictions with respect to which it has this Agreement in effect, and in which, on the basis of the information in the CbC Report, one or more Constituent Entities of the MNE Group of the Reporting Entity are either resident for tax purposes, or are subject to tax with respect to the business carried out through a permanent establishment.[40]

Section 5 of the aforementioned Convention states: "all information exchanged is subject to the confidentiality rules and other safeguards provided for in the Convention, including the provisions limiting the use of the information exchanged." Further, section 5 provides that no transfer pricing adjustments will not be based on the CbC Report. Inappropriate adjustments in contravention of this section made by local tax administrations will be conceded in any competent authority proceedings. Last but not least, to the extent permitted under applicable law, a Competent Authority will notify the Coordinating Body Secretariat immediately of any cases of noncompliance, including any remedial actions, as well as any measures taken in respect of noncompliance.

### 12.6.2 US Final Regulations on CbC Report

The US, though a signatory to the Convention has chosen not to ratify the Multilateral Competent Authority Agreement (MCAA), rather intends to enter into competent authority arrangements for the automatic exchange of CbCRs with jurisdictions with which the US has an income tax treaty or tax information exchange agreement.[41] There is no obvious policy reason why the US did not proceed with the ratification of the Protocol to the MCAA. The objectives of the final regulations being similar to the aim of the Convention, the best policy approach would require the US to ratify the Convention. Such an approach would avoid court interpreting in solo the exchange of information article among various DTT into force. The US standing contrasts with its major business partners, such as the EU.

On May 25, 2016, the EU Council adopted rules on the reporting by multinational companies of tax-related information and exchange of that information between

40. OECD (2015): Multilateral Competent Authority Agreement on the Exchange of Country-by-Country Reports, section 2 Exchange of Information with Respect to MNE Groups, p. 18.
41. IRS Final regulations (2016): Country-by-Country Reporting, Preamble, Exchange of Information with Foreign Jurisdictions.

Member States. The directive implements the OECD anti-BEPS Action 13, on CbC reporting by multinationals, into a legally binding EU instrument. It covers groups of companies with a total consolidated group revenue of at least EUR 750 million. The directive requires tax authorities to exchange these reports automatically, so that tax avoidance risks related to transfer pricing can be assessed.[42] The directive requires multinationals to report information—detailed CbC—on revenues, profits, taxes paid, capital, earnings, tangible assets, and the number of employees.

42. Council of the EU, Press release 271/16- 25/05/2016.

# CHAPTER 13
# The EU Illegal Aid and Transfer Pricing

## 13.1 INTRODUCTION

While state aid is mostly studied under the EC Competition laws, recent Commission investigations of tax rulings and transfer pricing APAs granted by some State Members to well-known MNEs set the tone or the determination of the EU to combat BEPS within their boundaries. Yet, the concept of state aid has no equivalent in US laws. In the US, state governments are permitted to provide incentives to businesses they want to bring in and very often, state governments make deals to entice corporate investments and job creations in their states.

Article 107(1) of the Treaty on the Functioning of the European Union (TFEU) states:

> Save as otherwise provided in the Treaties, any aid granted by a Member State or through State resources in any form whatsoever which distorts or threatens to distort competition by favouring certain undertakings or the production of certain goods shall, in so far as it affects trade between Member States, be incompatible with the internal market.

The term "state aid" encompasses any competitive advantage (1) selectively conferred to one business or group of businesses (2) by a EC State member or through State resources (3) which distorts or threatens to distort competition (4) and affects trade between the Member States (5):

- A tax measure would be considered as an illegal state aid if it differentiates between economic operators who, in light of the objective assigned to the tax system of the Member State concerned, are in a comparable factual and legal situation. The European Commission will find a selective advantage when a tax ruling "endorses a transfer pricing methodology for determining a corporate group entity's taxable profit that does not result in a reliable approximation of a market-based outcome in line with the arm's length principle."[1]

- The term "State resources" is broadly defined to encompass any measure with an impact on the state budget or where the state has significant control are included. Examples may include: tax exemptions, unsubstantiated tax rulings, and /or Advance Price Agreements.

As a matter of fact, a State Member seeking to grant a state aid measure must submit its proposal to the Commission before any execution.

According to Article 107(2) TFEU state aid would be deemed compatible when it has a social character. When a state aid is justified, it can be authorized by the European Commission in the course of the notification procedure.

Given the fact that state aid illegally granted to a business or group of businesses results in disgorgement of the undue advantage to be clawed back for the recipient, MNEs do need to consider the implications of their rulings, and for APA, and other clandestine deals with EU State member. Apple, Google, Microsoft, McDonalds, and Starbucks have been, or some are still, under the Commission investigations. Time has come for MNEs to rely on tax rulings, APAs from EU tax administrations to properly monitor and anticipate the challenges under TFEU Article 107. Since 2013, the European Commission has reviewed more than 1,000 tax rulings.[2] Most of them related to transfer pricing issues.

## 13.2 THE EU ALP

In a string of recent decisions, the Commission restated its interpretation of the ALP as follows:

> This arm's length principle necessarily forms part of the Commission's assessment of tax measures granted to group companies under Article 107(1) of the Treaty, independently of whether a Member State has incorporated this principle into its national legal system and in what form. It is used to establish whether the taxable profit of a group company for corporate income tax purposes has been determined on the basis of a methodology that produces a reliable approximation of a market based outcome. A tax ruling endorsing such a methodology ensures that that company is not treated favourably under the ordinary rules of corporate taxation of profits in the Member State concerned, as compared to standalone companies who are taxed on their accounting profit, which reflects prices determined on the market negotiated at arm's length. The arm's length principle the Commission applies in assessing transfer pricing rulings under the State aid rules is therefore an application of Article 107(1) of the Treaty, which prohibits unequal treatment in

1. European Commission Notice, paragraph 171.
2. DG COMP Working Paper on State Aid Tax Rulings, paragraph 6.

taxation of undertakings in a similar factual and legal situation. This principle binds the Member States and the national tax rules are not excluded from its scope.[3]

## 13.3 NEW STRATEGIES FOR MNEs

The time of stamp-approval for tax rulings and APAs is over. Moving onward, US MNEs operating in EU would need to attest and screen their tax rulings and APAs in light with TFEU Article 107:

> Review of transfer pricing rulings and APAS should include a robust inquiry into the underlying functional analysis and contracts, the selection of the transfer pricing method, choices made in applying the transfer pricing method (such as tested party, profit level indicator), the composition of the peer group in the benchmark study, the interpretation and use of collected data, among other things.[4]

## 13.4 THE STARBUCKS CASE ILLUSTRATION[5]

The Commission found that Starbucks' coffee roasting company, established in the Netherlands, was paying an unjustifiably high royalty (for coffee roasting "know-how") to a UK Starbucks entity that was not liable to pay corporate tax in the UK, or in the Netherlands. Meanwhile, the Netherlands Entity was also purchasing coffee beans from a Swiss Starbucks entity at an inflated price. The high royalty paid to the UK entity, coupled with the high prices paid to the Swiss entity, reduced the taxable base for the Netherlands Entity. The Commission held that the tax ruling issued by the Netherlands authority, endorsing Starbucks' arrangement, constituted illegal state aid (Figure 13.1).

The relevant facts of the case can be summed up as follows:

- Starbucks Manufacturing BV (SMBV) is the only wholly controlled Starbucks group entity outside of the US which roasts coffee. SMBV roasts, packages, and stores coffee beans, and performs related functions, such as acting as an intermediary distribution company for non-coffee items like Starbucks cups and napkins.

3. Commission Decision of 21.10.2015 on State aid which Luxembourg granted to Fiat, SA.38375, not yet published, paragraph 228; Commission Decision of 21.10.2015 in Case SA. 38374 (Starbucks), not yet published, paragraph 264; Commission Decision of 11.01.2016 in Case SA.37667 (Belgian excess profit rulings), not yet published, paragraph 150. *See also* Commission Notice, paragraph 172.
4. Laprévote, Francois-Charles & Nikolaas Van Robbroeck (2016): Three Years of EU State Aid Review of Tax Rulings: Taking Stock., p. 6.
5. SA.38374 (2014/C ex 2014/NN) implemented by the Netherlands to Starbucks, Commission Decision of 21.10.2015.

- On April 28, 2008, SMBV concluded an advance pricing agreement with the Dutch tax administration. The SMBV APA was binding for 10 years, from October 1, 2007 to December 321, 2017.
- The SMBV APA was concluded on the basis of Article 8b(1) of the Dutch Corporation Tax Act 1969.
- The APA applied a mark-up of 9 percent–12 percent of SMBV's operating expense to determine SMBV's arm's length remuneration for provision of roasting services and associated supply chain activities. Profits generated by SMBV in excess of that were transferred to Alki LP, a related UK limited partnership, as a tax deductible royalty for the license of IP needed to roast coffee beans.
- The Dutch tax administration accepted that the remuneration determined by Starbucks' tax advisor in the transfer pricing report for the functions performed by SMBV in the Netherlands (including risk assumed and assets used) constitutes an arm's length remuneration. Further, the APA provided that the royalty payment was deductible for corporate income tax purposes but not subject to Dutch withholding tax.
- SMBV set up in the Netherlands entered into various agreements that set out the contractual divisions of the roles and responsibilities of SMBV and its counterparties. The three agreements relevant for this decision are the Roasting Agreement between SMBV and Alki LP, the Green Coffee Purchase Agreement between SMBV and SCTC, and the Supply Agreement between SMBV and the Shops.
- On August 1, 2006, Starbucks Corporation and Alki LP entered into a cost sharing agreement, which determined the direct rights of Alki LP to license and sublicense to third parties the right to: (i) operate Starbucks stores, (ii) operate and (iii) manufacture and/or distribute products using the Trademarks and Technology and Know-How.
- Under the CSA, Alki LP paid to Starbucks Corporation a royalty, service fees for services provided by Starbucks Corporation, and cost sharing payments for the development of certain intangible assets. The royalty payments consist of: (i) a buy-in royalty allocated to the trademark and business format IP and (ii) a permanent royalty allocated to the coffee knowledge IP.
- The taxable profits of SMBV in the Netherlands, which were determined based on the SMBV APA in reference to the operating expense of the company, were reduced by a royalty paid to Alki LP.
- According to the transfer pricing report submitted by Starbucks advisor, the "TNMM" was selected by the tax advisor to estimate an arm's length remuneration due to SMBV over other transfer pricing methods, because, in the specific set of Starbucks' circumstances; the net margin was less affected by transactional differences and functional differences, as in the case with measures employed in standard traditional methods.
- In applying the TNMM to SMBV's roasting activities, the tax advisor considered the relevant base for the net profit indicator to be the costs of the services

rendered by SMBV, in line with the CP, which was considered an appropriate methodology for supply chain and manufacturing services. However, the mark-up was only applied to those costs where, according to the tax advisor, SMBV added value. The transfer pricing report listed those costs as main operating costs, such as cost of personnel and depreciation, excluding COGS.

- The Commission decided to initiate the formal investigation procedure because it took the preliminary view that the SMBV APA, which accepted the remuneration proposed by Starbucks' tax advisor for the functions performed by SMBV in the Netherlands, concluded by the Dutch tax administration in 2008 appeared to constitute state aid within the meaning of Article 107(1) of the Treaty that is incompatible with the internal market.
- To compare the value of the royalty payment to royalty levels observed on the market set in terms of percentage of turnover, the Commission calculated the amount of the royalty paid by SMBV to Alki LP as a percentage of the sales of roasted coffee by SMBV to the Shops each year. According to those calculations, the royalty payment varies between 1 to 10 percent and 30 to 40 percent of SMBV's revenues from sales of coffee over the life of the SMBV APA, confirming the Commission's doubts about the fluctuation of the royalty.
- The Commission considered that a comparison to CUTs using the CUP method, in particular the IP licensing arrangements in several roasting and manufacturing and distribution agreements Starbucks had concluded with third parties, demonstrated that the arm's length value of the royalty paid by SMBV to Alki LP for the roasting IP should be zero. In other words, no royalty should be due for that IP in that specific relationship, since SMBV did not derive any benefit from the use of the roasting IP licensed from Alki LP.
- The Commission observed, first, that the characteristics of the property transferred under the roasting IP arrangement between Alki LP and SMBV was identical to the property transferred in the transactions between Starbucks and the third parties in the roasting agreements listed in Recitals (148) to (150). Both sets of transactions consisted of roasting technology, coffee blends, and roasting curves.
- Starbucks assumed more functions vis-à-vis the third parties than Alki LP vis-à-vis SMBV.
- The Commission rejected the claims that any effective risk transfer takes place from SMBV to Alki LP through contractual arrangements. Therefore, any component of the royalty meant to compensate for an entrepreneurial risk transfer cannot be justified. That the level of the royalty payment was not justified by the amounts Alki LP pays for technology to Starbucks US under the Cost Sharing Agreement.
- The payments from Alki LP to Starbuck US under the CSA did not appear to be set at arm's length. In particular, regarding the acquisition of the IP relating to business format and brand, Alki LP paid in aggregate EUR [30–40] million for the acquisition of this IP, as of 2005, while that IP was sold by Alki LP for EUR 1–1.5 billion in 2014. That difference in values indicated that that arrangement

did not reflect an arm's length remuneration for the IP; the payments under the permanent royalty could therefore be seen as compensating for the sale of the brand in the same transaction for a value that was too low.

- Since the transfer pricing report failed to examine or analyze whether the price charged for the green coffee beans by SCTC to SMBV was at arm's length, the methodology proposed in that report to determine SMBV's taxable profits departed from a methodology that lead to a reliable approximation of a market-based outcome in line with the ALP. Since the application of that methodology leads to a lowering of SMBV's tax liability under the general Dutch corporate income tax system as compared to non-integrated companies whose taxable profits is determined by the market, the SMBV APA, by accepting that methodology, should be considered to confer a selective advantage on SMBV for the purposes of Article 107(1) of the Treaty.

*Figure 13.1 Starbucks Structure in the Netherlands*

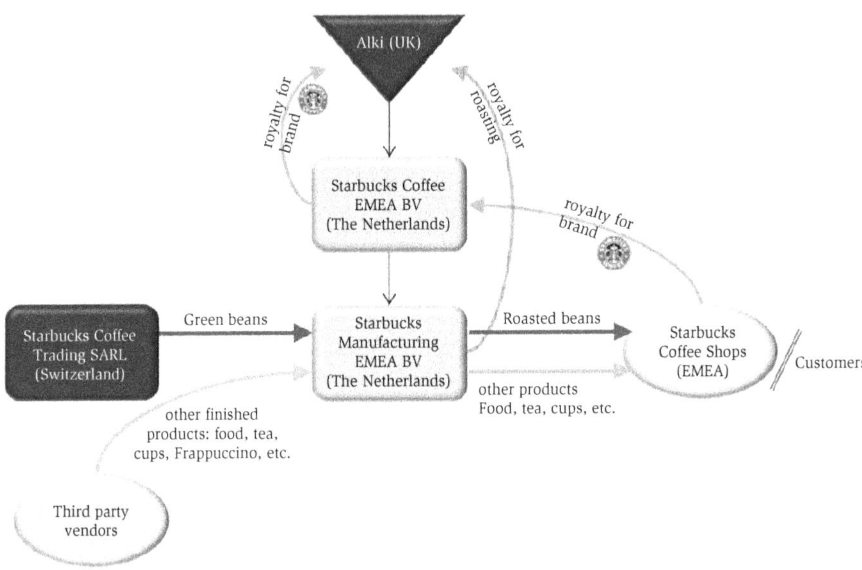


## 13.5 THE CRITICISMS OF THE EU STATE AID APPROACH

Several critics of the European Commission have challenged the perceived new approach by the Commission, among there are the US Treasury, some US Congressmen, as well some US scholars.

### 13.5.1 The US Treasury Criticisms

On August 24, 2016, the US Treasury Department released a White Paper in which the Treasury stated its concerns as follows:

- The European Commission's approach is new and departs from Prior EU Case Law and Commission Decisions. The Treasury stated that the European Commission investigations under the state aid have considerable implications for the US both for the US government and its companies.[6] There is the possibility that any repayments ordered by the Commission will be considered foreign income taxes that are creditable against US taxes owed by the companies in the US.

The US Treasury's interpretation of the European Commission under Article 107 is that:

> In the State aid cases, the Commission simply examined whether the measures at stake conferred a selective advantage on the companies under investigation, rather than separately assessing the existence of an advantage and the selective character of the measure, as it had done in prior decisions.[7]

Further, the US Treasury asserted that a foundational principle of EU state aid law is that advantage and selectivity are distinct elements. The EU Commission appears to have departed from this principle in the state aid cases.[8]

The US Treasury asserts that the tax benefits granted to US MNEs are not selective as they did not derogate from that common regime inasmuch as it differentiates between economic operators who, in the light of the objective assigned to the tax system of the Member State concerned, are in a comparable factual and legal situation. A derogation that is justified by the nature or general scheme of the system of which it is part shall not be deemed selective.[9] Further, the US Treasury asserts that there is no evidence that other multinational companies could not have obtained the same rulings as the companies now under investigation.[10]

- The European Commission should not seek retroactive recoveries under its new approach

The US Treasury asserts that rules of law must be clear and precise and predictable in their effect, so that interested parties can ascertain their position in situations and legal relationships governed by EU law. That any recovery of past allegedly unpaid tax would constitute retroactive enforcement of a newly adopted approach to state aid.[11] That none of the companies under investigation had identified the risk of state aid investigations in audited financial disclosures made prior to June 11, 2014. Until the

6. U.S. Department of the Treasury—White paper (August 24, 2016), p. 3.
7. U.S. Department of the Treasury—White paper (August 24, 2016), p. 6.
8. U.S. Department of the Treasury—White paper (August 24, 2016), p. 6.
9. U.S. Department of the Treasury—White paper (August 24, 2016), p. 10.
10. U.S. Department of the Treasury—White paper (August 24, 2016), p. 14.
11. U.S. Department of the Treasury—White paper (August 24, 2016), p. 14.

Commission had started its inquiries and investigations, neither internal review nor third-party review and audit of the affected firms by tax and audit professionals gave rise to any determination that their tax treatment could potentially be subject to state aid rules.[12] Furthermore, the US Treasury asserts that retroactive recoveries would be unwelcome when companies and Member States were not on notice that the Commission would take a new approach. Relying upon the German Coordination Centres case, the US Treasury asserts that recoveries can be avoided. However, the Treasury consents that the precedent cited (the German Coordination Centres) is distinct from the case of US MNEs under investigation. Indeed, under the German Coordination Centres case,[13] the German Government relied upon Commission's two previous public statements validating the Belgian scheme conferred a legitimate expectation on Germany and the aid beneficiaries. Still, the US Treasury asserts that although in the State Aid Cases the Commission did not issue any public statement that the tax rulings in question did not constitute state aid, the principle is the same.[14]

The US Treasury asserts that:

> The Commission's pursuit of retroactive recoveries is not only in tension with the G20's efforts to emphasize tax certainty, but also sets an undesirable precedent that could lead to other tax authorities, particularly those in developing countries that look to the EU as a model, to seek large and punitive retroactive recoveries from both US and EU companies.[15]

- The European Commission's new approach is inconsistent with international norms and undermines the international tax system

The US Treasury asserts that the Commission's actions undermine the international consensus on transfer pricing standards, call into question the ability of Member States to honor their bilateral tax treaties, and undermine the progress made under the BEPS project. Furthermore the US Treasury asserts that:

> The Commission has indicated neither the circumstances that will cause a "breach" of the arm's length principle nor when such a breach will be considered "manifest," leaving Member States and companies without meaningful guidance on how the Commission intends to apply its version of the arm's length principle.[16]

Further, the US Treasury asserts that:

> The Commission's new interpretation of State aid doctrine threatens to undermine the well-established basis of mutual cooperation and respect that many countries have worked hard to develop and preserve, particularly in connection with the BEPS project.[17]

12. U.S. Department of the Treasury—White paper (August 24, 2016), p. 15.
13. Commission v. Germany—Case No. C (2002) 3298.
14. U.S. Department of the Treasury—White paper (August 24, 2016), p. 16.
15. U.S. Department of the Treasury—White paper (August 24, 2016), p. 17.
16. U.S. Department of the Treasury—White paper (August 24, 2016), p. 20.
17. U.S. Department of the Treasury—White paper (August 24, 2016), p. 24.

### 13.5.2 The US Congress' Reactions: Fairness, and Double Tax Treaty Reliability Concerns

In a January 15, 2016 letter to Secretary Lew, the Chairman, Ranking Member, and other members of the US Senate Committee on Finance stated that the "US has a stake in these cases and has serious concerns about their fairness and potential impact on the US fisc,"[18] and that "these investigations raise serious questions about our ability to rely on bilateral tax treaties negotiated with EU Member States."

In a subsequent letter on May 23, 2016, the Senators added that their "concerns are driven not only by the initial cases, but also by the precedent they will create and their long-term implications."[19]

### 13.5.3 US Tax Scholar Reactions

Some scholars also have taken firm standing against the European Commission State aid investigation of US MNEs:

- In his open opinion published in the *Wall Street Journal*, Professor Graetz alleged that the EU Commission approach does not pass the smell test requirements of due process and the rule of law.[20] He called the undertaxed claims to fines.[21] Further Graetz asserts that the EC's Competition Directorate never before treated transfer pricing agreements for tax purposes this way.[22]
- Another US tax scholar, Itai Grinberg, asserts that the European Commission has breached the state members tax sovereignty by challenging legal certainty they have provided to MNEs through tax rulings that do not even seem to be selective; and using the state aid provision under Article 107 of the TFEU is novel and unprecedented.[23] Further he asserts that the remedy state aid provision under Article 107 is deeply inappropriate when applies to foreign multinationals.[24] He advocates that the US triggers IRS section 891 to retaliate against the EU Commission.

18. Letter from U.S. Senate Committee on Finance to Jacob J. Lew, U.S. Secretary of the Treasury (January 15, 2016), http://www.finance.senate.gov/imo/media/doc/Finance%20Committee%20Members%20Push%20for%20Fairness%20in%20EU%20State%20Aid%20Investigations.pdf.
19. Letter from U.S. Senate Committee on Finance to Jacob J. Lew, U.S. Secretary of the Treasury (May 23, 2016), http://www.finance.senate.gov/imo/media/doc/Hatch,%20Wyden,%20Portman,%20Schumer%20Continue%20Push%20for%20Fairness%20in%20EU%20State%20Aid%20Investigations.pdf.
20. Graetz, Michael (2015): Behind the European Raid on McDonald's, Wall Street Journal, December 3, 2015.
21. Graetz, Michael (2015): Behind the European Raid on McDonald's, Wall Street Journal, December 3, 2015.
22. Graetz, Michael (2015): Behind the European Raid on McDonald's, Wall Street Journal, December 3, 2015.
23. Grinberg, Itai (2016): A Constructive U.S. Counter to EU State Aid Cases, Tax Notes International (2016).
24. Grinberg, Itai (2016): A Constructive U.S. Counter to EU State Aid Cases, Tax Notes International (2016).

### 13.5.4 The Shortcomings of the Criticisms

Looking objectively through the issues, Professor Daniel Shaviro states: "it is not established solely by the fact that most of the probes' targets, thus far, have been U.S. companies,"[25] contrary to the allegations of some US scholars. Another confusion raised by US scholars lies on the fact that they are confusing or calling inappropriately these "underpaid taxes" fines retroactively applied. Finally, advocating IRS section 891 as a retaliatory weapon against the UE Commission is counterproductive. It is a fact that most US MNEs are deriving the bulk of their profits from the overseas operations rather in the US ones. Opening the pander box of IRC section 891[26] against the very countries where these US MNEs are prospering would trigger an international tax battle without any end at sight.

### 13.5.5 The New Area of Study and Cooperation

#### *13.5.5.1 A New Area of Study*

European antitrust policy is developed around two central rules set out in the TFEU: Article 101 and Article 102:

- Article 101 of the TFEU prohibits agreements between two or more independent market operators which restrict competition. Article 101 covers both horizontal agreements (between actual or potential competitors operating at the same level of the supply chain) and vertical agreements (between firms operating at different levels). The most flagrant illustration of illegal conduct infringing Article 101 is the creation of a cartel between competitors, which may involve price-fixing and/or market sharing.
- Article 102 of the TFEU prohibits firms that hold a dominant position on a given market to abuse that position, for example by charging unfair prices, by limiting production, or by refusing to innovate to the prejudice of consumers.

However, very few scholars have linked Articles 107 and 108 of the TFEU which cover state aid within the overall frame of the TFEU competition laws. They are often discussed separately. The recent state aid raid launched by the EU Commission has caught many MNEs and their advisory as by surprise. Moreover, the application of Article 107 of the TFEU in the field of taxation seems new to many. The TFEU defines

25. Shaviro, Daniel (2016): The U.S. Response to OECD-BEPS and the EU State Aid Cases, New York University Law and Economics Working Papers, p. 2.
26. Section 891 provides:

> Whenever the President finds that, under the laws of any foreign country, citizens or corporations of the United States are being subjected to discriminatory or extraterritorial taxes, the President shall so proclaim and the rates of tax imposed by sections 1, 3, 11, 801, 831, 852, 871, and 881 shall, for the taxable year during which such proclamation is made and for each taxable year thereafter, be doubled in the case of each citizen and corporation of such foreign country.

state aid as an advantage in any form whatsoever conferred on a selective basis to undertakings by national public authorities. Therefore, a tax ruling or any other tax arrangement selectively granted to an enterprise, or a tax reduction for which only a specific company is eligible, therefore excluding its competitors, may fall within the ambit of Article 107. State aid law can be applicable in two different cases:[27] (i) a state aid measure granted to one or several beneficiaries through a fiscal measure granting an advantage, such as an exoneration, and (ii) a tax-relief or even a specific depreciation rule.

The arrangements made whether through a tax ruling, an inefficient transfer pricing model fall within the ambit of Article 107 anytime they infringe or distort competition within the EU Zone.

### *13.5.5.2 A New Area of Cooperation*

Under Article 108(2) TFEU where the EU Commission has serious doubts about the aid's compatibility with EU state aid rules, or where it faces procedural difficulties in obtaining the necessary information, the Commission can initiate and communicate its investigation to the relevant Member State. It summarizes the factual and legal bases for the investigation and includes the Commission's preliminary assessment, outlining any doubts as to the measure's compatibility with EU state aid rules. However, the Commission is not required to inform the beneficiary of the aid. Moreover, if the commission concludes, at this stage, that an illegal aid has been granted, the Commission requires the Member State to recover the aid with interest from the beneficiary (unless such recovery would be contrary to a general principle of EU law). In this case, the Commission opens a "recovery case" to enforce the implementation of its decision. If the Member State does not comply with the decision in due time, the Commission may refer it to the European Court of Justice (ECJ), without initiating an infringement procedure under Article 258 TFEU.

In the context of globalization, it would be more appropriate for the Commission, at least, in the initial state of the state aid investigation to inform and exchange the data with the tax authorities of the beneficiary for a better coordination of tax abusive schemes. But this needs to be worked out and agreed upon by the Commission and its key partners such as the US Treasury. Otherwise, the home of the MNEs involved would be upset, mainly when the ramifications of the EU Commission affect elements of their tax policies or would require foreign tax credit, as in the cases of US MNEs under investigation. This can be solved diplomatically, without the use of any escalating disposition from the US such as IRC section 891.

As Daniel Shaviro argued, although US international tax policy should mainly be driven by the US interests, a willingness to cooperate and pursue common goals, especially with peer countries such as those in the EU serves the US interests as well.[28]

27. Cotrelis & Asocciates, Rules regarding State aids.
28. Shaviro, Daniel (2016): The U.S. Response to OECD-BEPS and the EU State Aid Cases, New York University Law and Economics Working Papers, p. 2.

The EU Commission state aid challenge provides an opportunity for scholars across the border to investigate the new area of law where competition and tax law become intricate; one cannot be understood without the unveiling of the other. This can only be achieved through intensive cooperation and exchange between the two sides.

# CHAPTER 14
# Transfer Pricing in Business Restructurings

## 14.1 INTRODUCTION

Businesses restructure for different reasons including: cutting costs, promoting growth, shaking up a culture, or shifting strategic focus. Whatever the reason may be, business restructuring almost always involves making major structural changes in pursuit of better performance.[1]

The OECD defines business restructuring as the cross-border reorganization of the commercial or financial relations between associated enterprises, including the termination or substantial renegotiation of existing arrangements.[2] Put more starkly, business restructurings involve transfers of functions, assets and/or risks with associated profit/loss potential between associated enterprises.

In order to determine the arm's length compensation payable upon a restructuring to any restructured entity within an MNE group, as well as the member of the group that should bear such compensation, it is important to accurately delineate the transactions that comprise the business restructuring by identifying the commercial or financial relations and the conditions attached to those relations that lead to a transfer of value among the members of the MNE group.[3] This analysis must include an identification of the functions before and after the restructuring and an evaluation of the rights and obligations of the restructured entity under the pre-restructuring

1. Blenko, Marcia W., Mankins, Michael & Rogers, Paul (2010): The Decision-Driven Organization, Harvard Business Review.
2. OECD (2016): BEPS: Conforming Amendments to Chapter IX of the Transfer Pricing Guidelines, p. 3.
3. Accurate delineation of the transactions comprising the business restructuring requires performing a functional analysis that identify the economically significant activities and responsibilities undertaken, assets used or contributed, and risks assumed before and after the restructuring by the entities involved.

arrangement (including those existing under contract and commercial law) and of the manner and extent to which those rights and obligations change as a result of the restructuring.[4]

## 14.2 THE OECD APPROACH

On July 22, 2010, the OECD released a version of its Transfer pricing (TP) Guidelines, with a new Chapter IX covering business restructuring. Recently, on July 4, 2016, the OECD has released the Conforming Amendments to Chapter IX of the Transfer pricing Guidelines, prompted by the changes to the Guidelines set out in the 2015 BEPS Reports.[5]

The OECD has identified that a common element in business restructurings is to create a single entity as the "principal" or "entrepreneur" with economic ownership of the taxpayer's intangible property. The principal oversees the development, production, and sale of goods, either globally or in a designated region. Intangibles, key functions, and risks are centralized in the principal to streamline operations and create economies of scale.[6]

The OECD has characterized business restructurings as comprised of a combination of four distinct components:[7]

- Conversion of full-fledged distributors into limited-risk distributors, marketers, sales agents, or commissionaires for a foreign associated enterprise that may operate as a principal.
- Conversion of full-fledged manufacturers into contract manufacturers or toll manufacturers for foreign associated enterprise that may operate as a principal.
- Transfer of intangible property rights to create a centralized IP company within the group.
- The concentration of functions in a regional or central entity, with a corresponding reduction in scope or scale of functions carried out locally.

### 14.2.1 Business Restructuring and Transfer Pricing

The OECD requests that in case of business restructuring, value exchanged or transferred (i.e., tangibles, intangibles) be made at arm's length. The arrangement must be made or conducted at arm's length at the level of each entity involved taking into account its rights and other assets, expected benefits from the arrangement, and realistically available options:

4. OECD (2009): Transfer pricing Aspects of Business restructurings, CTPA, p. 22.
5. BEPS Report on Actions 8–10.
6. US Joint Committee on Taxation (2010): Present Law and Background Related to Possible Income Shifting and Transfer Pricing, p. 13.
7. OECD (2016): Chapter IX: Transfer Pricing Aspects of Business Restructurings.

> Under Article 9 of the OECD Model Tax Convention, the fact that a business restructuring arrangement is motivated by a purpose of obtaining tax benefits does not of itself warrant a conclusion that it is a non-arm's length arrangement.[8]

The OECD Transfer Pricing Guidelines apply to business restructuring under whenever there is either a transfer of something of value or a termination or substantial renegotiation of existing arrangements. It also discusses the pre- and post-restructuring arm's length.

### *14.2.1.1 Transfer of Something of Value*

#### *14.2.1.1.1 Tangible Assets*

Business restructurings can involve the transfer of tangible assets (e.g., equipment) by a restructured entity to a foreign related party. Although it is generally considered that transfers of tangible assets do not raise any significant transfer pricing difficulty, one common issue relates to the valuation of inventories that are transferred upon the conversion by a restructured manufacturer or distributor to a foreign related party (e.g., a principal), where the latter takes title to the inventories as from the implementation of the new business model and supply chain arrangements.[9]

Example

- Patel Corp. was a fully fledged manufacturer and distributor. It purchased raw materials and manufactured wigs using its own tangibles and intangibles. Patel Corp. also assumed the marketing and distribution of all its wigs and related products.
- Subsequent to a business restructuring within the group it belonged, Patel Corp. has become a toll-manufacturer with limited marketing and distribution functions. Further, the new business model implemented by the Group the purchasing of raw materials, the distribution of the wigs and related products are assumed by related entities within the Group.
- Patel Corp. activities are reduced to purchasing wigs and related products once it has concluded a sale with customers.
- Patel Corp. was compelled to transfer all previously acquired raw materials and unsold wigs and related products to the related entities now in charge of.
- The ALPs shall apply to the transfer of all previously acquired raw materials and all unsold wigs by Patel Corp. to the two sister entities, under the best transfer pricing method under the circumstances.

8. OECD (2016): Chapter IX: Transfer Pricing Aspects of Business Restructurings, paragraph 9.8.
9. OECD (2016): Transfer pricing Aspects of Business restructurings, p. 15.

#### *14.2.1.1.2 Intangible Assets*

Transfers of intangible assets raise difficult questions both as to the identification of the assets transferred and as to their valuation.[10] Identification can be difficult because not all valuable intangible assets are legally protected and registered and not all valuable intangible assets are recorded in the accounts. Relevant intangible assets might potentially include rights to use industrial assets such as patents, trademarks, trade names, designs or models, as well as copyrights of literary, artistic or scientific work (including software) and IP such as know-how and trade secrets. They may also include customer lists, distribution channels, unique names, symbols, or pictures.[11]

The Guidelines provide that:

> The determination of an arm's length remuneration for the subsequent ownership, control and exploitation of the transferred intangible should take account of the extent of the functions performed, assets used and risks assumed by the parties in relation to the intangible transferred, and in particular analysing control of risks and control of functions performed relating to the development, enhancement, maintenance, protection, or exploitation of the intangibles.[12]

Further, the valuation of IP becomes complex whenever an intangible has been transferred at a point when its valuation was highly uncertain or hard to value.

#### *14.2.1.1.3 Ongoing Concern ("Goodwill")*

Business restructurings sometimes involve the transfer of an ongoing concern. The transfer of an activity in this context means the transfer of the total bundle of assets (possibly including contractual rights, workforce in place, goodwill) and liabilities associated with performing particular functions, including the inherent risks. The determination of the arm's length valuation for a transfer of ongoing concern does not necessarily amount to the sum of the valuations of isolated elements that are part of the transfer. In effect, transfers of ongoing concerns between independent parties often take account of any possible goodwill. The valuation of a transfer of an ongoing concern should reflect all the valuable elements that would be remunerated between independent parties in comparable circumstances.[13] Valuation methods that are used in acquisition deals between independent parties may prove useful to value a transfer of activity, including goodwill, between associated enterprises.[14]

10. OECD (2016): Chapter IX: Transfer Pricing Aspects of Business Restructurings, paragraph 9.5.
11. *Supra*, p. 28.
12. OECD (2016): Chapter IX: Transfer Pricing Aspects of Business Restructurings, paragraph 9.6.
13. OECD (2016): Chapter IX: Transfer Pricing Aspects of Business Restructurings, paragraph 9.6.
14. *Idem*.

##### *14.2.1.1.4 Outsourcing*

In outsourcing cases, it may happen that a party voluntarily decides to undergo a restructuring and to bear the associated restructuring costs in exchange for anticipated savings. For instance, assume a taxpayer that is manufacturing and selling products in a high-cost jurisdiction decides to outsource the manufacturing activity to a related party situated in a low-cost jurisdiction. Further to the restructuring, the taxpayer will purchase from its related party the products manufactured and will continue to sell them to third-party customers. The restructuring may entail restructuring costs for the taxpayer while at the same time making it possible for it to benefit from cost savings on future procurements compared to its own manufacturing costs. Independent parties at arm's length do implement this type of outsourcing arrangement and do not necessarily require explicit compensation from the transferee if the anticipated cost savings for the transferor are greater than its restructuring costs.[15]

#### *14.2.1.2 Termination or Substantial Renegotiation of Existing Arrangements*

The termination or renegotiation of contractual relationships in the context of a business restructuring may cause the restructured entity to suffer detriments such as restructuring costs (e.g., write-off of assets, termination of employment contracts), re-conversion costs (e.g., in order to adapt its existing operation to other customer needs), and/or a loss of profit potential. Although it is commonly accepted that at arm's length, indemnification should be paid to the restructured entity, the determination of such an indemnification is not easy to compute.[16] The analysis of whether an indemnification is at arm's length should be made on the basis of the accurate delineation of the arrangements before and after the restructuring and the options realistically available to the parties.[17] Another aspect that may be necessary to examine in assessing whether the conditions of an arrangement in relation to an indemnification clause are arm's length, is the remuneration of the transactions that are the objects of the arrangement and the financial conditions of the termination thereof, as both can be interrelated.[18]

#### *14.2.1.3 The Pre- and Post-restructuring Transfer Pricing*

The OECD asserts that the ALPs and the Guidelines thereof shall apply akin to post-restructuring transactions:

15. *Supra*, p. 33.
16. OECD (2016): Chapter IX: Transfer Pricing Aspects of Business Restructurings, paragraph 9.7.
17. *Idem.*
18. OECD (2016): Chapter IX: Transfer Pricing Aspects of Business Restructurings, paragraph 9.8.

> Comparable situations must be treated in the same way, regardless of whether or not they came into existence as a result of a business restructuring of a previously existing structure.[19]

The OECD distinguishes two distinct situations: (i) where before-and-after comparisons can be made because the transactions prior to the restructuring were not controlled, and (ii) where the before-and-after comparisons relied on transactions undertaken by controlled entities. In the first case, the arm's length range would be determined by comparison between related and unrelated entities engaged in similar and identified transactions. This is the mere application of the comparable unrelated entities and the adjustments thereof. However, in the second situation, the OECD stresses out that the arm's length range shall not be based upon Article 9 of the OECD rather be based on the economically relevant characteristics of the transactions at stake. This would lead to tax administrations second guessing what would have happened in the absence of any restructuring. In a sense, any business restructuring has the potential to create intangible such as goodwill which increases the value of the restructured business after-fact. Therefore, the OECD approach seems less elaborated and further explanations would be needed.

### 14.2.2 OECD Steps and the Determination of the Arm's Length Value

The first step consists of identifying the actual controlled transaction undertaken by the related parties within a business restructuring. This step is followed by the finding of a comparable unrelated transaction. The OECD provides five comparability factors:[20]

- the characteristics of the property or services performed;
- the functions performed by the parties, taking into consideration assets used and risks assumed;
- the contractual terms;
- the economic circumstances of the parties; and
- the business strategies pursued by the parties.

### 14.2.3 Intangibles with Uncertain Value at the Time of the Restructuring

Transfer of intangibles with uncertain value at the time of the restructuring poses another difficulty, as it raises the question whether the valuation at the time of the transfer was an arm's length valuation determined in good faith on the basis of information reasonably available at that time. The OECD offers several approaches.

19. OECD (2016): Chapter IX: Transfer Pricing Aspects of Business Restructurings, paragraph 9.8.
20. OECD, TP Guidelines, Chapter I, 1.36, p. 43.

One option consists of using anticipated benefits which take into account all foreseeable and predictable economic factors as a means for establishing the pricing at the outset of the transaction. Also, it is possible that independent enterprises back up the aforementioned option by providing a pricing based upon a particular projection of the intangible.

## 14.3 THE US APPROACH

US transfer pricing rules provide no specifics concerning restructuring. Thus, the OECD rules aforementioned would be applicable in determining the arm's length price within an MNE restructuring dealings.

In the US, the term "business restructuring" refers to the realignment of functions and risks between various entities in the supply chain.[21] A taxpayer's supply chain is the system that moves a product or service from supplier to customer. The supply chain may include entities that are related parties, unrelated parties, or both.[22] The Treasury and the IRS watch after restructuring dealing to make sure that the entity participating in the supply chain transact or deal at arm's length. The JTC conducted a public hearing which look after some specific business restructuring where transfer pricing and income shifting are most commonly to occur, such as: (i) distributor conversion, (ii) contract manufacturing conversion, (iii) specialization of operations, and (iv) centralized ownership of intangible property rights.

### 14.3.1 Distributor Conversion

In a distributor conversion, the principal (i.e., MNE, or another subsidiary) becomes responsible for the sale—after restructuring—but does not perform the sales function itself.[23] Very often, foreign subsidiaries of the MNE is converted into low-risk distribution service entities (limited-risk distributors, commissionaires, and/or commission agents), or the MNE may form new entities to provide for product distribution to serve expanding markets. In substance, the MNE or an affiliate of the MNE is merely involved in facilitating the sale and delivery of finished products and the collection of payment after the conversion. For services and risks assumed each affiliate shall be entitled to proper payments. Transfer pricing manipulation may occur through the related entities dealings.

### 14.3.2 Contract Manufacturing Conversion

Through contract manufacturing conversion, an MNE establishes a contract manufacturing arrangement with a second entity, usually an existing full-risk manufacturing

21. US Joint Committee on Taxation (2010): Present Law and Background Related to Possible Income Shifting and transfer pricing, p. 11.
22. *Idem.*
23. *Idem.*, p. 14.

subsidiary within the group. The former manufacturing subsidiary then becomes a low-risk service provider under the control of the MNE. Functions, risks, and ownership of the intangibles related to the product are centralized or shifted to the MNE (headquarter).[24] Such a centralized procurement allows the MNE to achieve economies of scale, sometimes, through transfer pricing manipulations.

### 14.3.3 Rationalization and/or Specialization of Operations

With rationalization of operations, the MNE takes high-value functions such as research and development, global marketing strategies, leaving minor functions to the stripped subsidiary. A post-restructuring transfer pricing study needs to be conducted in order to reflect both the services and functions transferred and those remaining, applying the ALP.

### 14.3.4 Centralized Ownership of Intangibles Rights

With a centralized ownership right of intangibles, the MNE or its wholly owned subsidiary centralizes the intangible property rights into a low-tax subsidiary, while allowing the full-group to enter into IP contract with the new entity owning the whole group's IPs.[25] Generally, the transfer of the IP would fall within the ambit of transfer pricing either through IRC section 482 or 367(d).

## 14.4 CRITICISM OF THE OECD/US APPROACHES

The approaches considered by both the OECD and the US are not voided of criticisms. The OECD analyzes that business restructuring are merely from the viewpoints of transfer of something of value or a termination or substantial renegotiation of existing arrangements, ignoring the core element of any business restructuring, which is decision-making process.[26] The determination as to how decisions have to be made after the restructuring weighs more value than the tax benefits that derived from the restructuring. Such a flaw is more evident within the US approach as the Joint Tax Committee (JTC) solely analyzes business restructuring from tax viewpoint exclusively. The JTC selected and examined solely cases where tax motivations were the driving force behind the restructuring—small but well publicized cases that overshadowed the very essence of business restructuring.

24. *Idem.*, p. 15.
25. *Idem.*, p. 16.
26. Ainsworth, Richard T. & Shact, Andrew B. (2011): Transfer Pricing & Business Restructuring-Intangibles, Synergies and Shelters, Boston University School of Law Working Paper No. 11-24, p. 4.

## 14.5 CASE STUDY

### 14.5.1 The McDonald Case[27]

This case describes the restructuring of McDonald group in Europe and the creation of McDonald's Corporation's franchise rights ("McD Europe") to which all franchising rights are conveyed. Under the new structure, McD Europe has two branches in the US ("US Franchise Branch") and Switzerland ("Swiss Service Branch"), respectively. McD Europe acquired beneficial ownership of a number of franchise rights intangibles ("franchise rights"). Subsequently, McD Europe allocated the franchise rights as well as the obligations to its US Franchise Branch. All royalties that were once received by McDonald's Corporation are now to be received by McD Europe through its US Franchise Branch (Figure 14.1).

- McDonald operates in the food service industry mainly through the franchising and operation of McDonald's restaurants.
- Outside of the US, McDonald's Corporation and its US affiliate, McDonald's International Property Company ("MIPCO"), license the right to develop and operate McDonald's restaurants on a market-by-market basis to entities which in most major markets are direct or indirect subsidiaries of McDonald's Corporation.
- In 2014 McDonald's recorded total revenues of USD 27 billion, of which USD 18 billion was from company operated sales and USD 9 billion from franchised revenues.
- On February 11, 2009, McDonald requested its first ruling from the Luxembourg tax authorities. According to the facts disclosed in the ruling request, McD Europe's US Franchise Branch assumed various economic risks associated with the development of the franchise rights and bears associated costs. Further, the second branch ("McD Europe's Swiss") licensed the franchise rights to franchisors in various European countries ("Master Franchisors") and provided management, support, development, and other similar or related services associated with the franchise rights. In exchange for those services, the US Franchise Branch reimbursed the Swiss Service Branch for all its costs and provides the Swiss Service Branch with a service fee equivalent to the costs of the Swiss Service Branch plus [...] percent.
- According to McDonald's tax advisor, McD Europe qualifies as tax resident in Luxembourg pursuant to Article 159(1) of the L.I.R., thus fully liable for corporate income tax in Luxembourg. However, as a Luxembourg tax resident, McD Europe was exempt from any taxation in Luxembourg under the provisions of the double tax treaty concluded by Luxembourg. Further, the profits generated by the US Franchise Branch will only be subject to possible taxation

27. Commission v. Luxembourg C (2015) 8343.

in the US and exempt from corporate income tax in Luxembourg by virtue of Articles 7 and 25 of the Luxembourg-US DTT.

- On March 30, 2009, Luxembourg confirmed in a tax ruling that McDonald's Europe Franchising, owner of McDonald's European IP and franchising rights, was not subject to tax in Luxembourg on profits it received from royalties paid by franchisees operating restaurants in Europe and Russia.
- Later that same year (2009), McDonald's reversed its first version of the key facts to the Luxembourg tax authorities, admitting that the profits of its US Branch were not subject to tax in the US because the US branch was not a PE under US law.
- McDonald's argued that notwithstanding the fact that there was no US PE under US law, under Luxembourg law and the Luxembourg/US tax treaty, McDonald's US entity would be a US PE, so the income should be exempt from Luxembourg tax under the treaty.
- On September 17, 2009, the Luxembourg tax authorities accepted the company's position in a second private, confirming again that McDonald's had no PE in Luxembourg and exempting all profits from taxation in Luxembourg.
- As a result, since 2009 McDonald's paid no tax on the royalty payments in either country. These untaxed profits amounted to more than EUR 250 million (USD 273 million) in 2013 alone.
- The two different accounts upon which the two rulings have been approved are, at best, questionable. Indeed, from Luxembourg tax perspective, the US activities of McDonald's Europe Franchising were characterized as creating a PE, while the same US activities of McDonald's Europe never raised to the level of creating a PE in the US.
- The Commission's preliminary decision, although, was that the Luxembourg tax administration should have only agreed to exempt income from corporate taxation to the extent that the income may be taxed in the US pursuant to the Luxembourg-US tax treaty. By instead reaching an erroneous interpretation of the treaty and law, Luxembourg conferred a selective advantage on McDonald's.
- The EU Commission went on to add: "where a tax measure results in an unjustified reduction of the tax liability of a beneficiary who would otherwise be subject to a higher level of tax under the reference system, that reduction constitutes both the advantage granted by the tax measure and the derogation from the system of reference."[28]
- The EU Commission pursued that: "a decision of a tax administration that departs from the general rules of taxation to the benefit of an individual undertaking in principle leads to a presumption of state aid and must be analyzed in detail. In particular, a tax ruling that has been issued in contradiction to the applicable tax provisions resulting in a lower tax liability for its addressee than what would have been the case if the general rules of taxation

28. EU Commission v. Luxembourg, Case C (2015) 8343, paragraph 74.

had been properly applied gives rise to a selective advantage to that undertaking."[29] Also, "since there is no possibility to tax the income of McD Europe in United States, as explained in the request for a revised tax ruling, the Luxembourg tax administration, being fully aware of this non-possibility of taxation, should not have agreed to the interpretation of the tax advisor which results in the exemption of the income attributed to the US Franchise Branch from corporate income tax in Luxembourg."[30]

- Therefore, the EU Commission concluded: "the tax ruling issued by the Luxembourg tax administration on 17 September 2009 in favour of McD Europe Franchising S.à.r.l. grants state aid to the latter and to the McDonald's Corporation as a whole within the meaning of Article 107(1) TFEU."
- Luxembourg has appealed the EU Commission's preliminary view and the case is still pending before the Commission for final determination.

29. EU Commission v. Luxembourg, Case C (2015) 8343, paragraph 80.
30. EU Commission v. Luxembourg, Case C (2015) 8343, paragraph 89.

*Figure 14.1 McDonald Europe Franchising*

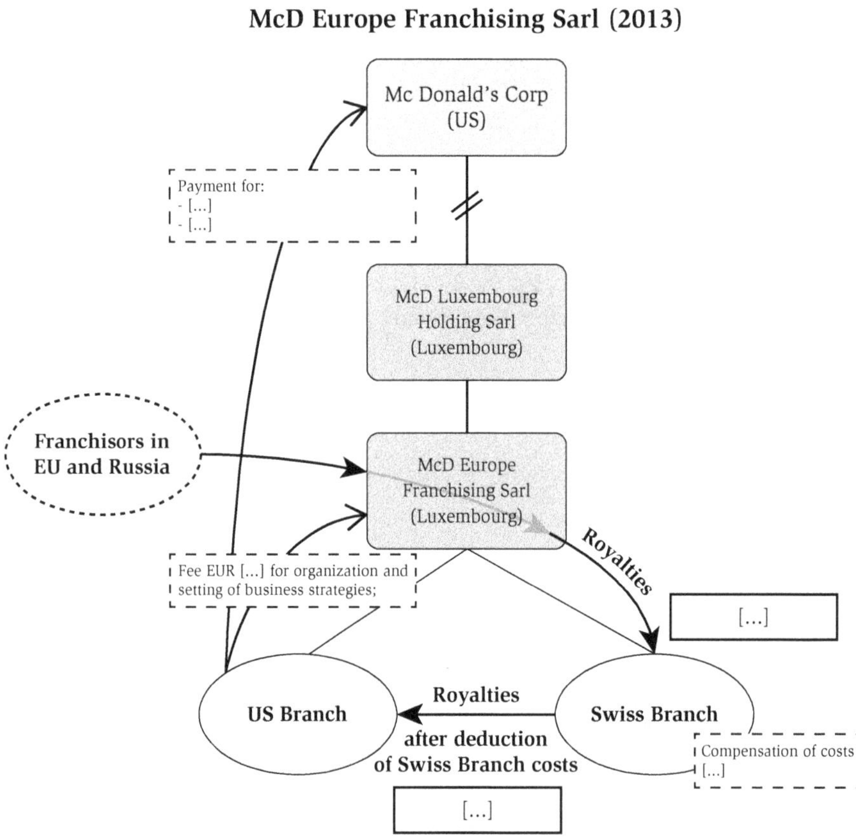


### 14.5.2 Luxembourg Tax Ruling Practice

The International Consortium of Investigative Journalists (ICIJ) revealed, on December 2014, that the Luxembourg tax authorities have delivered a substantial amount of rulings to more than 350 MNEs worldwide.[31] The tax inspectors approved without sound analysis hundreds of tax ruling per day, contrary to more meticulous tax services such as the IRS.

The Luxembourg tax ruling practice is plainly a fraud. Several multinational companies have channeled hundreds of billions of dollars through Luxembourg and saved billions of dollars in taxes. PepsiCo, IKEA, AIG, Coach, Deutsche Bank, Abbott Laboratories, and nearly 340 other companies have secured secret deals from Luxembourg that allowed many of them to slash their global tax bills. Some firms have

31. Rulings are decisions obtained from the Luxembourg tax administration which confirm the tax treatment of a particular transaction.

enjoyed effective tax rates of less than 1 percent on the profits they have shuffled into Luxembourg. The big-four auditing firms have been active in the practice. PricewaterhouseCoopers, for instance, has helped multinational companies to obtain at least 548 tax rulings in Luxembourg from 2002 to 2010.[32]

32. Luxembourg Leaks- ICJI, 2014.

# Bibliography

Ainsworth T. Richard & Shact B. Andrew (2011): Transfer Pricing & Business Restructuring-Intangibles, Synergies and Shelters, Boston University School of Law Working Paper No. 11-24, p. 4.

Amerkhil, Valerie (2006): Functional Analysis and Choosing the Best Method, ESC, 12-9.

Andrus, Joseph (2012): Transfer Pricing and the Arm's Length Principle, World Commerce review, June 2012. p. 28.

Atwood, T.J (2013): Are Worldwide Tax Systems Disadvantageous for Residents Firms Compared with Territorial Tax Systems?, Florida Tax Law Review, p. 8.

Avi-Yonah, Reuven (2009): The Rise and Fall of Arm's Length: A Study in the Evolution of US International Taxation, University of Michigan Law School-Law & Economics Working Papers Archive.

Avi-Yonah, Reuven (2009): Between Formulary Apportionment and the OECD: A Proposal for Reconciliation, University of Michigan Law School Scholarship Repository, p. 13.

Avi-Yonah, Reuven (2011): Formulary Apportionment—Myths and Prospects—Promoting Better International Policy and Utilizing the Misunderstood and Under-Theorized Formulary Alternative, University of Michigan law School Scholarship Repository, p. 381.

Avi-Yonah, Reuven (2011): Formulary Apportionment: Myths and Prospects—Promoting Better International Policy and Utilizing the Misunderstood and Under-Theorized Formulary Alternative, World Tax Journal, p. 373.

Avi-Yonah, Reuven (2012): Transfer Pricing Disputes in the United States, University of Michigan Law School Scholarship Repository, p. 42.

Avi-Yonah, Reuven and Clausing, Kimberly (2007): Reforming Corporate Taxation in a Global Economy: A Proposal to Adopt Formulary Apportionment,The Hamilton Project, pp. 12–15.

Avi-Yonah, Reuven (2016): Evaluating BEPS, NYU Tax Policy Colloquium, p. 5.

Clausing, Kimberly (2003): Tax-Motivated Transfer Pricing and US intrafirm Trade Prices, Journal of Public Economics 87, 2210–2222.

European Commission (2011): Proposal for a Council Directive on a Common Consolidated Corporate Tax Base (WP), p. 6.

Grinberg, Itai (2016): A Constructive U.S. Counter to EU State Aid Cases, Tax Notes International.

Graetz, Michael (2015): Behind the European Raid on McDonald's, Wall Street Journal, December 3, 2015.

Hunag, Chye-Ching (2013): The Fiscal and Economic Risks of Territorial Taxation, Center on Budget and policy Priorities, p. 7.

IRS Announcement and Report Concerning Advance Pricing Agreements, March 27, 2014, p. 2.

IRS Proposed Revision of Procedures for Advance Pricing Agreements, Notice 2013-79, p. 13.

IRS Proposed Revision of Procedures for Advance Pricing Agreements, Notice 2013-79, p. 9.

IRS Proposed Revision of Procedures for Advance Pricing Agreements, Notice 2013-79, pp. 8–9.

IRS Proposed Revision of Procedures for Advance Pricing Agreements, Notice 2013-79, p. 10.

IRS Proposed Revision of Procedures for Advance Pricing Agreements, Notice 2013-79, p. 11.

IRS Proposed Revision of Procedures for Advance Pricing Agreements, Notice 2013-79, p. 13

Kleinbard, Edward, D. (2012): The Lessons of Stateless Income, Tax Law Review, Vol. 65, pp. 99–172.

Laprévote, Francois & Nikolaas Van Robbroeck (2016): Three Years of EU State Aid Review of Tax Rulings: Taking Stock.

OECD (2009): Transfer Pricing Aspects of Business Restructurings: Discussion Draft for Public Comment.

OECD (2010) Transfer Pricing Guidelines, p. 33.

OECD (2010) Transfer Pricing Guidelines, p. 34.

OECD (2015): Model Legislation Related to Country-by-Country Reporting, Article 6(1).

OECD (2015): Model Legislation Related to Country-by-Country Reporting, Article 6(2).

OECD (2015): Model Legislation Related to Country-by-Country Reporting, Article 2.

OECD (2015): Model Legislation Related to Country-by-Country Reporting, Article 3(a).

OECD (2015): Model Legislation Related to Country-by-Country Reporting, Article 3(b).

OECD (2015): Model Legislation Related to Country-by-Country Reporting, Article 4(1).

OECD (2015): Model Legislation Related to Country-by-Country Reporting, Article 5.

OECD (2016), Guidance on the Implementation of Country-by-Country Reporting—BEPS Action 13, OECD/G20 Base Erosion and Profit Shifting Project, OECD, Paris. www.oecd.org/tax/guidance-on-the-implementation-of-country-by-country-reporting-beps-action-13.pdf.

OECD (2016): BEPS: Conforming Amendments to Chapter IX of the Transfer Pricing Guidelines.

Osborne, David (2011): Deterring Transfer Pricing Abuse: Changing Incentives as a Practical Alternative to a Global Tax Regime, Washington University Global Studies Law Review, Volume 10 Issue 4, p. 825.

Prysuski, Martin & Srini Lalapet (2005): A Comprehensive Look at the Berry Ratio in Transfer pricing, Tax Notes International, Volume 40, Number 8, p. 762.

Saint-Amans, Pascal (July 22, 2013): Testimony of the Director, Centre for Tax Policy and Administration, Organization for Economic Co-operation and Development (OECD) Before the United States Senate Committee on Finance, p. 6.

Saint-Amans, Pascal (July 22, 2013): Testimony of the Director, Centre for Tax Policy and Administration, Organization for Economic Co-operation and Development (OECD) Before the United States Senate Committee on Finance, p. 3

Shaviro, Daniel (2016): The U.S. Response to OECD-BEPS and the EU State Aid Cases, New York University Law and Economics Working Papers.

US Congress (2007): Report to the Congress on Earnings Stripping, Transfer Pricing and U.S. Income Tax Treaties, p. 45.

U.S. Department of the Treasury—White paper (August 24, 2016).

United States Senate—Permanent Subcommittee on Investigations (April 1, 2014): Caterpillar's Offshore Tax Strategy, p. 7.

United States Senate—Permanent Subcommittee on Investigations (April 1, 2014): Caterpillar's Offshore Tax Strategy, p. 95.

United States Senate—Permanent Subcommittee on Investigations (April 1, 2014): Caterpillar's Offshore Tax Strategy, p. 4.

United States Senate—Permanent Subcommittee on Investigations (April 1, 2014): Caterpillar's Offshore Tax Strategy, p. 6.

United States Senate—Permanent Subcommittee on Investigations (April 1, 2014): Caterpillar's Offshore Tax Strategy, p. 18.

United States Senate—Permanent Subcommittee on Investigations (April 1, 2014): Caterpillar's Offshore Tax Strategy, p. 21.

United States Senate—Permanent Subcommittee on Investigations (April 1, 2014): Caterpillar's Offshore Tax Strategy, p. 41.

United States Senate—Permanent Subcommittee on Investigations (April 1, 2014): Caterpillar's Offshore Tax Strategy, p. 43.

United States Senate—Permanent Subcommittee on Investigations (April 1, 2014): Caterpillar's Offshore Tax Strategy, p. 46.

United States Senate—Permanent Subcommittee on Investigations (April 1, 2014): Caterpillar's Offshore Tax Strategy, p. 50.

United States Senate—Permanent Subcommittee on Investigations (April 1, 2014): Caterpillar's Offshore Tax Strategy, p. 51.

United States Senate—Permanent Subcommittee on Investigations (April 1, 2014): Caterpillar's Offshore Tax Strategy, p. 56.

United States Senate—Permanent Subcommittee on Investigations (April 1, 2014): Caterpillar's Offshore Tax Strategy, p. 62.

United States Senate—Permanent Subcommittee on Investigations (April 1, 2014): Caterpillar's Offshore Tax Strategy, p. 94.

United States Senate—Permanent Subcommittee on Investigations (April 1, 2014): Caterpillar's Offshore Tax Strategy, p. 81.
US Senate Committee —Permanent Subcommittee on Investigations—Apple Inc, Memorandum, p. 4.
US Senate Committee —Permanent Subcommittee on Investigations—Apple Inc, Memorandum, p. 5.
US Senate Committee —Permanent Subcommittee on Investigations—Apple Inc, Memorandum, p. 25.
US Senate Committee—Permanent Subcommittee on Investigations—Apple Inc, Memorandum, p. 26.
US Senate Committee—Permanent Subcommittee on Investigations—Apple Inc, Memorandum, p. 28.
United States Senate Permanent Subcommittee on Investigation—Microsoft, (September 20, 2012).
Wegman, Jerry (2015): Sales Factor Formulary Apportionment of Global Profits as an Alternative System of Taxation of to the Current U.S. Federal Corporate Income Tax, pp. 2, 12.

# Table of Cases

# Glossary

A

**Advance Pricing Agreement Arrangement (APA)**: An arrangement in respect of certain specified transactions that determines in advance the appropriate criteria for determining transfer pricing. The agreement may be made by the taxpayer unilaterally with the tax administration or may be a bilateral or multilateral agreement involving the tax administrations of other countries.

**Affiliated Parties**: Affiliated parties are entities linked by a common interest normally defined in terms of a certain level of shareholding or other criterion.

**Allocation Key**: An allocation key is used to allocate costs of a service provider among other related entities for the purposes of computing the arm's length fee under the Cost Plus Method using an indirect charge approach. The allocation key may be a quantity such as turnover, employee numbers, working hours or floor space.

**Arm's Length Principle (ALP)**: The arm's length principle is an international standard that compares the transfer prices charged between related entities with the price of similar transactions carried out between independent entities at arm's length. An adjustment may be made to the extent that profits of a related party differ from those that would be agreed between independent entities in similar circumstances.

**Arm's Length Range**: The arm's length range is a range of values from which an arm's length price may be selected, arrived at by applying an appropriate transfer pricing method.

**Artificial Profit Shifting**: The allocation of income and expenses between related entities or between branches of a single legal entity with the aim of reducing the total tax payable by the group.

**Associated Enterprise (AE)**: Associated enterprises are enterprises under common control. T is will generally be the case where the same persons participate directly or indirectly in the management, control or capital of both enterprises.

**Average**: When a transfer price is found to be outside the arm's length range the transfer pricing rules of some countries require the price to be adjusted to the average value (usually the median) of the range.

## B

**Basic Arm's Length Return Method (BALRM)**: The basic arm's length return method assigns an estimated arm's length rate of return to the sale, licensing or transfer of intangible property. The method was proposed in a White Paper in the US in 1988 but has not been adopted in US transfer pricing legislation. Some aspects of the method are, however, present in the comparable profits method. The method focuses on the returns realized on the assets or costs used in performing each function by a related party, and examines the return of uncontrolled entities performing the same functions at arm's length.

**Benefit Test**: In considering the arm's length return for intragroup services the benefit to the recipient of the services, if any, should be taken into consideration. If no benefit is received by the recipient of the services this would indicate that no remuneration should be paid for the services.

**Berry Ratio**: The ratio of gross income to operating costs, sometimes used to establish the arm's length price using the Transactional Net Margin Method.

**Best Method Rule**: A rule requiring the taxpayer to use the transfer pricing method that results in the most reliable measure of the arm's length price in the circumstances. The rule does not give priority to the same transfer pricing methods in all circumstances.

**Bilateral APA**: An agreement between a taxpayer and the taxing authorities of two countries in advance of a transaction. Such an agreement benefits the taxpayer because it confirms that the taxpayer will not be subject to double taxation - that is, paying tax on the transaction to both the US and a foreign nation.

**Business Restructuring**: The cross-border redeployment of functions, assets and risks by a multinational entity.

**Buy-in Payment**: A Payment made by a new entrant to an existing CCA for obtaining an interest in any results of past CCA activity.

**Buy-out payment**: compensation a participant who withdraws from an existing CCA may receive from the remaining participants for an effective transfer of its interests in the results of past CCA activities.

## C

**Comparability Adjustments**: Adjustments made to improve the accuracy and reliability of the comparables to ensure that the financial results of the comparables are stated on the same basis as those of the tested party.

**Commodity**: Is any tangible personal property of a kind that is actively traded or with respect to which contractual interest are actively traded.

**Comparability Analysis**: An analysis carried out to compare the controlled transaction with the conditions that prevail in transactions at arm's length between independent entities. This involves an understanding of the economically significant characteristics of the controlled transaction and a comparison of the conditions of the controlled transaction with those of the comparable transactions.

**Comparability Factors**: Factors taken into account in determining the level of comparability of the controlled and comparable transactions. These are attributes of the transactions or parties that could materially affect prices or profits, including the characteristics of the property or services, functional analysis, contractual terms, economic circumstances and business strategies pursued.

**Comparable Adjustable Transaction**: Controlled and uncontrolled transactions are comparable if either none of the differences between them could materially affect the arm's length price or profit or, where such material differences exist, reasonably accurate adjustments can be made to eliminate their effect. A comparable transaction to which such comparability adjustments can be made is a comparable adjustable transaction.

**Comparable Data**: These may be internal comparables, i.e., transactions between the tested party and independent parties, or external comparables, i.e., transactions between two independent entities that are not party to the controlled transaction.

**Comparable Profits Method (CPM)**: A transfer pricing method based on the comparison of the operating profit derived from related-party transactions with the operating profit earned by third parties undertaking similar business activities.

**Comparable Uncontrolled Price (CUP) method**: A method of pricing based on the price charged between unrelated entities in respect of a comparable transaction in comparable circumstances.

**Competent authority procedure**: A procedure under which different tax authorities may consult each other to reach a mutual agreement on a taxpayer's position.

**Contingent liabilities**: Obligations of a government whose timing and magnitude depend on the occurrence of some uncertain future event outside the government's control.

**Controlled transactions**: Transactions between or among enterprises that are related, associated with respect to each other.

**Cost Contribution Arrangement (CCA)**: A cost contribution arrangement is an arrangement between enterprises to share the costs and risks of developing, producing or obtaining assets, services or rights. The arrangement sets out the responsibilities and risks of the participants and the nature and extent of the interest of each participant in the assets, services or rights resulting from the arrangement.

**Cost plus mark-up**: A mark-up measured by reference to margins computed after the direct and indirect cost incurred by a supplier of property or services in a transaction.

**Cost Plus Method (CPM)**: The Cost Plus Method evaluates the arm's length nature of an intercompany charge for tangible property or services by reference to the gross profit mark-up on costs incurred by the supplier of the property or services. It compares the gross profit mark-up earned by the tested party with the gross profit mark-ups earned by comparable companies.

**Cost Sharing Arrangement (CSA)**: A cost sharing arrangement is the term used to describe a cost contribution arrangement between enterprises to share the costs and risks of developing intangible assets. The arrangement would normally set out the contributions of the participants and define their share in the results of the assets resulting from the arrangement.

D

**Disregarded payment**: Refers to payment that is deductible under the laws of the payer jurisdiction and is not recognized under the laws of the payee jurisdiction.

**Divisional structure**: is a type of organizational structure that groups each organizational function into a division. These divisions can correspond to either products or geographies.

F

**Financial instrument**: Includes any arrangement that is taxed under the rules for taxing debt, equity or derivatives under the laws of the payee or the payer jurisdictions.

**Fiscal devaluation**: A revenue neutral shift from employers' social contributions toward value-added tax.

**FOGEI**: taxable income derived from the extraction of minerals from oil or gas wells based on the Fair Market Value (FMV) of the minerals in the immediate vicinity of the well.

**Foreign currency gain**: Any gain from a section 988 transaction to the extent such gain does not exceed gain realized by reason of changes in exchange rates on or after the booking date and before the payment date.

**Foreign currency loss**: any loss from a section 988 transaction to the extent such loss does not exceed the loss realized by reason of changes in exchange rates on or after the booking date and before the payment date.

**Functional Analysis**: An analysis involving the identification of functions performed, assets employed and risks assumed with respect to the international controlled transactions of an enterprise. The functional analysis seeks to identify and compare the economically significant activities and the responsibilities undertaken by the independent and associated enterprises.

**Functional structure**: is a common type of organizational structure in which the organization is divided into smaller groups based on specialized functional areas, such as IT, finance, or marketing.

G

**Global Formulary Apportionment (GFA)**: A method with which to allocate the global profits of an MNE group amongst the associated enterprises on the basis of a multi-factor weighted formula. Possible factors are property, payroll and sales or other factors that may be defined while adopting the formula.

**Gross Profit**: The result of deducting from total sales the cost of sales, including all the expenses directly incurred in relation to those sales.

H

**Hybrid branch**: as an entity with a single owner that is treated as a separate entity under the relevant tax laws of a foreign country and as a branch (i.e., DRE) of a CFC that is its sole owner for US tax purposes.

**Hybrid instruments**: Instruments treated as debt for foreign law purposes and equity for US purposes, in the context of conduit financing arrangements.

**Hybrid mismatch arrangement**: An arrangement that exploits a difference in the tax treatment of an entity or instrument under the laws of two or more tax jurisdictions to produce a mismatch in tax outcomes where that mismatch has the effect of lowering the aggregate tax burden of the parties to the arrangement.

**Hyper-inflationary currency**: the currency of a country in which there is cumulative inflation during the base period of at least 100 percent as determined by reference to the consumer price index of the country listed in the monthly issues of the "International Financial Statistics" or a successor publication of the International Monetary Fund.

**I**

**Independent enterprises**: Refers to enterprises which are not related each other.

**Intangibles**: Intangibles are property that has no physical existence but whose value depends on the legal rights of the owner. Examples of intangibles are intellectual property such as patents, copyright and trademarks.

**Intentional Setoff**: A benefit provided by one associated enterprise to another that is deliberately balanced to some extent by different benefits received from that enterprise in return.

**Interquartile Range**: This term is used in the transfer pricing rules of some countries to describe the values between the 25th and 75th percentile of the range of arm's length results derived from application of a transfer pricing method. In some jurisdictions this range may be used as the arm's length range.

**Internal Comparables**: Transactions between one of the parties to a controlled transaction (taxpayer or foreign related enterprise) and an independent party.

**Intragroup Services**: Services carried out by one entity in a multinational group for another entity or entities in the same group.

**J**

**Journal**: the ability to transfer a stock position from one subaccount to another, using book entries for the two accounts to accomplish the transfer, without the need to sell the position to the market and immediately buy it back.

**M**

**Margin**: Refers to the portion of the purchase price that the customer must deposit in cash as initial equity in customer's securities trading account.

**Matrix structure**: is a company structure in which the reporting relationships are set up as a grid, or matrix, rather than in the traditional hierarchy. In other words, employees have dual reporting relationships—generally to both a functional manager and a product manager.

**Minerals**: means hydrocarbon minerals extracted from oil and gas wells, including crude oil or natural gas. The term includes incidental impurities from these wells, such as sulfur, nitrogen, or helium. The term does not include hydrocarbon minerals derived from shale oil or tar sands.

**Multilateral APA**: An APA entered into between the taxpayer and the tax authorities of more than two countries.

**Mutual Agreement Procedure**: A procedure whereby tax administrations of different countries consult to resolve disputes regarding the application of double tax treaties.

**N**

**Net profit indicator**: The ratio of net profit to an appropriate base (e.g., costs, sales, assets). The Transactional net margin method relies on a comparison of an appropriate net profit indicator fir the controlled transaction with the same net profit indicator in comparable uncontrolled transactions.

**Notice of deficiency**: A letter from the Internal Revenue Service that advises a taxpayer about delinquent taxes owed plus any penalties and interest. A notice of deficiency is sometimes also called a 90-day letter because it gives the taxpayer 90 days to dispute the tax assessment.

**O**

**OECD Guidelines**: Report by the OECD on transfer pricing entitled "Transfer Pricing Guidelines for Multinational Enterprises and Tax Administrations," published in July 1995, with additional chapters subsequently issued.

**P**

**Patent**: Legal protection of a product or process invented or developed by the holder of the patent.

**Permanent Establishment (PE)**: A taxable business unit. Exact definitions vary in different countries and according to different double taxation treaties.

**Primary adjustment**: An adjustment that a tax administration in a first jurisdiction makes to a company's taxable profits as a result of applying the arm's length principle to transactions involving an associated enterprise in a second tax jurisdiction.

**Profit Shifting**: Allocation of income and expenses between related corporations or branches of the same legal entity in order to reduce the overall tax liability of the group or corporation.

**Profit Split Method**: The Profit Split Method seeks to eliminate the effect on profits of special conditions made or imposed in a controlled transaction by determining the division of profits that independent enterprises would have expected to realize from engaging in the transaction or transactions.

**Profit Level Indicator (PLI)**: A measure of a company's profitability that is used to compare comparables with the tested party. A profit level indicator may express profitability in relation to sales, costs/expenses, or assets.

**R**

**Related Parties**: Related parties are entities under common management, control or ownership, or where one entity controls the other entity.

**Resale price method**: A method of pricing based on the price at which a product is resold less a percentage of the resale price.

**Residence**: Refers to where the income earner—the taxpayer—has its primary location, its place of "tax citizenship."

**Reverse hybrid**: Is any person that is treated as a separate entity by a related investor and as a transparent under the laws of the establishment jurisdiction.

**Royalty**: A payment (often periodic) in respect of property (often intangible), e.g., a sum paid for the use of patented technology.

**S**

**Source**: Refers to where income is earned or from where it is derived.

**Structured arrangement**: Is any arrangement where the hybrid mismatch is priced into the terms of the arrangement or the facts and circumstances of the arrangement indicate that it has been designed to produce a hybrid mismatch.

**T**

**Tax audit**: an examination of an organization's or individual's tax return.

**Tax avoidance**: the process whereby an individual plans his or her finances so as to apply all exemptions and deductions provided by tax laws to reduce taxable income. Through tax avoidance, an individual takes advantage of all legal opportunities to minimize his or her state or federal Income Tax, gift tax, or estate tax.

**Tax evasion**: Unlawful attempt to minimize tax liability through fraudulent techniques to circumvent or frustrate tax laws, such as deliberate understatement of taxable income or willful non-payment of due taxes. Whereas tax evasion is an offense (punishable by both civil and criminal penalties), tax avoidance is not.

**Taxpayer**: Any person who is subject to that in a jurisdiction whether as a resident or by virtue of applicable source rules.

**Tangible property**: Physical property, e.g., inventory, plant, machinery and factories.

**Tax Information Exchange Agreements (TIEAs)**: provide for the exchange of information on request relating to a specific criminal or civil tax investigation or civil tax matters under investigation.

**Territorial tax regime**: A country which limits its tax base by excluding income earned outside its own territory, by reference to the other territories in which it is earned. In practice there is no pure territorial tax regime.

**Traditional transaction methods**: Refers to: (i) the comparable price method, (ii) the resale price method, and (iii) the cost plus method.

**Transactional profit method**: A transfer pricing method that examines the profits that arise from particular controlled transactions of one or more of the associated enterprises with respect to each other.

**Transfer pricing**: practice whereby companies use transactions between different corporate units to shift income between jurisdictions for the purpose of reducing the company's overall tax burden.

**Treaty abuse**: Refers to situations in which the result of a certain operation is in contradiction with the treaty.

**Treaty shopping**: Relates to situations in which an individual benefits from a treaty without being the legitimate beneficiary of it.

**U**

**Uncontrolled transactions**: Transactions between or among enterprises that are independent with respect to each other.

**W**

**Worldwide tax regime**: Refers to a tax system which includes as a taxable basis, all of a taxpayer's income, regardless of the origination. A worldwide tax system would generally grant credits to recognize other countries' legitimate taxation. There is no pure worldwide tax regime.

# Index

www.ingramcontent.com/pod-product-compliance
Lightning Source LLC
Chambersburg PA
CBHW071243230926
51849CB00001B/216
*9789041191960*